# The Science *and* Theology *of*
# Godly Love

# The Science *and* Theology *of*

# Godly Love

*Edited by* MATTHEW T. LEE *and* AMOS YONG

PRESS
*DeKalb, IL*

© 2012 by Northern Illinois University Press

Published by the Northern Illinois University Press, DeKalb, Illinois 60115

Manufactured in the United States using acid-free paper.

Design by Julia Fauci

Library of Congress Cataloging-in-Publication Data

The science and theology of Godly love / edited by Matthew T. Lee and Amos Yong.

   pages    cm

Includes bibliographical references and index.

ISBN 978-0-87580-449-1 (cloth : alk. paper) — ISBN 978-1-60909-057-9 (e-book)

1. God—Worship and love. 2. God—Love. 3. Religion and science. I. Lee, Matthew T., editor of compilation. II. Yong, Amos, editor of compilation.

BV4817.S377 2012

231'.6—dc23

011046897

# CONTENTS

**Introduction**   3

MATTHEW T. LEE, MARGARET M. POLOMA, AND STEPHEN G. POST

PART I—THEOLOGY AND GODLY LOVE

## One
### Godly Love
*Why We Cannot Endure without It*   17

STEPHEN G. POST

## Two
### Agape, Self-Sacrifice, and Mutuality
*An Exploration into the Thought of Jonathan Edwards
and the Theme of Godly Love*   33

MICHAEL J. McCLYMOND

## Three
### Imago Dei and Kenosis
*Contributions of Christology to the Study of Godly Love*   56

PETER ALTHOUSE

## Four
### Violence and Nonviolence in Conceptualizations of Godly Love   77

PAUL ALEXANDER

## Five
### Testing Creaturely Love and God's Causal Role   94

THOMAS JAY OORD

PART II—SOCIAL SCIENCE AND GODLY LOVE

Six

**Methodological Agnosticism for the Social Sciences?**
*Lessons from Sorokin's and James's Allusions to Psychoanalysis,*
*Mysticism, and Godly Love*    121
RALPH W. HOOD JR.

Seven

**Godly Love from the Perspective of Psychology**    141
JULIE J. EXLINE

Eight

**Sociology, Philosophy, and the Empirical Study of Godly Love**    157
MARGARET M. POLOMA

Nine

**Socialization, Empirical Studies, and Godly Love**
*A Case Study in Survey Research*    183
MARK J. CARTLEDGE

Ten

**Toward a Grounded Theory of Godly Love**
*Latino/a Pentecostals*    200
ARLENE SÁNCHEZ WALSH

**Conclusion**    217
AMOS YONG

**Contributors**    233
**Index**    235

# *The* Science *and* Theology *of*
# Godly Love

# INTRODUCTION

*MATTHEW T. LEE, MARGARET M. POLOMA,*

*AND STEPHEN G. POST*

"He makes his angels winds, his servants flames of fire."
—Hebrews 1:7 (NIV 1984)

"Saints live *in* flames; wise men, next to them."
—E. M. Cioran, *Tears and Saints*[1]

The topics of religious experience and benevolence are endlessly fascinating and complex by themselves, but when they are combined, the complexity of the subject matter increases exponentially. The authors have been studying these topics for decades, from scientific, theological, and philosophical standpoints. Every answer seems to reveal even more questions. At times, one might wonder about the wisdom of *studying* such phenomena at all, because they cannot be fully understood cerebrally—at arm's length. This might be one reason why so much scholarship on the topic is reductionistic, attempting to "explain away" the connections between religious experience and benevolence by pointing to psychological neuroses at the individual level or collective effervescence at the social level.[2] If benevolent servants of God are indeed "flames of fire," as the first quote from our epigraph suggests, then it is easy to see why the "wise" might prefer to keep their distance for fear of getting burned themselves.

It is also easy to see how this distance might be fatal to the effort to truly understand how and why religious experience and benevolence are related. One way that scholars have kept their distance is by operating within their own academic silos, ignorant of the conceptual frameworks and methodological approaches that comprise the wider intellectual landscape. This well-worn lament provides the impetus for the collection of theological, interdisciplinary, and methodological essays found in this book. If social scientists refuse to take theology seriously in developing their methodologies, then it should come as little surprise when poorly designed studies find that religious experience and benevolence are not related, that some other variable actually accounts for the apparent relationship. And if theologians are uninterested in what empirical study has revealed about how ordinary people actually experience religion, it is easy to see why some theological traditions have become irrelevant in many social circles—not just secular ones but religious as well.

All of the contributors to this book have benefited from contact with scholars on the other disciplinary shore of the science/theology divide. In a precursor to the current volume, sociologists Matthew T. Lee and Margaret M. Poloma have promoted psychologists Peter Hampson and Eolene Boyd-MacMillan's notion of "hospitality" between science and theology as a way to "move beyond the relativism of particularistic truth claims of individual disciplines."[3] But even this seemingly innocuous stance is not without controversy, and a lack of hospitality has led to missed opportunities for deeper understanding.

In the final analysis, what is needed is that all-too-rare virtue of humility and its intellectual counterpart, open-mindedness. The very structure of our scholarly institutions seems to work against these ideals, as scholars compete to get their pet ideas accepted while denigrating the work of others in a zero-sum game that can be anything but hospitable. Just as individuals struggle for dominance in a particular field, so do disciplines attempt to declare themselves preeminent and silence the voices of competing fields of study.

This book grew out of an attempt to move beyond such barriers. This does not mean that the authors have decided to change their disciplinary address, but rather that they have been humble enough to listen to others and open-minded enough to learn something new. The subject matter requires this willingness. The religious experience/benevolence nexus transcends artificial academic boundaries that seek to divide fluid realities into more manageable dichotomies like natural/supernatural, micro/macro, cognition/emotion, or altruism/egoism. Such distinctions can be useful at times for limited purposes, but the map is not the terrain.

At an early stage in the conversation to design a set of integrated, interdisciplinary research studies that eventually became known as the Flame of Love Project, theologian Stephen G. Post posed a foundational question to Matthew T. Lee and Margaret M. Poloma: "To what extent can emotionally powerful experiences of a 'divine flame of love' move us beyond our ordinary self-interests and help us express unconditional, unlimited love for all others, especially when our human capacities seem to reach their limits?" To begin working on an answer—and a single definitive answer is unlikely—these three scholars secured funding from the John Templeton Foundation and convened a group of twenty-two eminent social scientists and theologians to conduct a multifaceted four-year investigation. This involved the creation of a think tank that met biannually to direct the project and reflect on findings; a national study of altruistic exemplars in the broadly defined pentecostal tradition based on qualitative, face-to-face interviews; a national telephone survey of a random sample of American adults (including both the religious and the nonreligious); five major subprojects, each codirected by a social scientist and a theologian, some of which limited data collection to the United States, while others included international research sites; an intensive, two-week summer reading seminar at Calvin College in 2009 focused on our core concept; a public seminar offered for college credit in 2010 at Vanguard University of Southern California; and a series of writing projects. Our goal was to build a new field of study around the core concept of Godly love. Drawing on Poloma's earlier work (with social psychologist Ralph Hood), Godly love is defined as *the dynamic interaction between divine and human love that enlivens and expands benevolence*.[4]

This volume is a central part of the initial phase of this field-building exercise. Coedited by a social scientist and a theologian, this work serves as an introduction to a new field of study as well as a call for further research. It presents ten methodological perspectives on the study of Godly love written by leading social scientists or theologians involved in the inaugural phase of the Flame of Love Project. The editors have attempted to involve social science and theology in an interdisciplinary dialogue that will advance the study of Godly love. They have therefore selected both social scientists and theologians as contributors. The charge to the authors was to present material from their specific disciplines that might inform the interdisciplinary study of Godly love. They each describe a line of scholarship in their chosen discipline—and often draw on multiple disciplines—and relate this work to the topic of Godly love.

The initial grant proposal for the Flame of Love Project offered a comparative analysis of the Abrahamic faiths. But during the proposal review process, the authors were advised that the first stage of the project should focus on one of the faiths, to more deeply understand Godly love within a single tradition before branching out. The decision was clear: begin the study with Christianity—and particularly with its "Great Commandment" to love God and love neighbor as self—and save Islam and Judaism for a future phase. Christianity is obviously quite diverse, so to get a foothold our initial project focused on the pentecostal/charismatic tradition (broadly defined as "spirit-filled" Christianity, given its emphasis on supernatural activity and being filled with the Holy Spirit), in part because Poloma's foundational work on Godly love grew out of research on a neopentecostal group. But there is no reason to limit the study of Godly love to Christianity, and there is every reason to believe that including the Abrahamic faiths and beyond will enrich our understanding of the relationship between religious experience and benevolence. Indeed, our national telephone survey conducted in 2009 was based on a nationally representative, randomly selected sample of American adults from all religious backgrounds, including those who claim no religion at all. Some of the chapters in this book reflect our initial focus on pentecostalism—Yong, for example, is a pentecostal theologian and his concluding chapter reflects this standpoint—but others address groups such as Catholics, or Christians in general. The general issues each chapter raises about Godly love have broad applications.

### The Diamond Model of Godly Love

Over the years the authors and others participating in the Flame of Love Project have received much constructive criticism regarding our organizing concept. For example, our attempt to clarify that the reference to "divine love" in our definition involves a claim about human perception rather than ontological reality has upset some theologians who would not add this qualifier. On the other hand, some social scientists remain concerned about any reference to the divine. But the concept of Godly love has proven quite helpful in *providing a framework for a dialogue* among various branches of social science and theology, which often seem to have a difficult time speaking to each other. It has had great appeal to laypersons and scholars alike, thanks to its simplicity and connection with the well-known Great Commandment. The concept is actually just a starting point, to be developed and refined through empirical analysis and theological reflection. It is not an ideology that must be uncritically accepted, as the chapters of this book illustrate.

An earlier work developed an initial visual representation of the interactions involved in Godly love in order to clarify the meaning of the concept. This helpful illustration of the dynamic and interactional nature of the concept includes the key perceived interactions (see fig. 1). This conception is

FIGURE 1—The Diamond Model of Godly Love

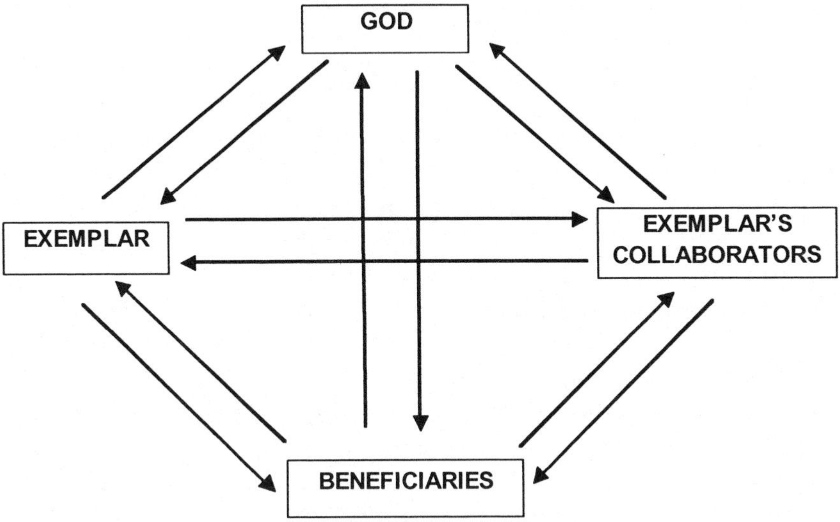

```
                    ┌──────────┐
                    │   GOD    │
                    └──────────┘


  ┌──────────┐                      ┌──────────────────┐
  │ EXEMPLAR │                      │   EXEMPLAR'S     │
  │          │                      │  COLLABORATORS   │
  └──────────┘                      └──────────────────┘


                ┌──────────────────┐
                │  BENEFICIARIES   │
                └──────────────────┘
```

premised on the existence of "exemplars" of Godly love—people who have lived out the Great Commandment to an unusual degree and have been recognized by their community for their benevolent acts. An exemplar of Godly love is the "flame of fire" mentioned in the epigraph. Researchers funded by the Flame of Love Project have interviewed over two hundred such people across the United States and throughout the world—as well as their collaborators, many of whom serve as exemplars in their own social networks. Their ability to persevere in a life of altruism despite substantial trials and tribulations (sometimes involving mortal danger) is inspiring. Regardless of financial setbacks, deteriorating personal health, impossible odds, or  repeated failures, these "flames of fire" have persevered in what they perceive to be a divine calling to serve others. Some of the difficulties Flame of Love Project interviewees experienced include contracting a life-threatening illness in a developing nation, watching an orphaned infant die in one's arms for lack of milk, working in situations involving extreme suffering, being abducted by a paramilitary group, and various kinds of financial collapse. What keeps them going in the face of such circumstances?

As displayed in the figure, an exemplar may draw strength and empowerment from a number of interactional partners, including God. In fact, our research has suggested that positive interactions with a loving God are essential to preventing burnout or other reasons for desisting from a life of altruism, for at least some people. These interactions are the foundation of a process of learning to see beyond material circumstances.[5] This is not to suggest that the religious have a monopoly on the ability to ignore overwhelming life conditions in the service of a cause. But it is at least conceivable that a loving relationship with God could serve as a resource in times of trial. In other words, no matter how bad existing conditions might be, Godly love exemplars may "know" in their heart that God's plan will come to fruition in the future and that their purpose is to help fulfill this plan regardless of the personal cost. As one of our interviewees put it: "The moment I met Jesus I was ruined. My life was not my own. Once you see Him, there is no turning back. I have seen His eyes. Now I can never turn away. If we die, we die for Him; if we live, we live for Him."[6] This sense of meaning and purpose transcends ordinary concerns about physical or emotional well-being and financial security.

God occupies a separate box in the Diamond Model, indicating that for the exemplar, and possibly the collaborators and beneficiaries, God is perceived to be an actually existing partner in interactions. Our national survey demonstrated that God is indeed a "significant other" for most people, not just exemplars. The arrows in figure 1 indicate that interactions potentially flow in two directions. Any of the individuals represented in the lower triangle of this "diamond" model can interact with God, for example, by treating God as the object of their love (possibly in terms of adoration), but also by being the beneficiary of God's love. An exemplar may pray to God (represented by the left arrow from exemplar to God), and God may respond (represented by the right arrow). In the fully specified model, all participants are involved in two-way interactions. In this ideal case, exemplars are involved in two-way interactions with God, collaborators, and beneficiaries, and this is likely to lead to much more effective forms of benevolence than would be the case if some of these interactions were one-way or absent entirely. This raises intriguing empirical questions. For example, do exemplars who "go it alone" without the help of human collaborators experience limited effectiveness and higher rates of burnout? Similarly, are those who are not involved in give-and-take relationships with beneficiaries less likely to meet the needs of those they claim to serve, and do they instead impose "solutions" that are neither helpful nor appreciated? These are the kinds of observations and concomitant questions that have emerged over the course of the Flame of Love Project.

The strength of interactions can be depicted with different kinds of arrows connecting the boxes (e.g., a thick arrow for particularly strong interactions, a dotted line for marginal interactions). Lines can be removed to indicate the absence of interactions at a particular point in time. For example, one of our exemplars experienced a "spiritual darkness" during which he perceived no interactions with God. Regardless of whether God was "really" interacting with him during this time, his perception was that no interaction was taking place. Therefore, the model would show no lines between the exemplar and God. During this time he was also involved in no benevolent service (beyond the normal and expected types of prosocial behavior required for human interaction), so those lines were also removed. Importantly, in an earlier phase of his life he experienced strong interactions with God but was not involved in the benevolence that resulted in his identification as an "exemplar." In this case, the lines at the top of the Diamond Model were present, but the lines at the bottom were absent. This illustrates how the experience of Godly love varies over time within a single life. The model provides a visual representation that is helpful for thinking about the importance of different kinds of interactions over the life course.[7] The diamond shape is a starting point, but the concept of Godly love is flexible enough to allow for other conceptualizations.[8]

One important conversation that has emerged from reflection on the Diamond Model concerns the image of God, and whether God should be placed in a box at all, which suggests separateness, as opposed to serving as the ground of being or creator/sustainer of life. Theologian Paul Alexander prefers keeping the box to represent God's immanence, but also using a large circle representing God's transcendence in a way that encompasses the entire Diamond Model. In chapter 4, Paul Alexander also makes a case for a nonviolent God. He argues that if "benevolent" service to others uses violence as a means, it cannot be properly called "Godly love," because God is not violent and does not encourage violence. This is an interesting and important issue. The empirical research for the broader Flame of Love Project did not include this explicit limitation, but Alexander's theological work leads to an important empirical question in his chapter: "Would social scientific research discern significant differences between those who perceive God as consistently nonviolent and never supportive of human violence and those who conceptualize God both as capable of violence and occasionally supportive of human violence?"

This is one example of how social science can seek answers to important theological questions. Alexander concludes: ". . . perhaps conceptualizing Godly love as nonviolent action can encourage human nonviolent action for peace with justice because when one acts, even sacrifices, for the good of others one can know that such action corresponds to and is empowered by the very nature of the creator and sustainer of all universes."

In other words, the image of God is important, and Godly love research must pay explicit attention to this issue. In chapter 10, religious studies professor Arlene Sánchez Walsh reminds us that the experience of Godly love is culturally conditioned, with some groups having intense, emotional interactions with God and others having more cognitive "interactions." For example, one group of Latino/a pentecostals that she studied has had powerful emotional experiences of a personal God, which motivated community service rather than social justice expressions of benevolence. A very different group of Latino/a pentecostals have focused on social justice advocacy instead of community service and lacked the strong emotional experience of a personal God. Walsh writes:

> The narrative quality that often comprises people's religious lives is missing, and therefore the common response when one thinks of Godly love—of a transcendent moment where the divine radically alters the way one's life is going, a narrative that Christianity has relied on for over two millennia—is absent. . . . If we are to truly say Godly love is experienced differently among different groups of people, then the results of that Godly love may be expressed differently and possibly arrived at without the dramatic effects of a Damascus-like encounter with God.

In the end the Diamond Model of Godly love can accommodate these two groups of Latino/as. The social meaning of the phrase "relationship with God" is very different, and the nature of the perceived interaction with God is also very different, but there is still something there in both cases that can be called an interaction. Taking these interactions seriously—and the authors suggest that the concept of Godly love does this effectively and flexibly—will help us better understand the relationship between religious experience and benevolent service to others.

As our discussion suggests, the Flame of Love Project began within a particular theological tradition, which assumed a specific image of God: the Christian "God of love" who is knowable through emotionally and affectively moving encounters. This is not the Neoplatonic image of an impassive "unmoved mover" that was so prominent for much of the history of Christianity.[9] Rather, this is a God that suffers with creation and desires personal relationship. It is more appropriate to speak of "theologies" rather than theology, and—recognizing that others may disagree—the authors of this introduction, as well as the editors of this book, have decided that the best approach is to situate our project within the work of a particular theological tradition.[10] Our interviewees do claim to have experienced the God of love, but many also were quite familiar with the God of wrath—particularly in childhood. But almost without exception, their understanding shifted throughout their life course from the image of a judgmental God to that of a loving God, just as theology made this shift more generally over the twentieth century.

Thus, at the broadest level the theological tradition that provided the starting point for the Flame of Love Project is grounded in the principle articulated by sociologist Christian Smith that the "center and sustainer of all reality is a thoroughly loving God. God is Love."[11] This is a personal God who is a significant actor in the daily lives of many contemporary Christian believers and reflects the *lived religion of experience*, rather than simply *adherence to a system of belief* or a collection of doctrines. Similarly, in the book that gave the Flame of Love Project its name, evangelical charismatic theologian Clark Pinnock wrote of the Holy Spirit and love within a Trinitarian framework as one and the same: "If Father points to ultimate reality and Son supplies the clue to the divine mystery, Spirit epitomizes the nearness of the power and presence of God. St. John of the Cross (b. 1542) aptly calls the Spirit a living flame of love and celebrates the nimble, responsive, playful, personal gift of God."[12]

Sadly, after serving on our research team from the time of our first formal meeting, Clark Pinnock passed away in 2010 while the chapters for this book were being compiled, and his chapter was never finished. Pinnock's scholarly legacy is a wealth of theological wisdom that continues to inspire and influence research and reflection on Godly love. Following theologian Jürgen Moltmann's argument that "Spirit is the loving, self-communicating, out-fanning and out-pouring presence of the eternal divine love of the triune God," Pinnock sought to bring the Holy Spirit back from the margins of the church and recover a more experiential form of spirituality.[13] Insofar as the Holy Spirit has been neglected or suppressed, Pinnock argued, so also has the celebratory experience of unlimited love as a lively divine gift. The experience has an ineffable quality that is felt through the heart, and is more a source of transformation than information.

This is the image that the project started with, but the concept of Godly love, and the Diamond Model, can easily accommodate other images—even the Neoplatonic God of the previous era. Yet should a concept like Godly love have any a priori normative foundations? This is ultimately a theological question, not a scientific one. Godly love is not just about altruism or benevolence; it includes God as a perceived interaction partner. So it makes a great deal of sense for us to pay close attention to what theologians have had to say about God and religious experience, as well as how ordinary people understand and experience God. Perhaps a better question might be, What difference does it make in terms of benevolence to start with a particular normative foundation? Is this helpful in terms of fostering understanding, or does it produce blind spots that hinder reaching this goal? One response is to point out that neither the Diamond Model nor the definition of Godly love itself precludes the use of any particular image of God, theological perspective, or normative foundation. The project drew inspiration from Pinnock's theology, as well as the work of pentecostal theologian Frank Macchia, but this was simply a starting point that enabled us to explore a particular kind of experience of Godly love.[14]

The Flame of Love Project quickly expanded to include other standpoints. It has not gone far enough at this point, but the authors welcome the work of others who use different lenses. This book provides a set of resources for scholars who wish to take up this call. How exactly do Muslims, Jews, Hindus, Buddhists, or members of other traditions experience "divine love," and what impact does this have on their benevolence to others? Which pathways in the Diamond Model are the most important for each group, and how does the nature of the interactions represented in this model vary?

## Overview of the Book

All of the contributors to this volume took the concept of Godly love and the Diamond Model seriously as they reflected on the content in their individual chapters. Some of the essays are truly interdisciplinary, while others are more specific to one discipline. But regardless of the home discipline, all of the chapters make an important contribution to the study of religious experience and benevolence. The first part of the book presents five essays written by theologians, and the second part contains five essays authored by social scientists.

The first five essays raise questions that have implications beyond theology. Is Godly love essential to human well-being and possibly even survival (Stephen Post's chapter 1)? Does Godly love require self-sacrifice or mutuality (Michael McClymond's chapter 2), self-emptying (Peter Althouse's chapter 3), or nonviolence (Paul Alexander's chapter 4)? How are we to understand the causal role of God in human behavior (Thomas Oord's chapter 5)? How we answer these questions will shape the direction of future work, both empirical and theological.

Turning to the social science essays, what is the consequence of studying Godly love within the strictures of methodological atheism, and what are the alternative possibilities (Ralph Hood's chapter 6)? How might we study Godly love using the methods of psychology (Julie Exline's chapter 7) or survey research (Mark Cartledge's chapter 9)? How might sociology and philosophy move the study of Godly love forward by directing attention to different—and perhaps competing—"faces" or "dimensions" of love (Margaret Poloma's chapter 8)? How is our understanding of Godly love impoverished by lack of attention to important group differences, for example the standpoints and experiences of different groups of Latino/a pentecostals (Arlene Sánchez Walsh's chapter 10)? And, finally, stepping back to engage the chapters of this volume all together, what are the real possibilities for the dialogue between social science and theology on these issues (Amos Yong's conclusion)?

All the essays in this book raise issues that deserve sustained reflection by anyone with a specific interest in the new field of study built around the concept of Godly love. But the essays will also reward those with more general interests in religious experience, benevolence, the relationship between the two, or the possibility of dialogue between theology and social science. Our experience over the last four years in studying Godly love with nineteen other scholars associated with the Flame of Love Project has convinced us that this interdisciplinary dialogue is both possible and essential to fully appreciating the topic. This is not to suggest that the conversation is devoid of disagreement (compare the very different understandings of the meaning of motivation in chapters 5 and 7).[15] And although few social scientists will accept Thomas Oord's proposition that we can infer the existence of divine causes by observing human action, there is much in his essay that will interest both social scientists and theologians who have an interest in understanding the different ways in which theologians conceptualize such causal mechanisms.

As Arlene Sánchez Walsh notes in her essay, the study of Godly love "cannot be conducted in a vacuum." Social scientists must carefully attend to the work of theologians or risk missing the meaning of the social behaviors they seek to understand. Similarly, theologians must move beyond the official theologies of scholars and churches to understand the lived theologies of ordinary people as revealed in social scientific studies. These are often divergent. The theological, interdisciplinary, and methodological essays in this book remind us that no single standpoint is likely to be able to capture a topic as complex as Godly love. But if we are humble enough to extend hospitality to others with different standpoints, we will be in a much better position to appreciate and value this complexity.

## Notes

The three authors of this introduction serve as co-principal investigators for the Flame of Love Research Project, which provided the impetus for the essays in this book. The project was funded by the John Templeton Foundation. To its great credit, the Templeton Foundation continues to see the value of having a serious dialogue between science and theology and has sponsored projects, like ours, that otherwise would not receive funding. Points of view expressed in this book do not necessarily represent those of the foundation. The authors thank Amos Yong for helpful comments on an earlier version. Some of the material in this introduction has been adapted with permission from Matthew T. Lee and Margaret M. Poloma, *A Sociological Study of the Great Commandment in Pentecostalism: The Practice of Godly Love as Benevolent Service* (Lewiston, NY: Edwin Mellen Press, 2009).

1. E. M. Cioran, *Tears and Saints* (Chicago: University of Chicago Press, 1995), 14.

2. Lee and Poloma, *A Sociological Study of the Great Commandment in Pentecostalism*, ch. 1.

3. Ibid., 57.

4. Margaret M. Poloma and Ralph W. Hood Jr., *Blood and Fire: Godly Love in a Pentecostal Emerging Church* (New York: New York University Press, 2008), 8. See also Margaret M. Poloma and John C. Green, *The Assemblies of God: Godly Love and the Revitalization of American Pentecostalism* (New York: New York University Press, 2010).

5. Lee and Poloma, *Sociological Study of the Great Commandment*, 88.

6. Heidi Baker, *Compelled by Love: How to Change the World through the Simple Power of Love in Action* (Lake Mary, FL: Charisma House, 2008), 124.

7. These models are displayed in Lee and Poloma, *Sociological Study of the Great Commandment*, 117.

8. For an extended discussion of these possibilities, see the video recording of a presentation by Matthew T. Lee titled, "The Diamond Model of Godly Love," given at Vanguard University of Southern California on October 22, 2010. This presentation was part of the public seminar featuring the work of the Flame of Love Project titled, "The Great Commandment: Theology & Social Science in Dialogue." This video, along with the rest of the seminar, can be downloaded at http://itunes.apple.com/us/podcast/the-great-commandment-theology/id404915128.

9. Theologian Frank D. Macchia has referred to the shift from the image of an impassive, distant God to a loving and suffering God as one of the major theological revolutions of the twentieth century. He delivered a public presentation on this subject on July 22, 2009, as part of the Flame of Love Project's summer reading seminar at Calvin College. The title of his talk was, "The God behind *The Shack*: Recent Revolutions in the Theology of God," which references the popular Christian novel *The Shack* by W. Paul Young. This novel provides a vivid description of the loving and suffering God at the heart of this theological revolution.

10. Ronald J. McAllister, "Theology Lessons for Sociology," in *Religious Sociology: Interfaces and Boundaries*, ed. William H. Swatos Jr. (New York: Greenwood, 1987), 27–39, at 33.

11. Christian Smith, "Why Christianity Works: An Emotions-Focused Phenomenological Account," *Sociology of Religion* 68 (2007):165–78, at 171.

12. Clark Pinnock, *Flame of Love: A Theology of the Holy Spirit* (Downers Grove, IL: InterVarsity Press Academic, 1996), 9.

13. Jürgen Moltmann, *The Spirit of Life: A Universal Affirmation*, trans. Margaret Kohl (Minneapolis: Fortress Press, 1992), 289.

14. Frank D. Macchia, *Baptized in the Spirit: A Global Pentecostal Theology* (Grand Rapids, MI: Zondervan, 2006).

15. Thomas Oord's theological chapter argues that individuals are in touch with the real motives for their behavior; Julie Exline's chapter suggests that psychological research has discovered that this is not the case.

# Part I

Theology and Godly Love

# GODLY LOVE

## Why We Cannot Endure without It

### STEPHEN G. POST

Adherents of the Abrahamic traditions self-report experiences of God's love, but these experiences do not necessarily inspire the powerful universal benevolence that characterizes agents of "Godly love" who have truly been shaped and formed by such experiences. Those who achieve Godly love demonstrate this in activities beyond tribal insularities as they engage in the impassioned service of *all humanity without exception*—what is commonly referred to in the context of the American civil rights movement as "the Beloved Community." Experiences of monotheism at their best undermine the deification of family, tribe, ruler, class, race, fellow believers, and all things that are obstacles to universal benevolence when they are afforded absolute rather than relative value. Moral genius emerges from the spirituality of God's love when it explodes through human in-group tendencies to an affirmation of a shared humanity, sentient life itself, and our generative planet Earth.

When the dynamic expansion to universal benevolence occurs, we bear witness to "Godly love," which is God's love deeply and enduringly interwoven with the somewhat recalcitrant substrate of evolved human nature so as to enable activities consistent with the Beloved Community. This dynamic is visible in the exemplary lives of those who manifest highly creative self-giving love with no concern for reciprocal gain, reputational benefits, or even inner satisfaction—though the latter seems an inevitable by-product that should be welcomed as such. God's love is often described as an invisible emotional energy that can be seen only in the lives of those who actively manifest Godly love. We know them by their fruits.

We urge the study of Godly love across the Abrahamic traditions because of what is at stake when Godly love is distorted and exacerbates conflict. To encourage such study, we deploy and elaborate on Sorokin's social scientific approach, because of its helpfulness in conceptualizing Godly love and associated rituals that allow for its optimal expressions.

## The Filters of Destruction

This expansive dynamic can be inhibited, misdirected, or perverted by theologies that deny moral status and the protective umbrella of "do no harm" to some segment of humanity, especially when such theologies are buttressed by hierarchical pressures and rituals of exclusivity. The results will be reliably destructive. Much of modern political history in the Abrahamic nations of the world has been shaped by spiritually impassioned individuals who, in God's name and with love-of-a-sort in their hearts, assassinate leaders who affirm the Beloved Community. From Gandhi to Rabin, great spiritual universalists have been eradicated by religious zealots for whom the idea of the Beloved Community is deemed a threat. Let us acknowledge that much evil has been done by those who, while sometimes deeply inspired by faith and religious experience, have little sense of the universality of God's love, however genuinely experienced. The spirituality of God's love can be intensely destructive when distorted by poor teachings or manipulated by hate mongers. This is why many people embrace the treatises of neo-atheism and wait for a world where there will be no religions. Clearly, the world needs religions-at-their-best in order to shape the spiritual experience of God's love in directions that are beneficial rather than harmful. Many will remain ambivalent or decidedly hostile toward religions, because these varied manifestations of organized spirituality can bring out the very worst in people as well as the very best.

The ultimate purpose of the Abrahamic faiths is to transform the emotional and spiritual energy of experiences of God's love into Godly love on the interpersonal and intersocietal levels. The violation of this purpose through teachings and rituals that encourage something less than universal love, especially when accompanied by hostile views of outsiders, is the seedbed of a great deal of the most rampant evil in the world. Destructive religions are not worth having, but religions both destructive and creative are a permanent and essential feature of human experience. Therefore, our focus must be on those aspects of religions that help transpose God's love into Godly love.

God's love is often described as absolutely unlimited in its inclusiveness, and therefore as extending the circles of insularity. The question is how we can more often experience this love in such a way that it deeply interweaves with our limited human capacities and drives us toward the Beloved Community, rather than away from it. We are of course always finite creatures bounded by time and space, so in the strictest sense we can never fully express Godly love. Also, we generally need communities that allow us to form self-identity in particularity. But we can interact with all those we encounter in a way that is inclusive and benevolent, and we can have an activist vision when it comes to healing the world wherever we happen to be.

A self-reported experience of God's love may be inauthentic and even feigned, or it may be genuine but distorted by human fallibility and fault. It cannot be a simple matter for God to continue to love humankind. Each generation violates the command of love in all possible ways. People whom God has inspired and in whom much divine trust is placed through experiences of God's calling routinely give way to distractions that divert them from what they know are divine intentions. Temptations abound in the forms of materialism, the abuse of power, infidelity, sloth, and greed. We all know of spiritual leaders who, inspired by moving experiences of God's love to devote their lives to their religious vocations, ended up abusing children in scandals that rock the very church that serves as the great traditional repository of mysticism and sainthood. We know that callings are abandoned and covenants broken. No wonder that by biblical accounts, an essentially loving God gets frustrated and angry with us all. Thus did the Protestant reformers eschew all perfectionism in Christian ethics and see the divine command to love as an indictment that would spur us to the confession of sins. In this they were following the lead of St. Paul, and they found a friend in St. Augustine.

So what of the Osama bin Ladens of the world? In his case, a wealthy secular youth who enjoyed a rather wild life came to experience Allah in a way that clearly transformed his life in a spiritual-religious direction. Regrettably, what may have been a calling to real Godly love was distorted and twisted by a brand of Islamic fundamentalism that easily teaches the annihilation of those who do not accept its view of God's purposes. This influence, along with the acculturation to violence in the Afghan conflict with the Soviet Union, left bin Laden hopelessly caught up in a life of wanton destruction. How many Islamic terrorists, had they had just a single non-parent mentor in youth who modeled and taught Godly love and the Beloved Community, would have lived exemplary lives of healing peace?

Human beings are especially malleable in these youthful years, and they make every imaginable desperate detour in growing up. They are so easily influenced by new ideas and people. Had circumstances been just a little different, they might have encountered just the right person to turn their lives in the direction of Godly love. So it is that the self-reported experience of God's love is actually quite susceptible to distortion.

## Why Godly Love Matters

The future of humanity is inextricably bound up with Godly love. Neither secularism nor fundamentalism can move us forward in a salutary direction. The former fails to recognize the perennial human need to find meaning in something beyond the human from which our value is bestowed, while the latter tends to exacerbate religious arrogance and demonize those who believe differently. Human prospects for a better future are tied up with Godly love—that is, with the successful transposition of God's love to human actions of universal benevolence. There is no other option that is so pervasive and motivationally powerful.

Reason alone can result in good, but the twentieth-century experiment with secular rationality was one in which every kind of demonic tyrant tried to fill the void of Godlessness, as did the religion of science. It is commonly said, "When God goes, the half-gods arrive." Secularism does not fill "the God-shaped hole" in the human heart, and it leaves inner emptiness in its wake. On the other hand, fundamentalism in each Abrahamic tradition results in such radical exclusion of those who believe differently than those in "my" tradition that there is no firm basis for peace in the world. Many a good committed Christian theologian has been excoriated by Christian fundamentalists for simply acknowledging that there may be some good in other faith traditions.

Believers in all faiths need to take the idea of God as love seriously. We think of the power of God and wage wars in God's name. We think up definitions of God that, even if inspired, are still products of the human mind and fail to make love central. When religions have put doctrine and force above love, they have created a history of massive evil from torture to terror, from coercion to conflict. Religious wars have been manifestations of a human tribalism and arrogance that brings out the worst in us. We forget that God is love, and we glorify our violence.

There is absolutely no substitute for a return to the deeper arc of God's love in the Abrahamic traditions. This love, when effective in our lives, gives rise to social change through the active affirmation of the dignity and worth of all human beings without exception. *Dignity* comes from the

Latin word for "worth." The psalmist wrote that man is "just a little lower than the angels" in the divine hierarchy of being. Dignity is about the nobility, majesty, wonder, and greatness of each human being in relation to God's love, despite degrees of decline, frailty, and mortality. Such dignity arises directly from the assertion that we human creatures are all within the special concern of God's love. These days we hear speeches about this dignity, but not about why we have it. When we manifest Godly love our dignity is at its very highest. All sustainable human hope rests in Godly love—in God's love overcoming human obstacles so as to become active in the Beloved Community.

Hatred, hostility, and revenge are emotions strong enough to overwhelm our deeper sense of Godly love. The pseudo-spirituality of hatred is contrary to all genuine spirituality, which is always an adventure in love. The love of power can sometimes overwhelm the power of love, so we must be humble and on guard to prevent this. How little we know about God, but we can still experience God's love. Most of religion and spirituality lies in rightly inspired healing emotions. The world will never know sustained peace in the twenty-first century without all religions living up to their inherent ideals of a Godly love that applies to all humankind without exception. Only by taking God's love much more seriously than we do—even to the point of a profound love of ancient enemies—can we expect to avoid increasing destruction.

### The Crisis of Our Time

Each of the Abrahamic faith traditions offers guidance on how we may grow toward identifying with a shared humanity rather than a mere fragment thereof, and on how each of us may come to see ourselves in the other; each tradition at its best seeks to shape a normative religious experience that guides its adherents toward recognition of a common humanity with believers on different spiritual paths. However, each tradition also contains restrictive elements that focus in a purely insular direction that may devalue or demonize nonadherents. We do not assume that the Abrahamic traditions are identical in this regard. Yet each tradition can enunciate its commitment to love of a shared humanity more vividly and can be enhanced in the practice of such extensive love through the nascent interventions that we hope to develop.

This theme of love for humankind is present in the sacred writings and the ideals of all the Abrahamic religions. To a significant degree, however, these great traditions have struggled to maintain their relevance, especially as secularism has partly eroded their confidence in the sacred.

The spiritual void left behind has found potent spiritualities anxious to fill the lacuna in a rising tide of fundamentalism, which has had a marked tendency toward an arrogant, narrow absolutism. The glorification of a favored identity (e.g., election, salvation) has made fundamentalism vulnerable to reifying the "otherness" of outsiders. This distorts the messages of love, unity, justice, compassion, kindness, and mercy that lie at the core of the great Abrahamic traditions.

Of course, tribalism is not something that we question in its constructive form. The Abrahamic faith traditions are keenly cognizant of, and defined by, notions of peoplehood or nationhood. It does not serve to lay indirect blame for the crisis of our age at the feet of a generic tribalism. Common sense calls us to delineate the morally functional and dysfunctional, the good and the bad, in ritually bounded and supernaturally sanctioned communities. The members of tribal clans live in relationship with each other not primarily on account of shared kinship but due to mutual affiliation with totemic entities, including beliefs, that defines the associative relations as sacred. These tribalisms are functional—they serve to reaffirm and elevate the holiness of a people and thus ideally inspire and enable greater and more successful acts of communal and worldly service to exemplify that holiness.

By contrast, the tribalism that loses sight of a shared humanity is prone to moral dysfunction. The tribal instinct as manifested within contemporary religious fundamentalists is not so much about affirming or elevating one's own holiness or sacred status for instrumental purposes as about judging and distancing oneself from otherness. The "other" is stigmatized, condemned, and avoided like the plague—and left to its reward in hell. In the contemporary world, systems of political economy have been used by fundamentalists in attempts to marginalize and even criminalize the "other."

This runs counter to the founding principles of the Abrahamic religions. Instead of engendering withdrawal within our tribal borders or, alternatively, militant reaction, our contacts with the "other" can present challenges of learning and growth. We can come to see in our brothers and sisters distinct reflections of our mutual oneness that perhaps we cannot see through our own cultural lenses. Engaging the divine in our fellow beings thus presents opportunities to better recognize our own divine nature. The enemy of progress is not tribalism per se, but rather the exploitation of tribalistic impulses dormant in respective religious traditions in order to marginalize, condemn, and attack other tribes, rather than to achieve allophilia.

If we are to survive as a species, perhaps even as a living planet, then our actions and those of our leaders and institutions must be guided by an ethic of mutual respect and love. This respect and love must extend to all humans and replace the predominant ethic, which defines social relations, local and global, in terms of concepts such as power, control, competition, possession, and dominance. In other words, the Abrahamic traditions need to take the vision of a God of unlimited love that defines them at their best with utmost seriousness.

In a time when inter-religious rage, fragmentation, and violence among the three Abrahamic faith traditions are so visible in our world, rethinking Godly love is critical to the human future. When Zionists step on Palestinians, when Islamic extremists set about the task of destroying infidels, or when Christianity fails to respond to "the Jewish problem" in Nazi Germany, we realize that at their worst religions can blind us to the plight of those who believe differently than we do, despite all the dynamics of God's love.

We eschew the secular assumption that people in these traditions can or should take off their particular religious identities like clothes removed before a shower. The enlightened modernist may think in such terms, but most human beings around the world define themselves—their core identity, their values, their ultimate commitments—in terms of faiths that are absolutely essential. We take seriously what William James termed the "will to believe." So our task is to study and enhance the universal of love for all people without exception—the Beloved Community—through the windows of Abrahamic religious particularities.

## Exemplars of Godly Love

Before going further, let us capture a representative model of Godly love. God's love can never be fully implemented by a human creature, because we are finite and it is infinite. Thus, many who report on the experience of God's love refer to the notion of vocation, to some special task that they have been called on to pursue in love. They have received a "call" to love some particular constituency of the neediest, and they try to live out their lives accordingly.

In October 1999 the Institute for Research on Unlimited Love (www. unlimitedloveinstitute.com) was beginning to take shape through a conference convened in Cambridge, Massachusetts. Among the leading lights of Godly love who have been invited to speak through the institute about their lives was the remarkable Templeton laureate Dame Cicely Saunders, then 83 years of age, and known all over the world as the creator and founder of the hospice movement. Indeed, she took the name *hospice* from the medieval notion of a place where wayfarers might spend the night; and as she viewed dying as a journey, Dame Cicely first applied the word in the modern sense of a safe haven where people can die in love and grace, and without a tube in every orifice natural and unnatural. Dame Cicely, who flew in from St. Christopher's Hospice in London, began her dinner plenary address by stating that her entire life's work was guided by God and by her experience of divine love, however much the standard professional textbooks manage to leave this out. Indeed, Christian bookstores in England sometimes have entire sections on Dame Cicely, who gained nursing and medical degrees in the process of building up her credibility for a single task—that of enabling people who are dying to experience a sense of significance. No, they are not beyond "care" simply because they are dying, nor need they be warehoused in dehumanizing and depersonalizing highly technological settings as though a few machines could afford them a sense of self-worth. Dame Cicely changed the world and did so because she felt so deeply that God loves people who are dying and wants their final months to be opportunities to sense the significance of their lives. At the end of her talk, Dame Cicely said that God has never allowed her to retire, and that she still goes into St. Christopher's to change bedpans, to listen attentively and express love, and to do all the small chores of hospice life with great love. She died several years later, and across the globe virtually every news organization printed voluminous obituaries to a modern saint who gave significance even to those who could no longer be rescued from death.

Some people are called to an engaged spirituality that explicitly confronts social, political, and economic structures deemed unjust and contributory to the suffering of some needful group. Mahatma Gandhi, Martin Luther King, Abraham Heschel, and Bishop Desmond Tutu are obvious examples. Their moral appeal is to human dignity and human rights, and their endeavor is to effect structural change. The psychological dynamic involved in these efforts requires the persistent confrontation of entrenched powers that are recalcitrant to change. This is a calling that is left to the most courageous. When we read about such lives, we sense that the love manifested hinted at God's love, something about which all these exemplars taught.

Godly love cannot be reduced to any single modulation or expression. It is too responsive to particular needs for such expressive monism. Love is always a deeply emotional and intellectual affirmation of the significance of others, but there are various spokes that fan out from this hub in more specific forms. Godly love takes the form of compassion in response to suffering. It is a *celebratory* love that recognizes human achievements and virtue. Indeed, some theologians and mystics describe this love as even *mirthful*.[1]

Godly love is expressed as *loyal*. It is not an extinguishable project. Its sincerity and honesty in intention is demonstrated in fidelity and permanence over time. Constancy provides security and safety for human creatures. Godly love is a *forgiving* love, because human creatures all fall short. It is a *respectful* love, for it includes a quiet reverence for the mystery of other lives, and a freedom from the desire to manipulate.[2] It is a *listening* love, attentive to human prayers of supplication. It is a love of *confrontation*, holding creatures accountable for destructive and self-destructive actions. And it is a *creative* love, inspiring us to use our gifts for noble purposes.[3]

Whatever modulations of love are our own, they all add dignity to our lives, and they confer upon others the sense that their lives are worthy of love, and significant in God's eyes. Like the "body of Christ" described by St. Paul in 1 Corinthians 12, we all have different strengths and gifts. For some, Godly love will be better expressed as compassion for the suffering, while for others it will be better expressed as creativity. The body needs an ear as much as a hand, an eye as much as a nose. Each part has its own function, and we should respect one another's different gifts and talents.

Godly love emerges within each of the Abrahamic faiths as the true and highest norm for human spirituality and activity. In each tradition, such love is commanded. This is because however much Godly love is an effective energy that engages the heart, it is also an ideal from which we easily stray. As a Christian philosopher, the author will address here why the commandment to love others—all others—must be a commandment.

However much love has a warm and emotional quality to be love, it is also a commandment. John 13:34 reads, "I give you a new commandment, that you love one another. Just as I have loved you, you also should love one another" (NRSV). Does it not sound contradictory to think of something that must come from the heart as also something to be commanded? Actually, we do need to be firmly reminded and commanded to keep our hearts active in love. There is a lot in us that flat-out rebels against giving universal love. Some of us love those we like but despise, hate, or ignore those we do not like. Loving has to be stronger than liking. We send the message that those we do not like do not matter, and they feel insignificant as a result, even to the point of self-destruction. Witness the adolescent suicide victims of cyber-bullying. *The trouble with this is that we cannot love even friends and family well if we despise, hate, or ignore anyone.* When it comes to love, we have each of us to be one traveler. We cannot get on down the road if we leave half of ourselves behind to travel down the road of hostility and indifference. One person can be located on only one road, not two roads at the same time. People have to make a choice for love and decide that, given the relatively low state of this world, it is worth the effort. But we all need to throw ourselves into the journey without second thoughts and with full hearts. We need a command.

So, Godly love is shaped and formed for the author through Christianity. But we know that God can be working to increase the net balance of love in the world through other traditions, to the extent that they also manifest Godly love. Thus, the author is not a fundamentalist exclusivist who is busy condemning other traditions, but neither is he the too-easy pluralist who must by definition affirm even the most unloving aspects of other traditions in the name of difference. Fundamentalist intolerance and pluralist tolerance both fail. But there is a middle position, the position of "inclusivism," that allows us to affirm those elements of other traditions (and indeed, of our own tradition) that seem to be consistent with the Godly love revealed in the life of Christ.

### God's Love Is Not Human Love

God's love is not to be confused with human love.[4] It far exceeds any human emotion, even at our impressive best, because it is at a different level of magnitude and stability than anything human. This does not mean that human love lacks authenticity and immense importance within the natural order, or that it is not the substrate upon which divine love acts. Human love nevertheless pales in comparison to the overwhelming experience of pure divine love.[5]

As Sorokin suggested in his classic work *The Ways and Power of Love*, a first dimension of love is *intensity*.[6] Low-intensity love makes possible minor actions, such as giving a few pennies to the destitute or relinquishing a bus seat for another's comfort; at high intensity, much that is of value to the agent is freely given. Human love can be intense or weak at any given moment, for we are subject to the ups and downs of the heart. Divine love is *perfectly intense*, meaning that its energies are infinite and constant. Human love falls short.

Sorokin's second dimension of love is *extensivity*: "The extensivity of love ranges from the zero point of love of oneself only, up to the love of all mankind, all living creatures, and the whole universe. Between the minimal and maximal degrees lies a vast scale of extensivities: love of one's own family, or a few friends, or love of the groups one belongs to—one's own clan, tribe, nationality, nation, religious, occupational, political, and other groups and associations."[7] Our human love tends toward insularity and has a strongly myopic tendency unless it is enlarged by the power of God's love. Whom should we love? Everyone, though obviously we finite creatures must establish functional priorities in ordering love. Even in doing so, we can still be leaning out toward all humanity. The Greeks felt that love should be confined to those who are worthy of it. We should love someone as a friend, argued Aristotle, only if they are virtuous.

Sorokin next added the dimension of *duration*, which "may range from the shortest possible moment to years or throughout the whole life of an individual or of a group."[8] For example, the soldier who saves a comrade in a moment of heroism may then revert to selfishness, in contrast to the mother who cares for a sick child over many years. Romantic love, he indicates, is generally of short duration as well. Human love is notoriously fickle. It gives up on people when they have been wounded by life, or when they fail to measure up to some standard of achievement. Divine love is perfectly reliable and enduring; human love is not.

The fourth dimension of love is *purity*. Here Sorokin wrote that our love is characterized as affection for another that is free of egoistic motivation. By contrast, pleasure, advantage, or profit underlies inferior forms of love, and they will be of short duration. Pure love—that is, love that is truly disinterested and asks for no return, represents the highest form of emotion. Human love is at best a mix of other-regarding and self-regarding motives, whereas divine love is pure.

Finally, Sorokin included the *adequacy* of love. Inadequate love is subjectively genuine but has adverse objective consequences. It is possible to pamper and spoil a child with love or to love without practical wisdom. Adequate love achieves ennobling purposes and is therefore anything but blind or unwise. Certainly, love is concerned with the building of character and virtue, and will shun overindulgence. Successful love is effective. Human love is sometimes very destructive in its application. We destroy our children by loving them in ways that breed bad habits and irresponsibility. Divine love is perfectly creative, because it is perfectly wise.

Sorokin argued that the greatest lives of love and altruism approximate or achieve "the highest possible place, denoted by 100 in all five dimensions," while persons "neither loving nor hating would occupy a position near zero."[9] Gandhi's love, for example, was intensive, extensive, enduring, pure, and adequate (effective). Of special interest to Sorokin was the love of figures such as Jesus, Al Hallaj, and Damien the Leper. Despite being persecuted and hated, and therefore without any apparent social source of love energy, they were nevertheless able to maintain a love at high levels in all five dimensions. Such love seems to transcend ordinary human limits, which suggested to Sorokin that some human beings do, through spiritual and religious practices, participate in a love energy that defines God.

Sorokin was convinced that such perfect love can best be explained by *hypothesizing an inflow of love from a higher source that far exceeds that of human beings.* Those who were despised and had no psychosocial inflow of love to sustain them must have received love from above:

The most probable hypothesis for them (and in a much slighter degree for a much larger group of smaller altruists and good neighbors) is that an inflow of love comes from an intangible, little-studied, possibly supraempirical source called "God," "the Godhead," "the Soul of the Universe," the "Heavenly Father," "Truth," and so on. Our growing knowledge of intra-atomic and cosmic ray energies has shown that the physico-chemical systems of energies are able to maintain themselves and replenish their systems for an indefinitely long time. If this is true of these "coarsest" energies, then the highest energy of love is likely to have this "self-replenishing" property to a still higher degree. We know next to nothing about the properties of love energy.[10]

Sorokin believed that those people of great love who, when surrounded by adversity, sustained love were graced. Those who are high in all the five aspects of love reflect, he conjectured, a divine love energy.

Sorokin was a scientific optimist, hoping that enhanced understanding might unlock the "enormous power of creative love"[11] to stop aggression and enmity and contribute to vitality and longevity,[12] cure mental illness, sustain creativity in the individual and in social movements, and provide the only sure foundation for ethical life. Sorokin's general law is as follows:

> If unselfish love does not extend over the whole of mankind, if it is confined within one group—a given family, tribe, nation, race, religious denomination, political party, trade union, caste, social class or any part of humanity—such an in-group altruism tends to generate an out-group antagonism. And the more intense and exclusive the in-group solidarity of its members, the more unavoidable are the clashes between the group and the rest of humanity.[13]

In-group exclusivism has "killed more human beings and destroyed more cities and villages than all the epidemics, hurricanes, storms, floods, earthquakes, and volcanic eruptions taken together. It has brought upon mankind more suffering than any other catastrophe."[14] What is needed, argues Sorokin, is enhanced extensivity.

Sorokin placed his faith in science: "Science can render an inestimable service to this task by inventory of the known and invention of the new effective techniques of altruistic ennoblement of individuals, social institutions, and culture. Our enormous ignorance of love's properties, of the efficient ways of its production, accumulation, and distribution, of the efficacious ways of moral transformation has been stressed many times in this work."[15]

We wish to make progress in going "from tribal egoism to universal altruism," perhaps through "hatred and the holy war against the common enemies of mankind," including the capacity for hatred that lies within us all.[16] In other words, is progress most likely through the redirection of hatred? We need to identify and better understand the rituals in the Abrahamic faiths that create a subjunctive, or "as if" and "could be," universe that directs even radical religious particularity toward the love of a common humanity. So many rituals do signal commitment to fellow believers and trust between members. Unfortunately, there is a dark side to this unity in that the intragroup solidarity that religious commitment typically produces also plays a role in intergroup demonization and conflict.

## Two General Rituals of Godly Love Enhancement

Sorokin identified two rituals or practices that might hold out some promise in solving the perversion of God's love into the un-Godly love of Abrahamic conflict.

(1) REPETITION OF GOOD DEEDS ACROSS ABRAHAMIC BOUNDARIES— Sorokin had the mind of an engineer, surveying the vast scope of world religious traditions for techniques and rituals of "altruization." One technique he found to be quite universal was the *repetition of good deeds* as a method of personal transformation, especially with respect to those whom the agent dislikes:

> performance of friendly, helpful, and loving actions can be prescribed for any person and group at any stage of altruistic education. It can be recommended even when such a person or group profoundly dislikes the addressees, and does not have any enthusiasm for doing good deeds for them. An age-old experience, well confirmed by our experimental studies, shows that after a sufficient number of repetitions, the good actions, performed at first in a cold, unenthusiastic way, begin to exert (according to James-Lange theory) their influence upon the performer. "Cold" or mainly external good deeds awaken friendly emotions and affections, become hearty and spontaneously desired to be rendered. The inimical attitude towards an enemy begins to melt; cold service and cold co-operation turn into warm sympathy and good will. Eventually hate gives place to a sort of indifference, then to a real and warm friendship. Repetition of good deeds instills eventually love even towards one's enemy, as Jesus correctly stated.[17]

What Sorokin is saying, consistent with the James-Lange theory of emotional change, is that helping actions generally create an emotional shift-effect, and that therefore engaging in such actions even when they do not feel spontaneous is a good starting point for inner transformation. Of course, neither can such actions be forced. But there is more to it: "Besides changing the doer of good deeds, the technique also changes the addressees of the good actions. Even an enemy-addressee, 'bombarded by good deeds' of his previous antagonist, rarely remains unresponsive. The good deeds speak louder than good words."[18] Sorokin rejects the assertion that "the technique of good deeds" is a form of "appeasement," "impotence," and the like. And its political efficacy in the world of international tensions is generally considerable. So it is that Sorokin saw all works of self-giving love and generosity as rituals of reconciliation through a process that changes the heart of the giver and that of the recipient. To the extent that religions and spiritualities exhort, model, celebrate, and reward such actions of doing "unto others," they engage believers in a ritual dance of goodness. He considers "the technique of good deeds" as "possibly the most effective and the most accessible for everyone."[19]

(2) ALTRUISTIC PRAYER AND MEDITATION ACROSS ABRAHAMIC BOUNDARIES—Sorokin saw much value in altruistic prayer, and little in egoistic prayer. The altruistic prayer asks for benefits for all or for others, as exemplified in the Lord's Prayer, "Give *us* this day *our* daily bread." Here "us" refers to the Beloved Community.

"We of the Abrahamic traditions" must be the essence of prayer. "We work out our solution on conflict through Godly love"; as Sorokin writes, "Altruistic prayer strives to free the supraconscious in man from the shackles of his little egos for the union with the Supreme Supraconscious."[20] It can be vocal or silent, individual or collective. It is "one of the most accessible and fruitful ways for spiritualization and altruization of human beings and groups."[21]

### Let Us Hope

The world shows no signs of becoming greatly less religious; we as humans will always have a passion for an ultimate truth that provides a safe haven of emotional security. To the extent that truly divine love can be captured in the ritual worlds that religions create, and expressed in spiritual emotions such as forgiveness and compassion, we will have a human future. To the degree that religions fall short of Godly love, violence will overcome us all. Godly love alone can rightly align the world in harmony and peace, although it must do so through human agents who are so imperfect. There are too many who kill in God's name under the assumption that they alone know the unfolding purposes of God. Our human knowledge of such purposes should be regarded as profoundly limited.

Elizabeth Alexander of Yale University wrote a poem entitled "Praise Song for the Day," which she read at Barack Obama's presidential inauguration. One stanza reads: "Some live by *love thy neighbor as thyself*, others by *first do no harm* or *take no more than you need*. What if the mightiest word is love?"[22] Love is the fundamental emotional dynamic that moves us to "do unto others" in kindness and generosity. It is what makes our lives meaningful. In love, we affirm the value of others as well as of self, and we act creatively; in hatred, we diminish value and act destructively. We do not have in mind "love" in the modern sense that limits it to the nearest and dearest; rather, we are talking about a love of humanity that is typically at the core of our great spiritual and moral-political traditions. It is believed that such love, in infinitely vibrant creativity, underlies the universe.

A bold statement on the power of love in hard times was that of Franklin Delano Roosevelt in his Christmas Eve address of 1941. He wondered how men and women could rejoice in the spirit of love in a time of such concerted war against radical evil, with "sons and brothers" endangered. He asked, "How can we light our trees, how can we give our gifts, how can we meet and worship with love and with uplifted spirit and heart in a world at war, a world of fighting and suffering and death?" He answered, "Against enemies who preach the principles of hate and practice them, we set our faith in human love and in God's care for us and all men everywhere."[23] And it was with this affirmation of universal love, he said, that the sacrifices of sons and brothers could be properly solemnized and honored. FDR learned this from his Episcopal religious upbringing and extended the concept to the throes of conflict with a Nazi regime that preached the brutal elimination of so-called inferiors.

It is easy to lose hope in the power of love but for faith that in the sweeping drama of history God set the universe in motion and wrote the play so that love would be victorious in the final act, despite startling scenes of immense cruelty and hideous violence in which evil fills the stage. Thus, St. Paul linked together faith, hope, and love (1 Cor. 13:13). Without faith and hope, love does not hold our hearts in the darkness. Faith declares that despite all the cruel tyrants and wanton abusers of life, Godly love has already won the day. Hope sets its sights on a real future in accordance with God's promises.[24]

## Notes

1. See G. K. Chesterton, *Orthodoxy* (New York: Image/Doubleday, 1959 [1908]).

2. Margaret A. Farley, *Compassionate Respect: A Feminist Approach to Medical Ethics and Other Questions* (New York: Paulist Press, 2002).

3. Dorothy L. Sayers, *The Mind of the Maker* (San Francisco: HarperCollins, 1979).

4. Henri Bergson, *The Two Sources of Morality and Religion*, trans. R. Ashley Audra and Cloudesley Brereton (Garden City, NY: Doubleday, 1935 [1932]).

5. K. E. Kirk, *The Vision of God* (Harrisburg, PA: Morehouse, 1991 [1931]), abridged ed.

6. Pitirim Sorokin, *The Ways and Power of Love: Types, Factors, and Techniques of Moral Transformation* (West Conshohocken, PA: Templeton Foundation Press, 2002).

7. Ibid., 16.

8. Ibid.

9. Ibid., 19.

10. Ibid., 26.

11. Ibid.

12. Ibid.

13. Ibid., 459, italics in original.

14. Ibid., 461.

15. Ibid., 477.

16. Ibid., 459 and 464.

17. Ibid., 330.

18. Ibid., 329.

19. Ibid., 329.

20. Ibid., 335.

21. Ibid., 339.

22. Elizabeth Alexander, "Praise Song for the Day," *New York Times*, Jan. 20, 2009; http://www.nytimes.com/2009/01/20/us/politics/20text-poem.html (last accessed 10/6/11).

23. The American Presidency Project, http://www.presidency.ucsb.edu/ws/?pid=16073 (last accessed 7/9/10).

24. Jürgen Moltmann, *Theology of Hope: On The Ground and the Implications of a Christian Eschatology*, trans. James W. Leitch (Minneapolis: Fortress Press, 1993 [1967]).

# AGAPE, SELF-SACRIFICE,

# AND MUTUALITY

## An Exploration into the

## Thought of Jonathan Edwards

## and the Theme of Godly Love

### MICHAEL J. McCLYMOND

Mutuality seems to be the new emphasis among ethical theorists and investigators of human love. A recently published collection of essays from sixteen authors, entitled *Mutuality Matters: Family, Faith, and Just Love*, proposes the general thesis that "love is mutual" and that "the aim of all genuine love is 'to bring others more fully to life' by closely attending to one another."[1] While this volume focuses on family relationships, it raises questions that go beyond the domain of the family. How, exactly, does one person's love bring about another person's fulfillment? And how does that person's love relate to her or his own fulfillment? Might one person's fulfillment—or the fulfillment of a larger group—require the sacrifice of the self-interest and personal fulfillment of one individual or of a smaller group? A recent exchange of articles by J. Jeffrey Tillman and Don Browning in the journal *Zygon* considered the possibility of agape as involving or requiring "sacrificial" behavior. When Tillman claimed that Browning's ethics left no room for self-sacrifice, Browning responded by denying this interpretation and insisting that he sanctioned self-sacrifice under certain circumstances.[2] Whatever one's views regarding Tillman's and Browning's arguments, the contemporary debates over mutuality and self-sacrifice can enrich the discussion of Godly love by helping us to frame some pointed questions. To put the matter sharply: Is it appropriate to call upon certain persons to set aside their own interests for the sake of others? Or are appeals to self-sacrifice a covert means whereby one group may manipulate another to its own advantage? Does the very notion of self-sacrifice imply a mistreatment or abuse of the self that is sacrificed?

Traditional Roman Catholic understandings of love culminated in a notion of union with God and a communion or community of persons with one another. Mutuality is thus an intrinsic, rather than an accidental, feature in Catholic conceptions of love. The Jesuit theologian Edward Vacek, in *Love, Human and Divine* (1994), proposed that agape love may be differentiated and distinguished from philos (friendship love) and eros (passionate love), and yet he equally insisted that agape is not to be sharply contrasted with philos or eros.[3] In what Vacek calls his "pluralist thesis," agape may be defined as loving the other for the other's own sake, philos as loving the other for the sake of the relationship, and eros as loving the other for one's own sake. Each of the three represents one possible orientation of the self toward the other within a relational context. Vacek's analysis of love suggests that in any actual relationship between human beings there may be intervening moments of agape, philos, and/or eros. These differing forms of love may be intertwined in complex ways, so that it is difficult to separate one form of love from the others, or even to say at any given moment which form is predominant. For example, if an elderly man were diligently feeding, nursing, and caring for his ailing wife, then would this be an expression of unconditional, or agape, love? A responsive act of appreciation for the passionate eros of earlier years? A reflection of lifelong friendship? Or an act of self-love, since the husband knows that his wife may recover from her illness and be restored as a more adequate friend and partner once her strength and vitality returns? Finally, we might ask how it would be possible to disentangle the disparate forms of love in a situation such as this.

Traditional Protestant understandings of love moved in a different direction than Catholic thought. They centered on the love of God as supremely demonstrated and displayed in the death of Jesus Christ on the cross. On this view, the highest expression of love for any human being is to imitate the self-sacrificial act of Christ, when he set aside his own interests and inclinations to offer himself upon the cross. Jesus's prayer to the heavenly Father in the Garden of Gethsemane—"not as I will, but as you will" (Matt. 26:39)—represents the highest limit and exemplification of agape love.[4] Anders Nygren's influential study *Agape and Eros* (1932) proposed that agape, as a self-sacrificial kind of love, was necessarily opposed to eros, as a self-seeking and acquisitive love. Agape sought to give, eros to take. Agape was independent of desirable qualities in love's object, eros was based on such qualities. Agape was revealed through God's love in Christ, while eros was a naturalistic, pagan instinct with nothing gracious about it. On Nygren's view, Christian theology was on the wrong track for more than a millennium prior to Martin Luther, who unmasked the "*eros* religion" and the implicit paganism contained in Augustine's "*caritas*-synthesis." He went so far as to claim that Luther's "criticism of the Catholic idea of love is . . . irrefutable." To love the neighbor meant "completely dispossessing and annihilating self-love." Martin Luther wrote that "blessedness is this, to will the will of God and His glory in all things, and to desire nothing of one's own either in this world or the next."[5]

While suppressing self-love might go against human nature, what was humanly impossible was divinely possible. Through God's grace, people did not have to act in accordance with their natural instincts but could transcend them.[6] Nygren's themes were paralleled in certain Catholic mystics—such as Francois Fénelon and Madame Guyon—during the so-called pure love (*amour pur*) controversy at the end of the seventeenth century. Cornelius Jansen and the Jansenists of France adopted similar views. Jonathan Edwards's leading disciple, Samuel Hopkins, insisted that self-love was essentially sinful and identified Christian love with what he called "disinterested benevolence." In a manner reminiscent of Nygren, Hopkins found the essence of Christian love to consist in self-sacrifice. In fact, Hopkins's ideas caught on to such an extent with adherents of the "New Divinity" (i.e., Edwardsean theology) at the end of the 1700s, that some candidates for Congregational ministry in New England around 1800 were asked: "Are you willing to be damned for the glory of God?" In his private notebooks, Jonathan Edwards discussed and rejected the idea that anyone who loved God could or would "be willing to be perfectly and finally miserable for God's sake."[7] Love for God would lead the true saint to want to be with God forever, and not to be eternally separated from God. Yet Hopkins and others so strongly identified Christian love with self-sacrifice that they proposed this "damnation question" as an introspective test for the genuineness of one's agape love. Stephen Post offered an incisive analysis of Edwards's and Hopkins's views on self-love.[8] As we will see below, Jonathan Edwards strongly emphasized the theme of mutuality and yet also had much to say regarding Christ's sacrifice on the cross and the need for Christ's disciples to practice self-sacrifice as well. Edwards thus mediated between Catholic and Protestant thinking in a way that may be helpful for ethicists and for developing a richer, fuller picture of Godly love.[9]

## Love and Mutuality in Edwards

Divine and human love held a prominent place in Edwards's thought. Love for him was a *divine power* that actuated the three persons of the Trinity, drove God's redemptive purposes in history, awakened the human response to God, overcame the corrupting effects of sin, inspired dispositions and acts of self-giving, gathered the saints into community, counteracted the corrosive effects of pride, envy, and lust, and enabled human selves to see themselves more accurately and to act as parts of a larger whole. The theme of love linked into every other theme. The pastor of Northampton was an apostle of love. Though well known for his fearsome sermons, he also wrote much concerning the "lamblike, dovelike spirit and temper" shown in "love, meekness, quietness, forgiveness and mercy" that was the summit of Christian experience.[10] Earthly love, moreover, was an anticipation of heavenly bliss, as shown in the final sermon in *Charity and Its Fruits* (1738)—entitled "heaven is a world of love."[11] For Edwards, in the words of William Danaher, "the primary point of contact between the church's present reality and its eschatological fulfillment is . . . the life of love."[12]

To say that Edwards made love central is not to say that he made it simple.[13] Lurking below the surface of his writings are innumerable questions regarding the possible subjects and objects of love—for example, God's love for us, the human love for God, the human love of fellow humans (neighbor-love), the love of the brethren (fellow Christians), and the love of oneself. To make things more difficult, there is often a question in Edwards's writings—as in other authors—as to what sort of love is under discussion at a given time. A number of classic works—including Nygren's *Agape and Eros* and C. S. Lewis's *The Four Loves* (1960)—proposed a typology of various kinds of love with reference to ancient Greek and/or Latin terms.[14] According to the generally accepted terminology, *agape* applies to God's unconditional love for humanity and to the disinterested love of one's neighbor. *Eros* denotes the love of preferential desire for an attractive other—often but not necessarily sexual in character. *Philia* or *philos* refers to the love of friendship and mutuality. *Storge* is a loving instinct or affection shown in parental, familial, or tribal relationships. *Amor sui* refers to self-love, while *caritas* refers to the desire for communion with God as the proper end, or telos, of human life. As one can see, the five subject–object relations could each be factored according to the six different types, and thus the simple word *love* might in practice carry ten, twenty, or even more disparate meanings. The Greek and Latin words serve as useful shorthand to help interlocutors understand one another in speaking of "love."

What, then, of Edwards? We should note that he chose the term *charity* for the title of his leading treatise on love, *Charity and Its Fruits*, and seems to have been aware of the intellectual and theological background of the Latin term.[15] Like Augustine, Edwards insisted from his earliest period that all human beings seek happiness. The difference between—let us say—Adolf Hitler and Mother Teresa did not consist in the fact that one sought happiness and the other did not. Rather it lay in the disparate objects in which each considered his or her happiness to consist.[16] In *Charity and Its Fruits* Edwards underscored the compatibility between natural impulses and instincts that partially resembled true virtue and the gracious love, or agape, that came through regeneration and the indwelling Holy Spirit. Edwards's position accorded with Aquinas's dictum that "grace does not destroy nature but perfects it." Human love toward God always came as a response to God's gracious initiative. Yet God worked through and not against our innate and inescapable impulse toward happiness. C. S. Lewis quipped that only a "silly creature" would presume to say before God: "I love you disinterestedly."[17] Edwards's general understanding of love thus fit better with the Augustine–Aquinas–C. S. Lewis lineage than with the Luther–Guyon–Nygren tradition.

From the standpoint of Edwards's theology, the greatest problem with Nygren's view of love may have been its lack of *mutuality*. Inspired by Edwards's thought, Stephen Post has said that he is "skeptical of those who would detach love from some degree of self-fulfillment," since this led to "idealizations of one-way love" that pull away from "the Christian norm of mutuality or communion." This engenders a religious solitariness, and "the moral agent is placed in a kind of isolation, not unlike the lonely runners of marathons." Love, argued Post, needs a participatory context of giving and receiving to come to full fruition. Post comments: "Selfless, purely one-way love may be an understandable exaggeration of unselfishness, but its impact is essentially negative in that it undermines the circular flow of giving and receiving in which agape is sustained and supported."[18]

When Edwards described love in *Charity and Its Fruits*, he depicted not a solitary individual but a holy society of mutual action, participation, and enjoyment. The self experienced enlargement, or what Edwards called the "propriety" of one person in another, according to the words that Edwards cited from the biblical Song of Songs, "My beloved is mine and I am his"

(Song of Songs 2:16), and from the prayer of Jesus, "That they all may be one; as thou, Father, art in me, and I in thee, that they also may be one in us" (John 17:21).[19] Love, said Edwards, is "diffusive" and causes a person to view others as connected to oneself and indeed as parts of oneself. This is true of God's love for humanity in Christ, where Christ is a "public person" and can say regarding acts of mercy to the poor: "Inasmuch as ye have done it unto one of the least of these my brethren, ye have done it unto me" (Matt. 25:40).[20] It is no less true of the various human loves, whether the erotic love of man and woman, the familial affection of parents and children, or the phenomenon of benevolence for one in need. In each of these cases, the self is enlarged and joined with one or more others in a larger whole.

### The Vexatious Issue of Self-Love in Edwards

Edwards's stress on the mutuality of love raises the issue of self-love—a much-debated topic in Edwards's day.[21] Some viewed it as a positive and prudential concern for one's own happiness. Joseph Butler linked self-love to virtue. "When we sit down in a cool hour," wrote Butler, "we can neither justify to ourselves this or any other pursuit, till we are convinced that it will be for our happiness." Others saw self-love as neither praiseworthy nor blameworthy but simply as a fact of human life. David Hume held that the very notion of a "public good" arose because people sought to protect themselves. Still others—as noted already—saw self-love as sinful and blameworthy.[22] Edwards's notebook entry "Miscellany 530" (written in 1731–1732) grappled with this issue of self-love. It began with the query "whether or no a man ought to love God more than himself."[23] Yet Edwards questioned the question, noting the confusion that arose from using the term "self-love" in conflicting ways. He argued that self-love and love of God, in some sense, "are not things properly capable of being compared with one another: for they are not opposites, or things entirely distinct; but one enters into the nature of the other." "Self-love" in its "most extensive sense" was simply a "capacity for enjoyment or suffering," and so "'tis improper to say that our love to God is superior to our general capacity of delighting in anything." One cannot compare—as lesser or greater—one's love for a particular object of love with one's general capacity for love. That would be like asking whether a particular lightbulb is brighter or dimmer than one's own power of sight. Instead one should ask whether one lightbulb shines more or less brightly than another. So it was with degrees of love. If "self-love" was defined as a delight in one's own private good in distinction from the good of others, then one might compare its degree with the degree of one's delight in the good of others. So there was one sense in which "self-love" could be compared to the love for God (or any other love), and another sense it which it could not be so compared.

Edwards then made a terminological distinction. What he called "simple mere self-love" was "entirely distinct" from the love of God. What Edwards called "compounded self-love" involved a "principle uniting this person to another, that causes the good of another to be its good." This "second sort of self-love is not entirely distinct from love to God, but enters into its nature." Edwards concluded Misc. 530 with a corollary that suggested that he was responding to some kind of radical negation of the self: "Hence 'tis impossible for any person to be willing to be perfectly and finally miserable for God's sake."[24] Martin Luther discussed the so-called *resignatio ad infernum*—the willingness to be damned, if God so willed[25]—and the issue came up again among seventeenth-century Catholic authors and mystics, and once again with Samuel Hopkins. Yet Edwards's Misc. 530 implied that the *resignatio* was a logical as well as a religious mistake. A true saint, by definition, desired above all to be joined to God eternally. What sense, then, would there be in a saint who willingly embraced everlasting separation from God? And how could such a choice be pleasing to God?

*Charity and Its Fruits* (1738) treated self-love much as Misc. 530 did. In the present life, wrote Edwards, both "saints and sinners and all love happiness alike, and have the same unalterable propensity to seek and desire happiness." Even the saints and angels in heaven love their own happiness. For if they did not, then there "would be no happiness to them; for that which anyone does not love, he can enjoy no happiness in."[26]

As William Danaher argued, Edwards's idea of human self-love rested on his principle of divine self-love. Self-love was foundational for Edwards's trinitarian understanding of God as Father, Son, and Spirit, for the arguments of *End of Creation* and *Nature of True Virtue*, and even for Edwards's general conception of God's relationship with creatures. In loving creatures, God did not cease from loving himself but rather in some sense loved the image of his own excellence—however faint—as exhibited in creatures. For God's "love includes in it, or rather is the same as, a love to everything, as they are all communications of himself."[27] Presupposing such divine self-love, one could well ask whether God was a cosmic Narcissus in love with his own reflection. We might also ask *how* human beings should imitate God. Should they do so by loving God (as God does) or by loving themselves (as God does)?[28] Edwards offered two responses. First, in God there is no conflict between self-love and regard for others, any more than "the welfare of the head, heart and vitals of the natural body should be opposite to the welfare of the body."[29] Second, our imitation of

God need not involve a trade-off between regard for God and regard for self, since these two things imply one another.

In summary, then, Edwards's treatment of self-love shows that he considered a basic regard for self, or a desire for one's own happiness, to be a root principle in human life. Along with Augustine, Aquinas, and C. S. Lewis, Edwards may be classified as a eudaemonist—a theme explored by pastor-scholar John Piper in his Edwards-inspired writings on "Christian hedonism."[30] This does not mean that God gave any definite command for us to love ourselves. Instead, the command to "love thy neighbor as thyself" (Matt. 22:39) presupposes a basic, universal self-love. It is noteworthy that Edwards's earliest extant sermon—the first of more than twelve hundred sermon manuscripts he left behind—was titled "Christian Happiness," and had for its thesis that "a good man is a happy man, whatever his outward condition is."[31] His early sermons glowed with a conviction that the holy life is happy and the happy life is holy. Furthermore, the early writings show that human self-love has its analogue in the life of the blessed Trinity. In loving himself, God subsists as Father, Son, and Spirit. In loving himself, God creates the world, according to the argument of *End of Creation*.

### Edwards on Divine Love and the Virtues of Community

Edwards's *Charity and Its Fruits* (1738) has been called a "phenomenology of the Christian moral life."[32] Though anticipating certain features of *Religious Affections* (1747), it differed in stressing interpersonal dispositions and actions, set in a communal context. The unifying theme of *Charity and Its Fruits* lay in an Augustinian notion of love, *caritas*, or "charity"—"that disposition or affection by which one is dear to another." Edwards distinguished between "love of benevolence" and "love of complacence." For "benevolence is that disposition" whereby one "delights in the good of another." "Complacence," though, "presupposes beauty, for it is no other than delight in beauty; or . . . in the person or being beloved for his beauty."[33] By distinguishing yet not separating these two loves, Edwards offered a sanction for enjoyment in the moral life. To be sure, the beauty that Edwards had in mind was principally a spiritual rather than a physical beauty. Yet spiritual beauty brought pleasure no less than did physical beauty. This meant that enjoyment, no less than beauty, was a pervasive theme. If we add mutuality as a third aspect of love, alongside "benevolence" and "complacence," then we discover a rough analogy to the three kinds of love noted above. "Benevolence" corresponded to agape (seeking the good of the other), "complacence" to eros (delighting in and enjoying the other), and mutuality to philia or friendship (pursuing relationship with the other). For Edwards, these loves were not defined in opposition to one another but rather existed in a complex interplay.

In the first sermon of *Charity and Its Fruits*, Edwards laid out an *ordo amoris* that moved in measured steps from the divine to the human levels. "Love is the principal thing," he wrote, "which the gospel reveals in God and Christ. The gospel brings to light the love between the Father and the Son, and declares how that love has been manifested in mercy; how that Christ is God's beloved Son in whom he is well pleased." Note that the first thing that God or the gospel "reveals" was not God's love for humanity, but God the Father's love for God the Son. Next in sequence, Edwards proceeded to the answering love of the Son for the Father: "There is revealed the love which Christ has to the Father, and the wonderful fruits of that love, as particularly his doing such great things, and suffering such great things in obedience to the Father." This mutual love of Father and Son created a community of love that was not self-enclosed but open to the participation of creatures: "There it is revealed how the Father and the Son are one in love, that we might be induced in like manner to be one with them, and with one another, agreeably to Christ's prayer, John 17:21–23." Repeatedly here, Edwards used the verb *reveal* to capture the divine origin of the love he described: the gospel "reveals the wonderful love of God the Father to poor sinful, miserable men. . . . while we were wanderers, outcasts, worthless, guilty, and even enemies. The gospel reveals such love as nothing else reveals."[34] This brief overview of love ended where many other Christian theologians began—with God's love for sinners. Edwards saw all forms of love—heavenly or earthly—as originating in the inner life of God. Love between human beings, moreover, was not an abstract ideal of unselfish behavior or "equal regard." Instead it was a theological principle and practice rooted in the mutual love of Father and Son, and the gracious reconciliation of sinners to God.[35]

Edwards wrote that God the Father was the "original seat" of all expressions of love. For "love is in God as light is in the sun, which does not shine by a reflected light as the moon and planets do; but by his own light, and as the fountain of light."[36] God's love was "diffusive" by nature and so extended outward to engender community. Not until the saints attained to heaven was the love of God to be perfectly expressed and embodied in a glorified human community. Throughout *Charity and Its Fruits* heaven functioned as a controlling concept. There was nothing vague or ethereal about Edwards's notion of heaven. It was as tangible as a New England red-brick meetinghouse. Present-day dispositions and actions were gauged as to whether they concurred with, or departed from, the heavenly condition. There the "whole society" will "rejoice in each other's happiness, for the love of benevolence is perfect in them." The love of "complacence," too, will be fully realized since "there are no unlovely persons" in heaven and there is nothing anywhere to be seen that does not bring pleasure.[37] To the degree that the earthly church resembles this heavenly church, it conforms to God's purposes, and it gradually prepares itself for its eternal destiny.

Most of *Charity and Its Fruits* is given over to the "in-between" church, moving gradually and fitfully toward an eternal destination. As with Augustine's *The City of God*, with its "city of God" and "city of man," Edwards described the present age as a "large wilderness" with two radically different "countries" defined by the love of God or by self-interest. In this age, the church had to resist the lure of selfishness, jealousy, contention, schism, hatred, and deceit. Yet worse was the "world of confusion" among the unregenerate, where "all are for themselves, and self-interest governs" with no regard for "what becomes of others." In the absence of God's love, all seek "worldly good, which is the bone of contention among them," and all are "continually envying and . . . reproaching one another," so that the world is "full of injustice" and "cruelty without any remedy." By contrast, when the church lives out its divine calling, "all are highly esteemed and honored, and dearly loved by all."[38] Not only is love expressed within the church, but the church exerts a transformative effect on the surrounding society. A "Christian spirit" disposes "those who stand in a public capacity" to promote "the public good" and not to be "governed by selfish views in their administrations" in order to "enrich themselves . . . on the spoils of others as wicked rulers very often do."[39]

In the present age, Christians long for heaven and yet feel a lack of "liberty" in loving God, since each "is not holy enough, but is very far from it." Earthly loves are fleeting and uncertain, and the "sweetness of earthly friendship" is diminished by "difficulties" and "afflictions" such as "distance of habitation." Though friends bear one another's burdens, they can also impose burdens, since friendship "makes them sharers in others' afflictions."[40] In a fallen world, love's mutuality brings sadness as well as happiness.

While certain texts pressed toward a more arduous and solitary expression of love for God, the major thrust of Edwards's writings—especially in *Charity and Its Fruits*—was toward a notion of love embodied in community. Augustine had proposed the idea of loving the neighbor "in God." This meant that everything that one did with respect to a fellow human was to be gauged against an eternal yardstick, namely, the human vocation to heavenly blessedness with God. Edwards reaffirmed such a love for the neighbor "in God," and yet he highlighted its communitarian element. "The chief purpose of neighbor-love," in the words of Stephen Post, was "to raise the neighbor upward toward the divine and inward toward the fellowship of those who share in the vision of God."[41] For Edwards there was no human blessedness apart from a holy society of those joined to God. To draw near to God was to draw near to the fellowship of the saints. In the present age, the holy society was a community of mutual aid in pursuing the journey toward God.

### Love and Self-Sacrifice in Jonathan Edwards

The theme of self-sacrifice in Edwards is closely tied to his life situation, especially during the latter part of his life.[42] The religious revival that occurred in 1734–1735 in Edwards's own parish of Northampton, Massachusetts, made him an international Protestant celebrity. Edwards's *Faithful Narrative* (1737)—a description of the events that transpired in Northampton—was widely read and discussed in America, Britain, and Europe. During the Great Awakening of 1740–1742, Edwards took on the role of lead interpreter and mediating figure, defending the colonial revivals and yet criticizing their excesses. A series of impressive works during the 1740s solidified Edwards's reputation as the leading interpreter of religious revivals—*The Distinguishing Marks of a Work of the Spirit of God* (1741), *Some Thoughts concerning the Present Revival* (1743), *Religious Affections* (1746), and *Humble Attempt to Promote Explicit Agreement and Visible Union of God's People in Extraordinary Prayer* (1747). Yet as Edwards's public stature rose, he encountered troubles in his own backyard.

The parish of Northampton—on Edwards's view—went into spiritual decline, first in the late 1730s (after the 1734–1735 awakening) and then throughout the 1740s (following the 1740–1741 Great Awakening). As early as the 1730s, Edwards's letters "reveal a vein of circumspection and wariness that may have resulted from his disappointment after the revival of 1734–35." Then again in 1742 he wrote of the "abatement of the liveliness" of his congregation's "affections in religion."[43] The 1734–1735 revival had ended abruptly with the suicide of Edwards's uncle by marriage, Joseph Hawley.[44] Following this melancholy episode, Edwards perceived a widespread falling away from the intense, exuberant spirituality of the awakening. He could not escape the conclusion, in George Marsden's words, that "he had overestimated the extent of genuine awakening."[45]

One mark of spiritual decline was the return of the "frolicking" that was common among young people up through the early 1730s, when the revival brought a change in their behavior. Edwards's words in *Faithful Narrative* (1737) regarding "mirth and company-keeping" were eighteenth-century code language for youthful sexual promiscuity. Patricia Tracy and George Marsden noted that premarital sex seems to have been common in Northampton, and that it was tolerated by many in the older generation so long as marriage took place in case of pregnancy. A scandal ensued only if unmarried men got women pregnant and then failed to marry them. Edwards pressed for marriage in a case of fornication in his parish involving Elisha Hawley and a pregnant Martha Root, and yet the two families settled out of court without any marriage taking place.[46] These events revealed both an implicit sexual double standard—whereby young men often got away with their sexual escapades—and Edwards's own declining authority. While he did not treat sexual transgressions as greater than other forms of wrongdoing, he spoke of indulgence in lust as a clear expression of sinful self-love. In his own post-adolescent years, Edwards had practiced "sparingness" in diet. This was an ascetic self-discipline that he undertook—as his *Diary* shows—to combat his own evil desires.[47] In the midst of the revivals Edwards seemed to be at one with his people. Yet during each of the postrevival letdowns, the contrast between the ascetic, self-denying, saintly pastor and the Northampton congregation became increasingly apparent.

One theme that emerged in Edwards's writing in response to the pastoral situation was a stress on "perseverance" and "obedience"—sometimes combined in the phrase "universal persevering obedience"—as the mark of the genuine convert. As early as 1729–1730, a number of Edwards's private notebook entries discussed "perseverance," and yet the number of such entries mushroomed during the period from 1736 to 1739. So also with entries related to "obedience."[48] It is clear that the postrevival situation of the later 1730s brought Edwards to reflect on these themes. Previously he had stressed an immediate experience of the "divine and supernatural light" as a key element in attaining assurance of salvation. Yet now he emphasized that perseverance was a condition of justification and a means of assurance: "Not only the first act of faith, but after-acts of faith, and perseverance in faith, do justify the sinner."[49] In the winter of 1737–1738 Edwards preached a lengthy sermon series on the parable of the wise and foolish virgins (Matt. 25:1–13) to show that Christian practice was an essential sign of grace. Notebook entries from the late 1730s—"Signs of Godliness" and "Directions for Judging of Persons' Experiences"—exhibited Edwards's stress on holiness and his reluctance to accept reports of spiritual experiences at face value unless they were corroborated by Christian practice.[50] If Christian love was the true test of faith, then it was difficult to escape the conclusion that the Northamptonites were failing.[51]

The years following the Great Awakening may have involved an even greater spiritual drop-off than the late 1730s. Edwards sought to provoke his parishioners to spiritual rededication with a public covenant renewal ceremony in 1742. Yet the older generation continued to have conflicts and quarrels among themselves, while the younger people tended to "lasciviousness." The so-called Bad Book episode—in which young, unmarried men taunted women with knowledge they had gained from a gynecological manual—demonstrated that Edwards's converts who had once renounced the ways of sin were still living in them. Youth from prominent families defied Edwards and flouted his authority, as epitomized in Timothy Root's declaration, "I won't worship a wig."[52]

As the 1740s wore on, Edwards began increasingly to depict the Christian life in terms of self-denial and self-sacrifice. This theme can be viewed autobiographically—as an expression of Edwards's experience of pouring out his life and energy on behalf of ungrateful parishioners. Yet equally it was Edwards's prescription for anyone who wished, as he did, to be a faithful Christian. As Wilson Kimnach points out, Edwards's ordination sermons during the 1740s show a "focused and insistent" stress on "the heroism of the professional ministry."[53] At the center of his evocations of the Christlike minister was the figure of David Brainerd, immortalized in the *Life of David Brainerd* (1749). It was Brainerd, above all others, who exemplified Edwards's emerging themes of perseverance, obedience, separation from the world, solitariness (if need be), self-denial, asceticism, and self-sacrifice. Marsden went so far as to suggest that "Edwards was much more interested in the sacrifice involved in Brainerd's mission than in its success."[54]

Brainerd pursued a brief but meteoric missionary career in the wilds of Pennsylvania. His constant exertions in travel, preaching, and prayer among the Indians—and in the absence of English-style food, housing, and companionship—soon took their toll. The young missionary contracted consumption (i.e., tuberculosis) and died at age 29—in effect, a martyr to Christian missions. When Edwards preached his funeral sermon on October 12, 1747, he did not present Brainerd's brief life as a tragic story or as a missionary opportunity cut short. Instead, he presented Brainerd's life of self-sacrifice as a model to be emulated. In his eulogy he declared:

> He in his whole course acted as one who had indeed sold all for Christ, and had entirely devoted himself to God, and made glory his highest end, and was fully determined to spend his whole time and strength in his service. He was lively in religion, in the right way: not only, nor chiefly, with his tongue, in professing and talking; but lively in the work and business of religion. He was not one of those which are for contriving ways to shun the cross, and get to heaven with ease and sloth; but was such an instance of one living a life of labor and self-denial, and

spending his strength and substance, in pursuing that great end, the glory of his Redeemer, and perhaps is scarcely to be paralleled in this age, in these parts of the world. . . . He seemed to have remarkable exercises of resignation to the will of God. . . . He several times spake of the different kinds of willingness to die; and spoke of it as an ignoble mean kind of willingness to die, to be willing, only to get rid of pain, or to go to heaven only to get honor and advancement there. His own longings for death seemed to be quite of a different kind, and for nobler ends . . . And at one time or another, in the latter part of his illness, he uttered these expressions. . . . "I don't go to heaven to be advanced, but to give honor to God. 'Tis no matter where I shall be stationed in heaven, whether I have a high or low seat there, but to love and please and glorify God . . . If I had a thousand souls, if they were worth anything, I would give 'em all to God: but I have nothing to give, when all is done."[55]

Edwards's *Life of Brainerd*—probably the first full missionary biography ever published—emerged as the best-known of all Edwards's literary works. Never out of print in the two and a half centuries since its publication, it provided "the Protestant icon of the missionary, its ideal type."[56] William Carey, English Baptist missionary to India and a principal founder of modern Anglo-American missions, drew up a covenant for his missionary band that included the words, "Let us often look at Brainerd." According to one of his biographers, Carey so devoured Edwards's *Life of Brainerd* that it became almost a second Bible to him.[57] John Wesley published an abridged version of Brainerd's *Life* in 1768 (and then seven more separate editions), excising Calvinist passages but writing that Methodist preachers with Brainerd's spirit would be invincible. The list of missionaries who testified to Brainerd's influence is a *Who's Who* of Anglo-American missions: Francis Asbury, Thomas Coke, Henry Martyn, Robert Morrison, Samuel Mills, Robert M'Cheyne, David Livingstone, Adoniram Judson, Theodore Dwight Weld, Andrew Murray, and Jim Elliott. Joseph Conforti argues that the *Life of Brainerd*'s enormous impact on American missionaries is "summed up by the fact that when the American Board of Commissioners for Foreign Missions established its first Indian post, among the Cherokees in 1817, the missionaries named it Brainerd."[58]

Brainerd's fervent life of service to God offered a stark contrast to the tepid, indifferent attitudes that Edwards discerned in his own congregation in Northampton. Beginning at the end of the 1700s, Protestant missionary recruits emulated Brainerd's self-sacrificial life and showed a remarkable willingness to die in the cause of Christian evangelization. Early missionaries to West Africa often succumbed to malaria or other tropical diseases and expired within two to three years of arriving. Other global regions were equally deadly for many early missionaries. Inspired in no small part by Brainerd, missionaries during this period embraced the prospect—if not the likelihood—of an early death. Behind the figure of Brainerd was that of Jesus Christ—for Christians, the ultimate model, icon, inspiration, and demonstration of self-sacrificial love and the willingness to embrace death as a means of giving life. Evangelical Protestants of this era—whether missionaries or not—generally embraced a paradox of life-through-death: "Unless a kernel of wheat falls to the ground and dies, it remains only a single seed. But if it dies, it produces many seeds" (John 12:24).

## Reflections on Agape, Mutuality, and Self-Sacrifice

For reasons already suggested, most contemporary ethicists have distanced themselves from the understanding of love set forth by Anders Nygren and his followers during the mid-twentieth century. On Nygren's view, if a loving action terminates in a union of the human self with God, with another human being, or with a human community, then this outcome could be seen as a form of self-fulfillment. If love is defined purely in terms of self-sacrifice, and if it excludes all notions of self-fulfillment, then love seemingly must also exclude the notion of a union or mutuality of selves. Love must be a solitary endeavor. One recalls Stephen Post's comment regarding the "lonely runner of marathons." Indeed, Nygren's view verges toward a reductio ad absurdum. Even Jesus's sacrifice on the cross had, as a deliberate outcome, the establishment of a community of believers who were to believe in and accept Jesus's sacrifice on their behalf. According to biblical teaching, the resurrected Christ enjoyed fellowship with those he had died for, and Christ during his earthly life viewed the future benefit of the church, and his union with it, as an aim and aspiration of his sufferings. "For the joy set before him," says the Epistle to the Hebrews, Jesus "endured the cross, scorning its shame" (Heb. 12:2). It is difficult then to conceive of any form of agape love— even of a self-sacrificial type—that rigorously excludes all notions of union, community, or community of persons as a proper outcome and expression of love.

The advantage of Edward Vacek's view on agape, as compared with Anders Nygren's, lies in its more encompassing character. Vacek's theory, that is, can assimilate the insights of Nygren, while Nygren's theory cannot draw anything from Vacek. If one begins, as Nygren does, with a total antithesis between agape and eros, then one can develop a theology of love that gives prominent place to the theme of self-sacrifice. What becomes problematic, though, is an understanding of love in everyday life, where— as in the example of the elderly husband caring for his wife—it may be difficult if not impossible to distinguish the differing forms of love (i.e., agape, philos, eros) and to demonstrate exactly where one form of love leaves off and another begins. The totally pure act of agape—the completely self-sacrificial act—is more of a limiting case or an ethical ideal than a principle for ordinary situations, where complicating factors enter in, and love typically includes desire, mutuality, fulfillment, and self-interest, as well as self-denial.

Thomas Oord offers a helpful definition of love that moves beyond the limitations of Nygren's definition: "To love is to act intentionally, in sympathetic response to others (including God), to promote overall well-being."[59] One notes that this definition does not necessarily imply or require self-sacrifice. An action is defined as loving if it promotes the "overall well-being" of another person, whether or not it promotes one's own well-being. Oord leaves open the question as to whether loving acts involve self-denial or self-fulfillment. Elsewhere in his writings Oord states that self-sacrifice may be necessary for the expression of agape love under certain circumstances. The point in Oord, then, is that the relationship between agape and self-sacrifice is not necessary—as Nygren would have us believe—but is merely contingent.

It is understandable that ethicists have reacted against Nygren's theory of love and rejected its fixation on self-sacrifice. Yet it is important not to reject self-sacrifice altogether as something repellent, abusive, manipulative, or ethically indefensible. Experience shows us that mutuality among persons often comes at a price. A relationship can often be maintained or advanced only when someone is willing to set aside his or her own desires and interests for the sake of the other and for the sake of the relationship. Family relationships afford many illustrations. In relationships involving the highest levels of mutuality—and perhaps especially in such relationships—one person must sometimes carry the burden of laboring and serving, against his or her own inclinations, on behalf of the other. Parents of teenage children put up with the indignity of doors slammed, insults shouted, rules flouted, and curfews broken. Sometimes they deal with heart-wrenching issues such as teen pregnancy, gang violence, drug addiction, or suicidal behavior. It is the parents' commitment to maintaining the relationship with their children that sustains them through these difficulties. Over the course of a lifetime, much will change, and the child who was once an insufferable 15-year-old may prove, at age 25 or 35, to be an exemplary son or daughter.

In the marriage relationship, spouses routinely set aside their own desires and preferences to please the other. It would strike most observers as morally objectionable for one spouse to make all of the sacrifices in the relationship, while the other steadfastly refused to make any. Yet the need for self-sacrifice in marriage is too obvious a point to be belabored. The call for self-denial is woven into the fabric of the marriage relationship, so that people sometimes say that marriage is a "school for character." Mutuality comes at a price. When various forms of physical or mental disability occur in families or communities—for example, Alzheimer's disease, autism, debilitating illness, severe depression, eating disorders—then the maintenance of mutuality and community may indeed be a call for some persons to engage in continual self-sacrifice. The only way to avoid self-sacrifice in such instances would be for someone to opt out of the relationship, eschewing its burdens and also forfeiting its delights.

If parental and/or spousal relationships show that the idea of self-sacrifice makes secular sense, then it makes Christian sense all the more. The figure of Jesus—who gave himself self-consciously and voluntarily to suffer on the cross on behalf of others—lies at the center of New Testament teaching. It is hard therefore to imagine any convincing account of the Christian message that removes the notion of self-sacrifice. In the life of Christian discipleship, the setting aside of one's interests on behalf of others may become habitual. During the 1740s, David Brainerd's missionary work required him to live in the untamed wilderness of Pennsylvania and to suffer from cold, heat, exposure, inadequate food, isolation, and loneliness. Within a few years, Brainerd's exertions took a toll on his health and brought about his early demise. The hardships of life among the Native Americans he went to evangelize were the price he paid for fulfilling his calling.

For a contemporary example of self-sacrifice as a way of life, one might consider the case of Heidi and Rolland Baker.[60] Over the course of three decades, this couple embraced austerity as a way of life in Indonesia, Hong Kong, England, and Mozambique. With their two children in tow, they moved into one of the worst slums of Hong Kong and sat on the streets among the poor, to share their lifestyle, concerns, and point of view. They ate the dubious food given to them, lived in squalid conditions, and contracted a number of serious, though not fatal, illnesses as a result. Upon arriving in Mozambique, Heidi Baker cared for orphans, contracted a "flesh-eating" and antibiotic-resistant microbe, and was diagnosed with multiple sclerosis—a condition later declared to be healed after she received prayer at the Toronto Christian Fellowship. The later phenomenal evangelistic success of the Bakers' ministry—with thousands of new churches established in Mozambique—did not come apart from these long years of struggle, suffering, and deprivation. In light of the happy ending of the story, it is all too easy to project the outcome backward and—in good American fashion—to turn this into a triumphalistic story of inevitable progress and assured success. Yet if one reads the Bakers' narrative sequentially—without prematurely inserting the uncertain, unknown outcome—then it is not a pretty story at all. Their story is alarming, if not appalling. Much of what they did in their earlier years would have seemed foolhardy to most observers. The difficulties they experienced did not seem proportionate to any benefits that they were likely to bring to themselves or to anyone else.

The author's visit to the Bakers' ministry in Mozambique (as part of Flame of Love Project–funded research) shed light on this theme of self-sacrifice. Arriving at the Iris-Arco compound in the city of Pemba, among a team of about 40 others from North America, Britain, Norway, and South Africa, we found ourselves with adequate though not lavish accommodations, in bunk beds and with shared shower facilities. Then the water ran out. We soon learned that this happened often at Iris-Arco Ministries, and that nothing much could be done about it. We had to wait until the water truck returned to replenish the depleted tank that supplied water for our faucets and showers. While the prospect of going without running water for a few days might not seem like an occasion of great suffering (just think of Brainerd!) or like the inspiring stories of the martyrs and heroes of times past (read any page of Butler's *Lives of the Saints!*), the unexpected experience of having "creature comforts" suddenly stripped away led many of us to pine for home. Within days, our clothes became foul, with sweat oozing into the fabric, and then drying, moistening, and forming a crust. Apart from those living on the streets, North Americans do not ordinarily get to experience the tactile sensation of pulling on a grimy piece of clothing in the morning, knowing in advance that the filth on one's flesh will only increase over the course of the day.

After several days had passed, a number of team members began to peel off in ones and twos, heading down to a luxury hotel—outside of the Iris-Arco compound, and yet within easy walking distance—to pay for the privilege of showering in a rented room and getting freshened up. The author was not among those who went to the nearby hotel, but fully understood why many went there, and applauded the eventual arrival of the water truck as much as anyone. Local Mozambicans were not heading off to the hotel, of course, since the one-day rental price for the room was more than an average annual salary. At the end of our stay in Mozambique, the author was struck when Heidi Baker came to a breakfast at this nearby hotel as the invited guest of the visiting team, and she looked around and casually commented that she had not been there for a year or two. Many of us accustomed to the accoutrements of Western life would have chosen to get away to the hotel on a regular basis, were we living in Mozambique.

Yet Heidi and Rolland Baker, from their early years, chose to live out an "incarnational" ministry. Indeed, this seems to be one of the secrets of their work and their effectiveness among the Mozambicans—their all-but-total identification with the condition and way of life of the people that they came to serve. In earlier years, Heidi often slept on the floor of the dormitory, alongside the orphans she had come to serve. It is hard to see how she got much sleep, given the noise and hubbub that often lasted well into the night. The work of Iris Ministries, we were told, was so valuable that it was worth all the inconveniences. Running water and "creature comforts"—things we took for granted but did not know that we took for granted—were quite dispensable. The trip to Mozambique was thus instructive. It showed that a lifestyle of self-denial was sometimes a necessary price for fruitful service to others. Furthermore, it demonstrated that self-sacrifice did not necessarily take place through a dramatic, momentary, all-or-nothing decision—someone choosing death over life in martyrdom, abandoning a promising career, breaking off a romantic attachment, etc. Difficult sacrifices sometimes take place gradually, over long periods of time, when one pursues a vocation requiring an abandonment of comforts and prerogatives.

In summary, then, Jonathan Edwards's theology is helpful for those seeking to understand Godly love. It offers a conceptual framework that may help us to make sense of the interplay between love's mutuality and love's sacrifice. Its stress on both the delight and difficulty of agape love rings true to experience. Edwards's sermon "Heaven Is a World of Love" may be his most beautiful evocation of the theme of mutuality.[61] There he demonstrates that humanity's ideal condition—i.e., heaven—is not a matter of individual human beings in relation to God. Instead it is a condition of corporate fulfillment, in which some human beings are so united to others that their well-being is all but indistinguishable. Those in heaven rejoice and thrill and delight in the honor, happiness, and pleasure of another just as much as if this honor, happiness, and pleasure had come to them instead. What might seem the highest limit of human love—discovered only in the most intimate marriages or friendships of this life—Edwards presents as fully realized in heaven. Moreover, the total mutuality of heaven is a yardstick against which lesser forms of community may be measured. In Edwards's theology, though, community comes at a price. His own pastoral labors brought increasing conflict with his congregation during the 1740s—culminating in his humiliating dismissal in 1750, by a church committee that decided the issue with a majority of one vote. This experience allowed Edwards to see the Christian life as modeled on the suffering Christ. That authentic Christian living involves self-sacrifice is clearly shown by such people as David Brainerd and Heidi Baker. A convincing picture of agape in practice will neither set aside the importance of mutuality among persons nor exclude self-sacrifice as a possible prerequisite for mutuality.

## Notes

1. Herbert Anderson, Edwards Foley, Bonnie Miller-McLemore, and Robert Schreiter, eds., *Mutuality Matters: Family, Faith, and Just Love* (Lanham, MD: Rowman & Littlefield, 2004), 6, citing the words of Paul Wadell.

2. J. Jeffrey Tillman, "Sacrificial Agape: Sacrificial Agape and Group Selection in Contemporary American Christianity," *Zygon* 43 (2008): 541–56; and Don Browning, "Love as Sacrifice, Love as Mutuality: Response to Jeffrey Tillman," *Zygon* 43 (2008): 557–62. Browning writes: "Tillman is perceptive in suggesting that these three Protestant theologians and I, in our openness to certain insights from the contemporary social sciences, also have shown appreciation for features of Christian love often articulated by Roman Catholicism and neglected by classical Protestantism. . . . I do believe that Protestants have something to learn from certain Thomists and neo-Thomistic Catholic views of Christian love. But this does not mean that I discount a prominent role for self-sacrifice in my view of Christian love" (558).

3. Edwards Collins Vacek, S. J., *Love, Human and Divine: The Heart of Christian Ethics* (Washington, DC: Georgetown University Press, 1994).

4. Unless otherwise noted, all biblical references in this chapter are to the New International Version.

5. Martin Luther, *Lectures on Romans*, ed. Wilhelm Pauck (Philadelphia: Westminster, 1961), 163.

6. Anders Nygren, *Agape and Eros*, trans. Philip S. Watson (Chicago: University of Chicago Press, 1982 [1932]), 722, 131, 713, 722–23; cf. 217, 222. Karl Holl, in *The Reconstruction of Morality* (1948), agreed with Nygren and called Augustine a "corrupter of Christian morality" (cited in Burnaby, *Amor Dei: A Study of the Religion of St. Augustine* [London: Hodder & Stoughton, 1938], 255).

7. Jonathan Edwards, *The Works of Jonathan Edwards*, 26 vols. [online version, 73 vols.] (New Haven, CT: Yale University Press, 1957–2008), 18:75. Henceforth, this work will be cited by volume and page number as "WJE."

8. See Stephen G. Post, *A Theory of Agape: On the Meaning of Christian Love* (Lewisburg, PA: Bucknell University Press; London: Associated University Presses, 1990), 36–51; and Post's essay "Disinterested Benevolence: An American Debate over the Nature of Christian Love," *Journal of Religious Ethics* 14 (1986): 356–68.

9. On Edwards as a mediating figure between traditional Protestant and traditional Catholic ideas and interests, see Michael J. McClymond and Gerald R. McDermott, *The Theology of Jonathan Edwards* (New York: Oxford University Press, 2011), 695–705, 722.

10. Edwards, WJE, 2:344–45.

11. Ibid., 8:366.

12. William J. Danaher Jr., *The Trinitarian Ethics of Jonathan Edwards* (Louisville: Westminster John Knox Press, 2004), 237.

13. Authors on Edwards's views on love include: William Spohn, "Sovereign Beauty: Jonathan Edwards and the Nature of True Virtue," *Theological Studies* 42 (1981): 394–421; Paul Ramsey, "Editor's Introduction," in WJE 8:1–121; Stephen G. Post, "Communion and True Self-Love" and "Jonathan Edwards's Ideal of Perfect Communion," in *A Theory of Agape*, 17–51; William Spohn, "Spirituality and Its Discontents: Practices in Jonathan Edwards's *Charity and Its Fruits*," *Journal of Religious Ethics* 31 (2003): 253–76; William J. Danaher Jr., *The Trinitarian Ethics of Jonathan Edwards* (Louisville: Westminster John Knox Press, 2004), esp. 59–63, 136–37, 201–49; and Stephen A. Wilson, *Virtue Reformed: Rereading Jonathan Edwards's Ethics* (Leiden: Brill, 2005).

14. Anders Nygren, *Agape and Eros*; C. S. Lewis, *The Four Loves* (New York: Harcourt, Brace, Jovanovich, 1960). More recent works that continue Nygren's themes include Gene Outka, *Agape: An Ethical Analysis* (New Haven, CT: Yale University Press, 1972); Edmund S. Santurri and William Werpehowski, eds., *The Love Commandments: Essays in Christian Ethics and Moral Philosophy* (Washington, DC: Georgetown University Press, 1992). A historical work in the Augustine–Aquinas–Edwards–C. S. Lewis tradition on love—and in response to Anders Nygren—is John Burnaby's *Amor Dei* (cited above). A recent work that advances a multidisciplinary understanding of love is Thomas Jay Oord, *Defining Love: A Philosophical, Scientific, and Theological Engagement* (Grand Rapids, MI: Brazos Press, 2010).

15. Edwards read Latin well and avidly, and he was generally much more aware of the etymological background of Latinate terms than would be the case with most English-speakers today.

16. "All men," said Augustine, "desire to live happily." For "following after God is the desire for happiness; to reach God is happiness itself" (Augustine, "On the Morals of the Catholic Church," in *Basic Writings of St. Augustine*, 2 vols., trans. Whitney J. Oates [New York: Random House, 1948], 1:320).

17. Lewis, *Four Loves*, 14.

18. Post, *Theory of Agape*, 10, 12.

19. Paul Ramsey comments that "John 17:21–22 is the manifest fully unveiled meaning of goodwill among men" (WJE 8:26). See the references to this text in WJE 8:144, 443.

20. This quote is from the King James Version (1611). Edwards cites the scriptural texts given above in developing his teaching on "propriety" (WJE 8:380, 144, 443, 217, 267). On Christ as a "public person," that is, a corporate personality that includes others, see WJE 17:249; WJE 18:148, 150; WJE 20:475, 477; WJE 24:1214; and WJE 25:234. Edwards also writes of Adam as a "public person"—WJE 3:260, 396; and WJE 20:391.

21. The account here draws from Danaher's insightful treatment of self-love in Edwards in his *Trinitarian Ethics*, 59–63, 136–37, 269n72, and 270n74.

22. Joseph Butler, *Five Sermons Preached in the Rolls Chapel and a Dissertation*

*upon the Nature of Virtue*, ed. S. L. Darwell (Indianapolis: Hackett, 1983), 56; David Hume, *A Treatise of Human Nature*, ed. E. C. Mossner (New York: Penguin Books, 1984), 580–81; cited in Danaher, *Trinitarian Ethics*, 269n72.

23. Edwards, WJE, 18:73.

24. Ibid., 18:73–76.

25. See Martin Luther, *Luther's Works*, vol. 25: *Lectures on Romans* (St. Louis: Concordia, 1972), 379–84 (on Rom. 9:2–3).

26. Edwards, WJE, 8:255, 15.

27. Ibid., 6:365. Edwards continues: "So that we are to conceive of divine excellence as the infinite general love, that which reaches all proportionally, with perfect purity and sweetness."

28. *End of Creation* argued that there is nothing morally suspect in God's supreme regard (WJE 8:450–52).

29. Edwards, WJE, 8:452.

30. See John Piper, *The Pleasures of God* (Portland, OR: Multnomah Press, 2000), and *Desiring God: Meditations of a Christian Hedonist* (Downers Grove, IL: InterVarsity Press, 2004).

31. Wilson Kimnach in Edwards, WJE, 10:239; the sermon appears in Edwards, WJE, 10:296–307.

32. Paul Ramsey in Edwards, WJE, 8:61.

33. Edwards, WJE, 8:213, 542. The distinction between "benevolence" and "complacence" appears in Francis Hutcheson's *An Inquiry into the Original of Our Ideas of Beauty and Virtue* (1725), listed in 1738 in Edwards's "Catalogue" of reading (WJE 26:211–12), and cited several times in Edwards's corpus in either the 1725 or 1738 edition (WJE 3:224; WJE 8:562, 625, 698; WJE 23:235; WJE 26:47, 77, 91–92).

34. Edwards, WJE, 8:129, 143–44.

35. Gene Outka describes the "normative content" of agape, or neighbor-love, as "equal regard" or regard "for every person qua human existent" (*Agape*, 9; see 7–54). While Outka's definition does not contradict *Charity and Its Fruits*, it lacks Edwards's theological specificity. Outka generally follows a Kantian approach wherein the highest moral principle consists in a regard for persons as ends-in-themselves.

36. Edwards, WJE, 8:373.

37. Ibid., 375, 370.

38. Ibid., 392–94.

39. Ibid., 261–62.

40. Ibid., 389, 380–81.

41. Post, *Theory of Agape*, 12.

42. This section is based on McClymond and McDermott, *Theology of Jonathan Edwards*, 80–83, where we treat the "ethical-rigorist turn" in Edwards's preaching and writing during the 1740s and 1750s.

43. George Claghorn, "Editor's Introduction," in Edwards, WJE, 16:10,13.

44. For references, see ibid., 4:46, 109, 206.

45. George Marsden, *Jonathan Edwards: A Life* (New Haven, CT: Yale University Press, 2003), 189.

46. See Patricia J. Tracy, *Jonathan Edwards, Pastor: Religion and Society in Eighteenth-Century Northampton* (New York: Hill & Wang, 1980), 90–91, 106–111, 130–31, 160–66; Marsden, *Jonathan Edwards*, 189, 131; and Claghorn, WJE, 16:14–15.

47. Marsden, *Jonathan Edwards*, 107.

48. Thomas Schafer's index (WJE 13:142) shows that there were entries on "perseverance" (nos. 415, 428, 467) during the years 1729–1730; see WJE 13:474–75, 480, 508. The entries on "perseverance" appeared in increasing numbers in 1736–1739 (nos. 711, 726, 729, 744-corol. 1, 750, 755, 773, 774, 795, 799, 823); see WJE 18:340–41, 352–57, 387–88, 398, 403–4, 422–25, 496–97, 498–500, 534–35. On "obedience," see the entries from 1736 to 1739 (nos. 790, 819, 876); see WJE 18:474–88, 530–31, and WJE 20:119.

49. WJE, 18:355.

50. Minkema, "Edwards," 153, citing "Signs of Godliness" and "Directions for Judging of Persons' Experiences" in WJE 21:469–510, 522–24.

51. Marsden, *Jonathan Edwards*, 190.

52. Claghorn, WJE, 16:14; Marsden, *Jonathan Edwards*, 298–99.

53. Wilson Kimnach, "Editor's Introduction," in Edwards, WJE, 25:15.

54. Marsden, *Jonathan Edwards*, 332.

55. "True Saints, When Absent from the Body, Are Present with the Lord," Edwards, WJE, 25:250–52.

56. Walls, 253; for more on the Edwards–Brainerd legacy for missions, see John A. Grigg: *The Lives of David Brainerd: The Making of an American Evangelical Icon* (New York: Oxford University Press, 2009), 128–46, 164–87.

57. Stuart Piggin, "'The Expanding Knowledge of God': Jonathan Edwards's Influence on Missionary Thinking and Promotion," in David W. Kling and Douglas A. Sweeney, eds., *Jonathan Edwards at Home and Abroad: Historical Memories, Cultural Movements, Global Horizons* (Columbia: University of South Carolina Press, 2003), 273, 275–76.

58. Joseph A. Conforti, *Jonathan Edwards, Religious Tradition, and American Culture* (Chapel Hill: University of North Carolina Press, 1995), 75.

59. Oord, *Defining Love*, 15. Oord's definition of agape is a variation on the statement quoted above: "Agape is intentional sympathetic response to promote overall well-being when confronted by that which generates ill-being" (43).

60. The account given here is based on personal experiences and conversations with the staff and visitors of Iris Ministries in Pemba, Mozambique during May–June 2011, and on a reading of the Bakers' books—Rolland and Heidi Baker, *Always Enough: God's Miraculous Provision for the Poorest Children on Earth* (Grand Rapids, MI: Baker Book House/Chosen Books, 2003), and Heidi Baker, with Shara Pradhan, *Compelled by Love: How to Change the World through the Simple Power of Love in Action* (Lake Mary, FL: Charisma House, 2008).

61. Edwards, WJE, 8:366–97.

# IMAGO DEI AND KENOSIS

## Contributions of Christology
## to the Study of Godly Love

*PETER ALTHOUSE*

The concept of Godly love as defined in the introduction of this book leads to the hypothesis that human perceptions of divine love motivate persons to act in loving ways for the Other in works of social benevolence. Godly love is a new field of study in the social sciences that, in dialogue with theology, attempts to overcome the bias of "methodological atheism" with a more neutral approach of "methodological agnosticism"—in other words, a scholarly honest approach neither excludes nor assumes divine interaction as a scientific presupposition.[1] The theological disciplines have resources for exploring the divine–human interaction as well as the implications this interaction has in the social sphere. Although some theological approaches may in fact start from a fundament of "methodological atheism," for the most part there is a presupposition of divinity in theology. Moreover, theology insists that human experience of the divine is in some manner a divine encounter; otherwise, why bother with theology at all?[2]

The Christian faith takes the witness of Scripture as normative for theology, which is then organized thematically using the principles of reason.[3] In this process, certain biblical-theological themes emerge as important in motivating people to act. Two that have significance for constructing a theological method for the study of Godly love are the imago dei and kenosis. In the Christian faith the ultimate image of Godly love is divine kenosis, in which God became human flesh to suffer the way of the cross. The cross is the ultimate act of sacrifice for the Other, in that Jesus Christ, the messianic Son of the living God, suffers divine abandonment so that the world might be reconciled. The eschatological unfolding of the effects of the cross spreads into the world through divine mission, calling people to act for the good of the Other in accordance with the values of the kingdom. Correlate to kenosis is the image and likeness of God. The proposal here is for a relational understanding that insists that the image of God is fully realized in community, as the community of God seeks to live in likeness to the crucified Christ—offering oneself for the sake of the Other. Acts of benevolence, which can range from compassion and humanitarian action to social justice and creation care, reflect Godly love as people live in the likeness of the kenotic Christ. Although the concept of Godly love was not developed with kenosis or the imago dei in mind, these theological considerations should be more central to empirical investigations of Godly love, because there is a need for a normative framework in the evaluation of the extent to which a set of divine/human interactions truly reflect Godly love. In other words, the emerging field of study built upon the concept of Godly love has been normatively agnostic as well as methodologically agnostic, but from the standpoint of theology, kenosis and the imago dei provide a framework for making normative judgments about the character of benevolent acts.

We shall begin in reverse order with a theological investigation of the imago dei, first by framing the discussion according to the substantive and relational interpretations, two of the more dominant views in contemporary theology. We then engage in a detailed discussion of Karl Barth's theology of the divine image and its Christological orientation. The choice of Barth as a dialogue partner is based in his understanding of the image of God as a relational rather than substantive quality. Discussion will focus on kenosis as an important image of divine self-giving love in which the Son of God "empties" or "condescends" in the incarnation of Christ Jesus in order to take on human flesh and journey the way of the cross. This image has practical import in that for the Christian to imitate and be in the likeness of Christ, she or he must be willing to surrender or limit the desires of the self in order to love, help, and serve the Other. The conclusion will comment on how this theological construction can aid in the development of Godly love, specifically the practical implications of the theologies of kenosis and the imago dei on social acts of benevolence for the Other that must be rooted in self-giving humility as found in the likeness of the crucified Christ.

## Two Views on the Imago Dei

The Christian doctrine of the imago dei is rooted in the Genesis account of creation, specifically the creation of humanity. "Then God said, 'Let us make man in our image, in our likeness. . . . ' So God created man in his own image, in the image of God created them; male and female he created them" (Gen. 1.26–27, NIV 1984). Although Jewish theology does not appear to have expanded on this idea, the Christian fathers grappled with the anthropological and Christological meaning of the "image" and "likeness" of God.[4]

The substantive view has been the dominant position throughout Christian history, insisting that the image is idiosyncratic to humanity and claiming that it constitutes part of humanity's physical, psychological, or spiritual makeup. On a literal reading, image can be interpreted as humanity's physical ability to walk upright, or more symbolically interpreted as a psychological and/or spiritual capacity to reason, contemplate, or will. During the patristic and medieval periods of Christian history, the image and likeness of God were taken to be distinct but interconnected doctrines. On the one hand, image was taken to be the physical quality that makes humanity human. Origen, for instance, believed that the image was given directly in creation, whereas Irenaeus believed that Adam was endowed with reason and free will. On the other hand, the likeness was thought to be a spiritual or moral endowment. In other words, the divine likeness was for the purpose of spiritual growth in relation to God. For Origen, likeness was not something conveyed immediately in creation but something acquired over time and consummated in the new creation.[5] For Irenaeus, likeness was a supernatural endowment possessed through the activity of the Spirit. It was only embryonic and undeveloped in form, but would through the application of human free agency develop fully in righteousness as God intended. In the fall divine likeness was lost completely, and the image was corrupted but not completely lost, otherwise the human would no longer be human.[6] Medieval scholastics continued to extrapolate Irenaeus's view, seeing image as the natural capacity in humanity making humanity what it is, and likeness as a divine gift added to human nature. Stated negatively, the constitution of humanity remained, but the capacity to be holy and good was lost.[7]

With the Reformation the doctrine of the imago dei changed. As a biblical theologian, Luther read the image and likeness as a Hebrew parallelism and therefore as referring to the same thing. For Luther, all aspects of the image have been corrupted by the fall. No aspect of the image or likeness remains intact. Together, they are now a mere relic of what they once were. Calvin's position developed in a way similar to Luther's, but because a relic remains, knowledge of God is gained by probing the nature of the human self, since humanity is in the image of God, however tattered. For Calvin, the interconnectedness of God and humanity was found in the measure of holiness and in humanity's ability to reason.[8] Interestingly, Calvin's emphasis on reason is the point of departure for the modernist period, which located the image of God in this reasoning capability.[9]

The relational view of the imago dei has been developed primarily by Karl Barth. The relational view is better able to support current developments in the study of the field of Godly love, because the relational view makes communal life and giving to the Other the basis for a proper expression of love and social benevolence. The idiosyncratic view of the imago dei has the disadvantage of being too heavily invested in modernist notions of individual subjectivity, where desire—for experience, for success, for blessing, for the meeting of personal financial and emotional needs, etc.—is given primary relevance. In other words, the individualistic view of the image of God is prone to egoistic desire, whereas the relational view supports, at least potentially, a proper expression of altruistic acts, that is, acts that are not primarily motivated by personal gain.

## Christology and the Image of God in the Theology of Karl Barth

This author's starting point for integrating a theology of the image of God with the emerging field of Godly love is the evangelical theology of Karl Barth. In reaction to the German Liberal Protestant tradition in which he was schooled, Barth launched a new direction in theology that is now considered the beginning of postliberalism. German liberalism sought to articulate a universal, systematic theology grounded in nature and the human individual as an idiosyncratic predisposition, either as rational in structure (Kant) or as experiential (Schleiermacher). Barth, however, begins from the premise that dogmatic theology must be grounded in the self-revelation of the Word, that is, the Word made flesh in Christ Jesus, whose incarnation, death, and resurrection is attested to by the apostles as recorded in Scripture and is enlivened in the human heart by the activity of the Holy Spirit. The significance of this turn in theology is that Barth takes Scripture seriously, not as a source for excavating the religious in humanity that can be judged by some independent criteria, but as the normative basis for theological assessment and construction.[10] Specifically, Barth reads the Genesis account of the imago dei with fresh eyes that see human creation as relational and communal. In other words, Barth argues that the imago dei is constituted in the relationship and differentiation of male and female, rather than in an idiosyncratic predisposition of the individual that can be replicated as a universal constant. "It will be shown that divine likeness cannot actually exist for him in the continuance or even the progressive development of a deposited quality, but can only be the object of his hope in God his Creator."[11]

Thus, Barth distinguishes the image and likeness of God. The plural pronoun in "our image" is an important clue for a communal rendering of the imago dei in that "God's own sphere and being" is found in "us"—that is, the community of human relationships. Yet this image, this beingness that defines human creatureliness, is the prototype; that is, the Word is the agency of creation and the true image for humanity as a whole who is to be imitated. Correspondingly, likeness points to the contingency of human beings who live in relationship to one another as patterned after the divine image. "The being created in the likeness of this image is man. The rest of creation has this character of a copy or image only so far as has found its conclusion and climax in the creation and existence of man."[12] For Barth, the image is the Word of God who is the archetype of creation and who becomes incarnate in history. Humanity receives its likeness as a copy of the prototype—the Word.

A number of things should be noted in terms of Barth's reconstruction of the image of God. First, God is depicted not as a unified monad but as trinitarian. In other words, the threefold self-differentiation within the One God is taken seriously when grappling with God's image in humanity. What this means is that the divine image from which humanity has been fashioned is an expression of trinitarian relationship that gives to the other in perichoretic fellowship. "In God's own being and sphere," asserts Barth, "there is a counterpart: a genuine but harmonious self-encounter and self-discovery; a free co-existence and co-operation; an open confrontation and reciprocity. Man is the repetition of this divine life; its copy and reflection."[13] Because the imago dei in humanity is a reflection of the inner-trinitarian life of God, human existence is not defined in isolation but as social and relational. "He [man] is this first in the fact that he is the counterpart of God, the encounter and discovery in God Himself being copied and imitated in God's relation to man. But he is also in the fact that he is himself the counterpart of his fellows and has in them a counterpart, a co-existence and co-operation in God Himself being repeated in the relation of man to man."[14]

The second thing to note is that the image and likeness is found in "man," according to Barth, but is not a possession of "man," as something that is intrinsically inherent. The creation account does not indicate that the image of God is something that is possessed by Adam and therefore idiosyncratic to him, but that the image is of God, given by God as an act of grace, and assumes the uniqueness of trinitarian plurality in the differentiation of male and female.[15] The imago dei, then, as an act of grace of God's self-giving character, carries with it the relational quality of self-giving love.

Third, the image and likeness of God is found in human differentiation, specifically the differentiation of male and female. Barth's use of "man" (which is jarring in the current climate of gender inclusiveness but understandable in his early twentieth-century context) should be understood as the whole of humanity, not as individual; specifically, the image of God is found in the differentiation of male and female.

> The only thing that we are told about the creation of man, apart from the fact that it was accomplished by the Word of God in and after the image of God, is that "God created them male and female." . . . The only real differentiation and relationship is that of man to man, and in its original and most concrete form of man to woman and woman to man. Man is no more solitary than God. But as God is One, and He alone is God, so man is one and alone, and two only in the duality of his kind, i.e., the duality of man and woman.[16]

Not only does Barth reject the type of individualism as defined by Cartesian subjectivity in which the individual is understood as self-isolated from community and noncontingent with reference to the Creator, but he drives his point harder to argue that this differentiation of the sexes in man and woman extends into human community. The covenant God makes with humanity in creation is fundamentally based in the imago dei and establishes the relationship between God and humanity. But the imago dei also forms the human covenantal relationships with one another, based on our imitation of the imago dei that is the imitation of the relational God.[17] The implication of this new paradigm is important. It critiques the religious support for the social structures of patriarchy, thereby creating space for gender inclusivity.[18] Most importantly, the relational paradigm establishes the ground for human community. The locus of God's activity in the world, for Barth, begins in the church, the community of those who are called and elected as the body of Christ, who live together in dependence on Christ, and who give of themselves for the kingdom of God. This community is inclusive rather than exclusive, outwardly oriented in love for the lost, the downtrodden, and the suffering. It is a community for the Other, a theme to be taken up later in the discussion of Sorokin's distinction between in-group egoism and community altruism. Nevertheless, Barth was not uncritical of the troubled times in his world and developed his own political theology of liberation amidst the social upheaval of Nazi Germany.[19]

The final thing to note with regard to Barth's theology of the imago dei is the Christological orientation of the creation of humanity, in that Christ as the Word is the true image that is reflected in likeness. "It will be shown that man has reason to look for the man who will be different from him, but who for this reason will be real man for him, in the image and likeness of God male and female in his place and on his behalf, namely Jesus Christ and his community."[20] In this theological move, Barth eschews an individualistic framework that is prone to egoistic tendencies, and takes a more relational approach in the differentiation between men and women who together constitute God's image, and provides space for seeing divine interaction with the entire human race. The Word made flesh, the prototype of the imago dei, carries the divine image of the trinitarian and therefore relational God.

Generally, a distinction is made between Christian anthropology, in which the imago dei occupies a major theological place, and Christology, in which the likeness of God is found in the second Adam in whom humanity finds its identity and from whom humanity receives the likeness of God. However, the connection between the anthropological focus on image and likeness and the admonition by the apostle Paul to be in the likeness of Christ suggests that these two theological loci need to be more integrated. Certainly, Barth noted the interconnection of the two in the centrality of Christ as the revelation of God. Alister McGrath proposes that despite Barth's profound suspicion of natural theology, his project makes space for a Christologically infused natural theology.[21] The Christological focus of special revelation and natural theology for whom Christ is the head of creation provides connections between the Christian confession of Jesus Christ the Lord and creation as the work of the Lord for which Christ offered himself in love. Barth's work stands in contrast to Luther's equation of image and likeness as parallel expressions with the same meaning. It is also different from the patristic development of image and likeness in which the image is corrupted yet retains vestiges of itself, but likeness as moral infancy is lost. Barth distinguishes image and likeness in a way that makes reference to image as being retained in God, and likeness as imitation of that image.[22] The prototype to which Barth refers is key for understanding his position in that it is none other than the Word, the Son of God, who became incarnate as truly human. Thus, Barth sums up: "At any rate, the point of the text is that God willed to create man as a being corresponding to His own being—in such a way that He Himself (even if in knowledge of Himself) is the original and prototype, and man the copy or imitation."[23]

The apostle Paul makes this connection between Christ and image/likeness in his discussion of the First Adam and the Second Adam, and the interplay of this typological construction has implications for human community. Christ *is* the image of God (1 Cor. 11:7; 2 Cor. 3:18; 4:4; Col. 3:18; Heb. 10:1[24]), and those who constitute the body of Christ are to be in the likeness of Christ (Rom. 6:5; 8:3; Phil. 2:7; Heb. 2:17; 7:3; 1 John 3:2). Hans Urs von Balthasar puts it nicely by stating that because Jesus Christ is *the* image and likeness of God, "So we must be 'conformed' to his image (Rom 8:29; 2 Cor. 3:18); 'Just as we have borne the image of man of dust (Adam), we shall also bear the image of the man of heaven' (1 Cor 15:49). If the two tensions are combined ('image-likeness' and 'earthly-heavenly image'), complex fugues result; the two can be treated in relative isolation, but they can also be fused in such a way that the first motif is rooted in the second from the start."[25] For Barth, "man" was created in the image of the divine prototype, Christ, who is the image of the triune God, in such a way that *men and women together* constitute the copy of the prototype. To play with the theology a little, there is a reversal in the typology of the first Adam and second Adam in the sense that Jesus Christ is truly the first Adam from whom earthly Adam derives his image and likeness. "In other words, Adam is already Jesus Christ and Jesus Christ is already Adam. In the relationship of prophecy and fulfillment in which Paul conjoined the Old Testament with Jesus Christ, this identification is valid for all the self-evident differences. In this way Paul regarded the man Jesus Christ as the real image of God, and therefore as the real man created by God."[26] The significance of the Christological reading of the imago dei will become clear in the next section, in that Christ's humility and self-giving love is to be imitated and is the basis for human self-giving love in help for the Other. What this means in relation to the field of Godly love is that simply acting in benevolent ways does not in itself constitute Godly love if this is done for selfish or egoistic reasons—that is, to feel good about oneself, to advertise one's name for the sake of celebrity status, to gain a tax benefit. But when one acts in Christlike humility and operates according to the principle of self-giving love for the other, then and only then has Godly love been expressed. The basis for humility and self-giving in Christianity is divine kenosis, and this free act leads to the cross as God's ultimate sacrifice.

### Kenosis as the Divine Act of Self-Humiliation and Self-Giving

To be in the image and likeness of Christ in which both male and female together constitute the imago dei through community relations has implications for the field of Godly love. More specifically, the Christological hymn of Philippians 2:5–8 has implications for how being in the image and likeness of God works outward into human community in love for one's neighbor. Known as the theology of kenosis, the Philippians passage says that Christ "did not consider equality with God something to be grasped but made himself nothing, taking the very nature of a servant, being made in human likeness." *Kenosis* derives from the Greek and means "to empty." It has cognates such as Christ's self-emptying, humiliation, or condescension and relates to, but is distinguished from, the incarnation and hypostatic union of Christ, finding its ultimate expression in the event of the cross.

Although kenosis theology is as old as apostolic Christianity and has especially been developed in Eastern Christianity around the theology of theosis or deification,[27] it has been mediated in Western Christianity through the Lutheran Reformation and developed in the nineteenth century through Gottfried Thomasius's theology of kenoticism. However, for the patristic fathers kenosis was the way to support the Chalcedon position of the hypostatic union, which asserts that the Logos made flesh is both fully divine and fully human. Kenosis was the means by which the early fathers established the divinity of Christ.[28] The Reformers approached the question of divine kenosis from a philosophical position in which the paradoxical juxtaposition of divine and human attributes in Christ was not in reference to giving up something divine in order to assume human form, but the willful non-use of his divine powers as a human walking the face of the earth.[29] For Luther, Christ's work reflects his being so that in condescension sinful humanity could be united to God through him. But Christ's divine properties remain hidden: otherwise the revelation of divine majesty and glory would be more than creatures could bear. The theology of the cross was for Luther the place of ultimate condescension, the point where weakness makes foolishness of vain human attempts at self-glorification. As a servant Christ reigns through the suffering of the cross, making egoistic self-interest despicable. However, Jesus came to heal egoistic lust (understood as self-exaltation and self-glorification and not as sexual desire). "In this way he teaches people to serve others with a pure divine love which does not love in order to receive good things but in order to give good things to those who lack them."[30] Participation in Godly love, as will be discussed momentarily, eschews benevolent activity from egoistic desire. Rather, engaging in self-giving to the Other must derive from a place of sacrificial love that may very well involve personal or communal suffering, as Christ has suffered for us.

Nineteenth-century kenoticism has sparked a flurry of interest in the nature of divine self-limitation in Christ and has become a hotly debated topic. Initially, Lutheran theologian Gottfried Thomasius probed the question: what attributes did the Logos surrender to become human? The basis of this new endeavor was an apparent logical fallacy. According to the law of noncontradiction, something cannot both be and not be at the same time in the same respect. Therefore, infinity and finitude cannot exist simultaneously in the same location and the same respect without being illogical. At the same time, he was faced with the dilemma that if God were to surrender attributes essential to deity, then God would cease to be God. To resolve this problem, Thomasius made a distinction between essential and relative attributes. Essential attributes are those attributes that are essential to or rather constitute divinity, whereas relative attributes are those attributes that are related to the finitudes of creation. Omniscience, omnipotence, and omnipresence are relative to creation in that in primordial deity there would be no need to define these attributes as such. Only in creation are the omni attributes defined in relation to the limitations or finitudes of created knowledge, limited power, and bound presence. Consequently, the divine omnis are therefore not essential to deity as deity. Thus, the law of noncontradiction is not violated if one sees the omni attributes as not being essential to deity.[31]

In the latter half of the twentieth century, the question of divine kenosis moved beyond the locus of the hypostatic union with questions surrounding the full divinity and full humanity in Christ and began to probe the nature of kenosis for the triune life. If kenosis is central to divine being and not merely an economic activity in the second person of the Trinity, then what does it mean to say that the Father and Spirit have self-limited or self-emptied? Although Barth rejected nineteenth-century kenotic Christology, his theology employed kenotic language to represent God in Christ. Barth understood divine kenosis within a trinitarian framework in which the kenotic activity of God is not a relinquishment of divine attributes, but an intra-trinitarian event of divine love, a sovereign act of obedience in which the Father wills to send and the Son wills to obey. The identity of God is that of obedient self-emptying. "If, then, God is in Christ, if what the man Jesus does is God's own work, this aspect of the self-emptying and self-humbling of Jesus Christ as an act of obedience cannot be alien to God."[32] For Barth, the dialectic in the God-man is paradoxical, an "identity-in-difference" that reveals the mystery of God.[33]

For Jürgen Moltmann, kenosis is revealed in the cross as a trinitarian event in which the Father suffers the giving up and abandonment of the Son and the Son suffers the abandonment of the Father. But kenosis begins with creation, which for Moltmann is a covenantal act and therefore cannot be separated from salvation. In its most radical form kenosis theology has been used as an argument for establishing the death of God,[34] but for Moltmann the abandonment was not the death of God but a death in God and therefore touches the intra-trinitarian relations of the Godhead.[35] Kenosis speaks to the identity of the triune God so that the crucified God is "the image and therefore the identification of the invisible God as one who participates fully in his creation."[36] In the sovereign and primordial decision to create, God willed the universe into existence, and in so doing also chose to self-limit to make space for the space-time structure of creation. "The *outward incarnation* presupposes *inward self-humilitation*."[37] This is a "primordial kenosis" of self-surrender in the inner-Trinitarian relations of divine persons to one another. There is also a restriction of omniscience that limits God's foreknowledge in order to allow for human freedom.[38] Thus, creation is an act of divine kenosis, led in the perichoretic (interrelational) dance by the Father, though with full participation of the Son and the Spirit. One can see the influence of kenotic theology on Moltmann, especially in terms of the restriction of the relative attributes in the creative-salvific process.[39]

However, Moltmann is also clear that in the trinitarian economy there is a kenosis of Spirit as well. In *The Spirit of Life*, Moltmann argues that in creation, the incarnation, and the crucifixion, the Spirit surrenders divine prerogatives by dwelling in time and space, mediating divine presence in creation.[40] Moreover, the Spirit actively participates in the event of the cross, enabling Jesus to follow the way of the cross, sustaining Jesus as he experiences the suffering of God-forsakenness, groaning with Christ in weakness as Jesus gives up the Spirit in death.[41] In abandonment, the Spirit's work in bringing forth the messianic Son and his kingdom is nullified and abnegated.[42] Thus, divine kenosis does not begin with the incarnation but with creation, and more importantly kenosis is a characteristic of the very nature of divine love expressed in the interrelations of the triune God for the Other. Because God is self-giving love, and humans are to live in the likeness of God, self-giving love must be seen as normative for human expressions of love for the Other.

### The Social, Ethical, and Political Implications of Kenosis for Mission

At this point, shifting from the philosophical and theological debates to probe the practical implications of a theology of kenosis will help to construct a theological view of Godly love. In particular, if being in the likeness of Christ means that human community imitates the kenotic mandate of Christ, then there are very real missional and ethical considerations for extending love into the world. Stated differently, the kenotic activity of God in Christ provides a powerful symbol for being in the likeness of God, so that our human activity of expressing love overflows from the mission of God in help, service, liberation, and justice for the Other in and to the world. Although the starting place for this effort is the church as the community that is the body of Christ and therefore preeminently shaped by the *imitatio Christi*, the mission of the church to the world embodies the love of God to the world. The implication here for the emerging field of Godly love is that benevolent acts enacted in self-giving humility, rather than benevolent acts in and of themselves, constitute Godly love.

A shift occurred in mission studies, starting with Karl Barth but taken up especially by the ecumenical dialogues of the World Council of Churches. David Bosch's *Transforming Mission* shifted the focus from missions as the activity that professional ministers do planting churches in other countries or providing for the needs of suffering people,[43] to mission as the mission of God in the sending of Jesus Christ into the world. Important is the all-inclusiveness of Jesus's mission, which practices forgiveness and solidarity with the poor (the focus of Bosch's third chapter). Bosch then outlines an ecumenical missionary paradigm in which the church is for the Other in its mediation of salvation, but also seeks justice and liberation. Although proclamation is important, it must coincide with social action in ways that respect the Other, even the faith stances of the Other. In fact, Bosch argues that the new mode of missional activity is ecumenical and interfaith dialogue. The kenosis of Christ and his ultimate sacrifice on the cross is the fulcrum on which the church's mission operates, through which the incarnation enfolds within itself the world as the eschatological reign of the risen Christ. "The scars of the risen Lord . . . constitute a model to be emulated by those whom he commissions. . . . It is a mission of self-emptying, of humble service—herein lies the abiding validity of Bonhoeffer's idea of the 'church for others.'"[44] Lest one think this mere sentimentality or a nice ideal that has no reality, Bosch goes on to argue that the reconciliation of the cross "demands sacrifice, in very different but also in very real ways, from both oppressor and oppressed. It demands the end to oppression and injustice and commitment to a new life of mutuality, justice, and peace. . . . [It] also means a ministry of love of enemies, of forgiveness."[45] Following up on Bosch's work, Bevans and Schroeder argue that both proclamation and social action to help those in need are acts of peace and justice. "Action on behalf of justice and participation in the transformation of the world fully appear to us as a constitutive dimension of the preaching of the Gospel, or, in other words, of the Church's mission for the redemption of the human race and its liberation from every oppressive situation."[46]

Imitation of Christ in kenotic love is not, nor should it be, for the sake of suffering, but rather suffering is something that must be resisted to be overcome, though something one is willing to assume for the Other. Currently a number of proposals are being offered to come to terms with the incarnational implications of kenosis and the cross. These are evident in the political theologies that have emerged such as with Barth and Moltmann and with numerous liberation, feminist, and ecological theologies. Barth, for instance, leveled his prophetic critique against the disparities of capitalism, which "fostered unwholesome collective relationships of exploitation and dependency," described as an "'almost unequivocally demonic process'—largely because of the ways in which capitalism exacerbates the worst agents of human nature, debases human culture, and, not least, obscures its own injustices."[47]

Moltmann's critique is even more unrelenting, beginning with *Theology of Hope* and *The Crucified God* and taking concrete form in his political and environmental writings.[48] *Theology of Hope* emphasizes the revolutionary character of Christian hope in which the power of the coming kingdom of God overcomes death and destruction in this world and brings sociopolitical transformation. *The Crucified God* looks to the theology of the cross as the basis for active resistance to the powers of sin and despair and spurs the Christian faithful to protest sinful practices in the social world to bring a more just society. The last chapter especially looks to the active resistance brought about by the cross, calling into question all forms of social power and civil religion that dehumanize human life. Moltmann states, "The crucified God is in fact a stateless and classless God. But that does not mean that he is an unpolitical God. He is the God of the poor, the oppressed and the humiliated. . . . Christians will seek to anticipate the future of Christ according to the measure of the possibilities available to them by breaking down lordship and building up the political liveliness of each individual."[49] While self-giving love starts with a personal act of love for the Other in compassion, it must also include love that is extended to the sociopolitical and economic spheres. The complexities of our world are such that the "powers and principalities" take on a life of their own and need to come under the eye of love for the Other. In other words, there needs to be a comprehensive approach to the poor, the suffering, and the downtrodden that goes beyond personal self-giving and must include the social and political powers of nations and states.

Likewise, liberation theologies that have been concretized in Latin America,[50] Asia,[51] Africa,[52] and the United States[53] attempt to address the disparity between those who are privileged and those who are disadvantaged by social systems. Not only are these theologies focused on class and economic systems, but they are also addressing issues of gender disparity[54] and ecological degradation.[55] As an example and in reference to Latin America, Leonardo Boff pushes for action on behalf of justice to bring about sociopolitical and economic transformation. "'The Gospel message contains . . . *a demand for justice in the world.* This is why the Church has the right, indeed the duty, to proclaim justice on the social, national and international level and to denounce instances of injustice.'" More telling, though, is his statement that "due to the incarnation of God in Jesus Christ, 'the attitude of man toward other men is integrated in his [or her] attitude toward God.' . . . In other words, the truth of our relationship with God is measured by the truth of our relationship with others."[56] How human beings help and care for other people—and "other" here is specifically focused on the poor and disadvantaged—is indicative of their relationship to God.

Miroslav Volf constructs a political theology rooted in divine, self-giving love, and while it favors the language of trinitarian self-giving love in the event of the cross, it is kenotic in its orientation. Volf draws on Moltmann's political theology of the cross in which God suffers with those who are suffering in order to give them rights and dignity. The suffering of the cross creates solidarity not simply to suffer with those who suffer, but more importantly to struggle on the side of those who suffer. "All *sufferers* can find comfort in the solidarity of the Crucified; but only those who struggle against evil by following the example of the Crucified will discover him at their side. To claim the comfort of the Crucified while rejecting his way is to advocate not only cheap grace but a deceitful ideology. Within the overarching theme of self-donation, however, the theme of solidarity must be fully affirmed, for it underlines rightly the partiality of divine compassion toward the 'harassed and helpless' (Matt 9:36)."[57] Suffering as understood within a kenotic framework is not self-deprecation but willingness to assume suffering (whatever that may be) to stand in solidarity with and help the Other who suffers. Using the analogy of embrace, Volf argues that liberation of the poor and oppressed must also include forgiveness for the oppressor (otherwise the liberator becomes the oppressor, as has been witnessed in human history) in which justice involves mutual embrace of the one seeking liberation and the one seeking forgiveness for acts of oppression.[58]

The task facing the church and what needs to be incorporated in the field of Godly love is how to develop a comprehensive picture of benevolence that includes perceptions of the divine (perceived or otherwise) expressed through love for the Other and the more organic inclusion of social systems in the process. A definition of benevolence in the field of Godly love needs to incorporate a broad-based and multidimensional praxis of liberation.

## Concluding Comments on Theology and the Study of Godly Love

What, then, do divine kenosis and the imago dei offer in the developing study of Godly love? Why is religion even necessary for inspiring people to altruistic acts? Do we even need to bring God into the picture when developing the field of Godly love?

The model of Godly love proposed by the Flame of Love Project (see chapter 1 of this book) is one in which the interaction between exemplars and/or collaborators presupposes a perception of interaction with the divine. As exemplars and/or collaborators perceive the reception of love through ritual interaction, they are then motivated to share that love with others who are beneficiaries of Godly love. In other words, altruistic acts of self-giving are motivated by perceptions of divine love and embrace so that altruists act in benevolent ways.[59] The language of theology (re) presents the divine in symbolic idioms in ways that inspire and motivate people to act. University of Notre Dame sociologist Christian Smith, for instance, argues that social narratives have the power to inspire and motivate social actors to act in specific ways. In other words, cultural symbols that form the narratives of life are no mere abstraction but have practical implications.[60] Language has the power to structure social reality.[61] The symbolic content of the theology of kenosis and divine image and likeness and the consequent call for persons to conform to the likeness of God as represented in the crucified Christ have important implications as social narratives for the enactment of Godly love, in terms of the manner in which benevolence is enacted and the ends to which benevolence is directed. Benefits for the Other can range from momentary acts of kindness for friends and family to extended acts of compassion, social transformation, and broad-based liberation from socioeconomic, ethnic, racial, gender, and even environmental oppression. The latter benefit must involve more than simply benevolent acts by individuals, but a collaboration of individual, economic, governmental, and global institutional powers.

Yet not all acts of social benevolence can be considered altruistic, and therefore they do not necessarily count within the field of Godly love. As previously stated, many who engage in benevolence do so for egoistic reasons—self-promotion, economic or social gain, etc. To count as Godly love, giving to the Other must emerge as a selfless act, one that involves personal and/or group sacrifice. For instance, although religious communities are important locales for the reception and expression of Godly love, the notion of community needs to be unpacked. Community cannot be defined exclusively as the in-group, whether this is defined as family, tribe, nation, institution, ethnicity, church, gender, or class. In *The Ways and Power of Love*, Harvard sociologist Pitirim Sorokin argues that altruistic behavior must move beyond in-group altruism, because the in-group produces egoistic aggression against those outside it. Love is more universal and oriented to the Other in the world than simply the tribal love of the group. He writes: "An exclusive love of one's own group makes its members indifferent or even aggressive towards other groups and outsiders. The members of 'my group, right or wrong' cannot help treating the rest of humanity as a mere means for their group."[62] Loyalty becomes the key concept for defining fidelity to the in-group in opposition and aggression to outsiders. However, when love is extended to other groups and the rest of humanity, tribal love and exclusive loyalty are exposed as bankrupt and egoistic selfishness. Benevolent behavior toward others, however, further produces and extends love. When human beings treat each other with love and respect, willing to help in spontaneous or intentional acts of self-giving, "then, and only then, altruistic love is extended over the whole of humanity. With such an extension of creative love, all exclusive tribal solidarities are cleansed of their egoistic poison."[63] Human community, then, needs to be understood as the whole community of the world over which love extends, and not merely the exclusive in-group of the family, tribe, or even church. A church focused solely on itself and its institutional needs has not embodied kenotic love and is therefore not an expression of Godly love.

Thus, humility and self-giving activity embodied in the theology of kenosis, image, and likeness establishes a normative framework for discerning and assessing benevolent activity. Admittedly, many people will have mixed motives in their expression of love and giving to the Other. The ambiguity of the human condition following the fall complicates the picture in that egoistic and altruistic intentions may be commingled, but the humility of self-giving love is a norm that needs to be cultivated. Nevertheless, the self-giving acts must reflect the self-giving God, who did not see divinity as something to be grasped but made himself low (Phil. 2:6). The opening of Philippians 2 notes the implications of kenosis when it says: "[M]ake my joy complete by being like-minded, having the same love, being one in spirit and purpose [as Christ]. Do nothing out of selfish ambition or vain conceit, but in humility consider others better than yourselves. Each of you should look not only to your own interests, but also the interests of others" (Phil 2:1–4, NIV 1984). Clearly, the image of divine kenosis has implications for benevolent acts for the good of the Other rooted in a stance of humble self-giving.

Sorokin not only proposes that love is a form of energy but establishes a method to quantify love and its outcomes. He argues that love could be measured according to its intensity, extensity, duration, purity, and adequacy. Intensity would measure the amount of energy involved in the act of love. Extensity would map the range of love, with self-love on the one side to love of all the world and the cosmos on the other. Duration would measure the interval of love, from mere seconds to longer sustained periods. Purity would measure love according to its egoistic and altruistic acts. And adequacy would measure the relationship between its intent and its outcome.[64] Kenotic love as symbolized in the love of the cross would especially fit the categories of intensity (the degree to which one is willing to give of oneself in order to love the Other), extensity (the range of love for family and friend to the love of creation), duration (how long one can kenotically love the Other), and purity (the degree to which love is self-serving or self-giving).

Juxtaposing kenosis with the imago dei suggests how the narrative image of the divine act of self-giving is exemplified in Jesus Christ, who likewise acts in sacrificial self-giving (exemplar) and inspires and motivates those who are committed to the way of Jesus Christ (collaborators) to act in altruistic and self-giving ways toward others who are relationally interconnected in community through the image and likeness of God (beneficiaries).

## Notes

1. See also Matthew T. Lee and Margaret M. Poloma, *A Sociological Study of the Great Commandment in Pentecostalism: The Practice of Godly Love as Benevolent Service* (Lewiston, NY: Edwin Mellen Press, 2009).

2. This is not to suggest a precritical naïveté. Certainly one can point to socio-psychological, socioeconomic, and cultural elements in any human experience, but there are spiritual elements as well. See George P. Schner, "The Appeal to Experience," *Theological Studies* 53 (March 1992): 40–59.

3. Reason here is understood in its broadest sense and includes various forms of rationality, philosophy, culture, and the social sciences.

4. Hans Urs Von Balthasar, *Theo-Drama: Theological Dramatic Theory*, vol. 2, *The Dramatis Personae: Man in God*, trans. Graham Harrison (San Francisco: Ignatius Press, 1990), 316–33. Balthasar posits that finite freedom defined within nature as rational is the quality to which image refers, though the question then arises about how freedom has been redefined by a modernist epistemology and collapsed into individualism (326–28).

5. Origen, *De Principiis*, 3.4.1: ". . . in his first creation man received the dignity of the image of God, but the fulfillment of the likeness is reserved for the final consummation. . . . The possibility of perfection given to him at the beginning by the dignity of the image, and then in the end, through the fulfillment of his works, should bring to perfect consummation the likeness of God." As cited by Alister E. McGrath, *Christian Theology: An Introduction*, 4th ed. (London: Blackwell, 2007), 361.

6. Irenaeus, *Against Heresies*, 5.6.1: "But when the Spirit here blended with the soul is united to [God's] handiwork, the man is rendered spiritual and perfect because of the outpouring of the Spirit, and this is he who was made in the image and likeness of God. But if the Spirit be wanting to the soul, he who is such is indeed of an animal nature, and being left carnal, shall be an imperfect being, possessing indeed the image [of God] in his formation (*in plasmate*), but not receiving the similitude through the Spirit, and thus is this being imperfect"; in Alexander Roberts and James Donaldson, eds., *Ante-Nicene Fathers*, vol. 1, *The Apostolic Fathers, Justin Martyr, Irenaeus* (1885; reprint, Peabody, MA: Hendrickson, 1994), 532.

7. Millard J. Erickson, *Christian Theology*, 3 vols. in 1 (Grand Rapids, MI: Baker Book House, 1983, 1984, 1985), 498–500.

8. Ibid., 501.

9. For instance, Ernst Troeltsch, *Protestantism and Progress: The Significance of Protestantism for the Rise of the Modern World* (Philadelphia: Fortress Press, 1986).

10. Karl Barth, *Church Dogmatics*, ed. G. W. Bromiley and T. F. Torrance, trans. J. W. Edwards, O. Bussey, and H. Knight (Edinburgh: T & T Clark, 1958), 185. Hereafter, CD followed by volume and number.

11. CD III.i, 190.

12. Ibid., 183–84.

13. Ibid., 185.

14. Ibid.

15. Ibid., 188, 202.

16. Ibid., 185–86.

17. Ibid., 186–87.

18. Ibid., 203.

19. See, for instance, George Hunsinger, *Disruptive Grace: Studies in the Theology of Karl Barth* (Grand Rapids, MI: Eerdmans, 2000), esp. chs. 1–4.

20. CD III.i, 190.

21. Alister E. McGrath, *A Scientific Theology*, vol. 1, *Nature* (Edinburgh: T & T Clark, 2002), 280–86. In assessing T. F. Torrance's critique of Barth, McGrath notes that "Barth is not denying the possibility or even the actuality of natural theology. His point is that natural theology 'is undermined, relativized and set aside by the actual knowledge of God mediated through Christ'" (281). In fact, Torrance argues in relation to Barth that natural theology is founded on a doctrine of creation and that therefore natural science and theology are "thoroughly compatible" (283) when Christ is seen as the head of creation.

22. CD III.i, 197.

23. Ibid.

24. The author is fully aware that Pauline authorship is disputed in some of these citations but, for symmetry, follows the canonical understanding of the Pauline tradition.

25. Von Balthasar, *Theo-Drama*, 324.

26. CD III.i, 203.

27. See, for instance, Vladimir Lossky, *In the Image and Likeness of God*, ed. John H. Erickson and Thomas E. Bird, intro. by John Meyendorff (Crestwood, NY: St Vladimir's Seminary Press, 1974), esp. 125–39.

28. Sarah Coakley, "Does Kenosis Rest on a Mistake? Three Kenotic Models in Patristic Exegesis," in *Exploring Kenotic Christology: The Self-Emptying of God*, ed. C. Stephen Evans (New York: Oxford University Press, 2006), 246–64; Daniel T. Knapp, "The Self-Humiliation of Jesus Christ and Christ-Like Living: A Study of Philippians 2:6–11," *Evangelical Journal* 15 (Fall 1997): 81–82; T. D. Herbert, *Kenosis and Priesthood: Towards a Protestant Re-Evaluation of the Ordained Ministry* (Milton Keynes, UK: Paternoster, 2008), 31–41.

29. Bruce L. McCormack, "Karl Barth's Christology as a Resource for a Reformed View of Kenoticism," *International Journal of Systematic Theology* 8 (Spring 2006): 223–51 (245).

30. Sammili Juntunen, "The Christological Background of Luther's Understanding of Justification," *Seminary Ridge Review* 5 (Spring 2003): 6–37, quote from 30.

31. For instance, see Ronald J. Feenstra, "Reconsidering Kenotic Christology," in Ronald J. Feenstra and Cornelius Plantinga Jr., eds., *Trinity, Christology and Atonement: Philosophical and Theological Essays* (Notre Dame, IN: University of Notre Dame Press, 1989), 128–52; Ronald Karo and Meelis Friedenthal, "Kenōsis, Anamnēsis, and Our Place in History: A Neurophenomenological Account," *Zygon* 43 (December 2008): 823–36; Thomas V. Morris, "Understanding God Incarnate," *Asbury Theological Journal* 43 (1988): 63–77, esp. 68ff.; Brian E. Marek, "The Gift of Himself: Kenotic Theology as a Window into Creation's Kinship with God," *Crux* 41 (Summer 2005): 11–21; Peter Forrest, "The Incarnation: A Philosophical Case for Kenosis," *Religious Studies* 36 (2000): 127–40; Kenneth Surin, "Some Aspects of the 'Grammar' of 'Incarnation' and 'Kenosis': Reflections Prompted by the Writings of Donald MacKinnon," in Kenneth Surin, ed., *Christ, Ethics and Tragedy: Essays in Honour of Donald MacKinnon* (London: Cambridge, 1989): 93–115; Larry D. Bouchard, "Moving in the Disjunction: Langdon Gilkey, Secularity, and the Emptiness of God," *American Journal of Theology and Philosophy* 28 (January 2007): 137–60.

32. CD IV.i, 193.

33. Herbert, *Kenosis and Priesthood*, 52–54.

34. The death of God theology can be traced back to the philosophy of G.W. F. Hegel, whose dialectical method proposed that the kenotic event of the cross in which Jesus was abandoned is the death of God. What he meant by this position was that the death of God is the death of transcendent philosophy and the secularization of religion corresponding with the dawn of modernity. See Thomas J. Altizer, "Modern Thought and Apocalypticism," in Bernard McGinn, John J. Collins, and Stephen J. Stein, eds., *Encyclopedia of Apocalypticism*, vol. 3 (New York: Continuum, 1998), 325–59.

35. Jürgen Moltmann, *The Crucified God: The Cross of Christ as the Foundation and Criticism of Christian Theology*, trans. Margaret Kohl (London: SCM Press, 1974), 207.

36. Herbert, *Kenosis and Priesthood*, 63.

37. Jürgen Moltmann, *The Trinity and the Kingdom: The Doctrine of God*, trans. Margaret Kohl (Minneapolis: Fortress Press, 1993), 119, author's emphasis.

38. Jürgen Moltmann, *Science and Wisdom*, trans. Margaret Kohl (Minneapolis: Fortress Press, 2003), 57, 64.

39. For Moltmann, the economy of creation and the economy of salvation are intrinsically bound together. See Jürgen Moltmann, *God in Creation: An Ecological Doctrine of Creation*, trans. Margaret Kohl (London: SCM Press, 1985).

40. Jürgen Moltmann, *The Spirit of Life: A Universal Affirmation*, trans. Margaret Kohl (Minneapolis: Fortress Press, 1992), 47.

41. Ibid., 62–68.

42. D. Lyle Dabney, "Naming the Spirit: Towards a Pneumatology of the Cross," in *Starting with the Spirit*, ed. Gordon Preece and Stephen Pickard (Australia: Australian Theological Forum, 2001), 28–58; also see T. David Beck, *The Holy Spirit and the Renewal of All Things: Pneumatology in Paul and Jürgen Moltmann* (Eugene, OR: Pickwick, 2007).

43. David J. Bosch, *Transforming Mission: Paradigm Shifts in Theology of Mission* (Maryknoll, NY: Orbis Books, 1991).

44. Ibid., 513–14.

45. Ibid., 514.

46. Stephen B. Bevans and Roger P. Schroeder, *Constants in Context: A Theology of Mission for Today* (Maryknoll, NY: Orbis Books, 2004), 369.

47. Hunsinger, *Disruptive Grace*, 46.

48. Besides Moltmann's *God in Creation*, see also his *God for a Secular Society: The Public Relevance of Theology*, trans. Margaret Kohl (London: SCM Press, 1997).

49. Moltmann, *Crucified God*, 329.

50. Hans Schwarz, *Theology in a Global Context: The Last Two Hundred Years* (Grand Rapids, MI: Eerdmans, 2005), 479–87.

51. These include theologians Kazoh Kitamori and Kosuke Koyama (Japan), Choan-Seng Song (Taiwan), Byung-Mu Ahn (Korean Minjung theology), and various theologies from the Indian subcontinent; see Schwarz, *Theology in a Global Context*, 510–21.

52. Theologians such as Desmond Tutu, John Mbiti, Kwesi Dickson, and Mercy Oduyoye; see Schwarz, *Theology in a Global Context*, 500–509.

53. In the U.S., it is primarily focused on the black theology of James Cone, Deotis Roberts, and Cornel West (Schwarz, *Theology in a Global Context*, 472–78), though it can include Hispanic theologies of liberation in the United States.

54. Feminist theologians include Luise Schottroff, Elisabeth Schüssler Fiorenza, Rosemary Radford Ruether, Mary Daly, Delores Williams, and Sally McFague, to name a few of the more prominent; see Schwarz, *Theology in a Global Context*, 487–500.

55. See Steven Bouma-Prediger, *For the Beauty of the Earth: A Christian Vision of Creation Care* (Grand Rapids, MI: Baker Academic, 2001), and *The Greening of Theology: The Ecological Models of Rosemary Radford Ruether, Joseph Sittler, and Jürgen Moltmann* (Atlanta: Scholars, 1995).

56. Leonardo Boff, *Church: Charisma and Power: Liberation Theology and the Institutional Church*, trans. John W. Diercksmeier (New York: Crossroad, 1992), 23–24, quoting the 1971 Synod of Bishops publication *Justice in the World*, 36, author's emphasis.

57. Miroslav Volf, *Exclusion and Embrace: A Theological Exploration of Identity, Otherness, and Reconciliation* (Nashville: Abingdon Press, 1996), 24.

58. Ibid., 220ff.

59. See the introduction of this book; see also Lee and Poloma, *A Sociological Study of the Great Commandment in Pentecostalism* (referred to in n. 1 above).

60. Christian Smith, *Moral Believing Animals: Human Personhood and Culture* (New York: Oxford University Press, 2003), 63–81.

61. See, e.g., the work of Peter L. Berger and Thomas Luckmann, *The Social Construction of Reality: A Treatise in the Sociology of Knowledge* (New York: Anchor Books, 1966); and Peter L. Berger, *The Sacred Canopy: Elements of a Sociology of Religion* (New York: Anchor Books, 1967).

62. Pitirim A. Sorokin, *The Ways and Power of Love: Types, Factors, and Techniques of Moral Transformation* (1954; reprint, Philadelphia: Templeton Foundation Press, 1982), 459.

63. Ibid., 461–62.

64. Ibid., 15–35.

# Four

# VIOLENCE AND NONVIOLENCE

# IN CONCEPTUALIZATIONS

# OF GODLY LOVE

## PAUL ALEXANDER

"What is God like?" . . . There are things only God may do. One of them is to use violence. . . . For the sake of the peace of God's good creation, we can and must affirm this divine anger and this divine violence. . . . God's violence, if it is to be worthy of God who "is love" (1 John 4:8), must be an aspect of God's love. . . . If peace is what we are after, then a critique of the religious legitimation of violence—the critique of bellicose gods—is . . . urgent. . . .

—Miroslav Volf, *Exclusion and Embrace*[1]

This chapter is a critique of theology that supports a violent and bellicose God. For although violence is often justified as loving action, as a Christian theological ethicist this author proposes that from a Christian perspective Godly love should be understood to be both active and entirely nonviolent. Nonviolence therefore becomes an important criterion for judging an action to be consistent with the concept of Godly love. This Christological argument emerges from a close study of the life and teachings of Jesus of Nazareth, who resisted evil actively and nonviolently and taught active and nonviolent resistance to evil. In some Christian theology Jesus Christ is considered to be the "incarnation" of God—God in the flesh, Dios con carne, that is, "God with meat." In Christian scripture Jesus is reported as saying, "the one who has seen me has seen the Father" (John 14:9). This strand of thinking about God leads to the claim that everything about the Father in particular or the Godhead in general is clarified in the Son, Jesus Christ. It is as if the shadows of understanding about the nature of God have been dispersed by the appearance of a floodlight (Jesus—God in the flesh). The author of Colossians reveals that he or she thinks this way about the clarity Jesus brings to our understanding of God: "He [Jesus] is the image of the invisible God" (1:15).

Following this particular Christian idea that Jesus is the image of the invisible God and that those who see Jesus also see the Father, it is possible that the nonviolent life and teachings of Jesus can be understood to be the life, teachings, and very nature of the invisible God, with no violent remainder. That is, "there is no *deus absconditus . . .* lying behind the *deus revelatus.*"[2] The Father, who is often considered to be a God who sometimes works violently and kills humans and other creatures, can be understood from this Christological perspective to be the God who always works nonviolently and who does not kill.[3] Jesus reveals that God is active yet not violent, and that active nonviolence is a faithful Christian way to understand Godly love, creation/the big bang, God's relation to evolution, the problem of evil, and human action for justice.[4] This middle way—active and working, yet nonviolent—avoids the twin perils of passivity and violence and follows closely the way of the *deus revelatus.*

### Godly Love in Jesus Is Nonviolent and Active

Numerous others have made the case that Jesus rejected violence and actively loved and forgave his enemies (and expected all of his disciples to do the same).[5] Even Reinhold Niebuhr, who argued for Christian participation in violence and killing, did not claim that Jesus taught violence or expected his followers to do violence. Niebuhr claimed that killing and violence are necessary for justice and that responsible Christians must sometimes kill people, but he did not ground his claims in Jesus Christ. Perhaps the strongest biblical and theological arguments for consistent Christian nonviolence arise from the Anabaptist traditions of which John Howard Yoder was a part and are presented persuasively in his work. Yoder's work provides background for the author's methodological starting point: the nonviolent and active love of Jesus Christ himself.

Yoder points out, "*Like our heavenly Father and like Jesus himself* (although our imitating Jesus is not the theme of the sermon) we are not to answer evil with evil but to love our enemies. Ever since Augustine, theologians have invested great ingenuity in dulling the edge of that call. Ever since Tolstoy at the beginnings of modernity, honest readers have had to admit that that is what Jesus meant, even if they do not intend to follow it."[6]

This chapter would traditionally be considered "Christo*centric*," since it begins with Jesus, but it is better considered "Christo*morphic*," so that the call to nonviolent active love is understood as a clear invitation for Christians (and others) to become reshaped by living out the implications of the narrative of Jesus. Jesus did no violence and his nonviolence has revelatory power with implications far beyond his own life. In this respect, this work is aligned with Nancey Murphy's argument that "what we see in nature is the same kind of nonviolent divine action that we see in Jesus . . . a view of divine action wherein Jesus' [nonviolent action] is the paradigm of all of God's interaction with creation, not a shocking exception."[7]

When Jesus said, "Love your enemies," he meant for this to include, *at minimum*, not killing or doing violence to them, just as he did not kill or do violence. Jesus, the incarnate God, the "image of the invisible God," did not kill or do violence to his own enemies but instead talked and ate with them, sought to make peace with them, prayed for them, and even forgave them while they were torturing and murdering him on the cross—"Father, forgive them, for they do not know what they are doing" (Luke 23:34, NIV 1984; all scriptural quotations hereafter are NIV 1984). 1 Peter, remembering the words of Isaiah, says that Jesus "committed no sin [violence], and no deceit was found in his mouth. When they hurled their insults at him he did not retaliate, when he suffered he made no threats. Instead, he entrusted himself to him who judges justly" (2:22–23). The early Christian communities remembered Jesus as a peacemaker, reconciler, lover of enemies, and one who overcomes evil with good—these are all positive actions that necessarily, in the view of the early Christian communities, meant being "nonviolent." Willard Swartley, in his important work *Covenant of Peace: The Missing Peace in New Testament Theology and Ethics*, tracks these emphases throughout the New Testament (NT) and convincingly argues "that the NT consistently not only supports nonviolence, but also advocates proactive *peacemaking*, consisting of positive initiatives to overcome evil by employing *peaceable means* to make *peace*."[8] Swartley notes that a recurring emphasis even among historical Jesus scholars is that Jesus was the initiator of a peace movement in the occupied territory of Palestine, for the "Gospels' evidence . . . marks Jesus as a Leader for peace and not a proponent for violence."[9]

However, some scholars argue that Jesus did violence and supported violence.[10] One example is Jesus driving out the animals from the temple in Jerusalem and overturning the tables of the moneychangers and animal peddlers, declaring this house which is to be a "house of prayer for all nations" you have made a hang-out for robbers! (Mark 11:17). Yet Jesus's "bold prophetic act" did no violence to humans.

Many have made the case that Jesus's rejection of violence did not mean he was passive or that he did not resist evil.[11] It is important to recognize that nonviolent resistance need not be passive. Jesus modeled both "[nonviolent] resistance and nonresistance."[12] Paul Keim, along with many others, makes the important point that refusing violence is not necessarily refusing action: "When God's character is expressed in terms of a negative—'nonviolent'—we may easily overlook the call for active, vigorous action in the world to alleviate suffering, to protect the dignity of human life in the face of daily humiliations and degradations, to stand in the breach, and to say 'No, over my dead body, no.'"[13]

## Nonviolent Godly Love, the Big Bang, and Evolution

A Christology of nonviolent Godly love can inform theology proper—the nature of God—and theology proper, so informed, does not contradict the big bang theory or the evolutionary process. Is the big bang an act of violence? Is the big bang an act of coercion? John Milbank argued that "Christianity recognizes no original violence," and Miroslav Volf agreed: "The creation of the world involved no violence."[14] But how do we account for the apparent coercion of God speaking to the little dime-sized mass, the singularity, that became all there is? Perhaps this universe is not the first one, and there are multiple ones before the singularity that became this universe. Nevertheless, a compelling argument can be made that God *suggested* the original big bang. If Jesus Christ is God, and God is noncoercive love, then it makes sense theologically to also call the big bang the "big suggestion" or the "big invitation." It did not have to be, for creation can say "no" to the Creator. Perhaps before the big bang actually occurred, God's previous suggestions were denied by the little ball of matter.

Christian theologians claim that God created *ex nihilo* (out of nothing).[15] An ex nihilo creation is a peaceful and noncoercive creation, for there was nothing to be coerced, nothing to be violated. There was nothing but God. Perhaps God said, "Let there be a small dime-sized mass of matter, a singularity." And there was a dime-sized singularity. And it was good. Perhaps God, who is love, and who is nonviolent and noncoercive, said to the dime-sized singularity, "Let there be this kind of a universe." And there was *not* a universe, for the singularity did not respond to the voice of God. And God suggested again, "Let there be this kind of a universe." And as God saw fit, God continued to say, "Let there be this kind of a universe," until the singularity submitted to the loving God's suggestion and exploded in what we now call the big bang approximately 13.7 billion years ago . . . or in a big bang billions or trillions of years before that.

The time in the story between the ex nihilo creation of the singularity and the event of the big bang is not a necessity in a nonviolent and noncoercive cosmology of Godly love, for ex nihilo creation is noncoercive. But its existence in the story foreshadows the way that God interacts with creation throughout the process of evolution and with humans throughout our history. But how can a dime-sized singularity of matter resist a suggestion by God? Nancey Murphy's discussion of indeterminacy and "free will" is helpful.

> God cooperates with, but does not overpower, the creature. . . . God's control over any particular event is limited . . . if God is to act in all events and entities, then God must act in the most elementary constituents of the universe, since these are among the entities that exist in the world. . . . God acts in all things by acting within the smallest constituent parts of the universe. According to contemporary science, these are subatomic "particles" such as quarks and electrons. The interesting feature of these entities, for present purposes, is the *indeterminacy* of their behavior. While indeterminacy and free will are not the same thing, indeterminacy will provide a valuable analogue for free will in an account of divine action. . . . God's scope for determining natural events is limited by respect for the integrity of these tiny creatures.[16]

Although Murphy may argue that God could in fact determine the *when* of the Big Bang without coercing the smallest parts of the singularity, consider the possibility that somehow even the singularity was free to resist God's invitation. This is implied by Murphy's contention that "all created structures must be viewed as joint effects of the divine will and the wills of created co-creators."[17] Perhaps the strings within the singularity, the created co-creators, could not explode into the big bang until they were in consensus with the Creator.

Regarding evolution, if life has evolved for 3.5 billion years on Earth, what has the God who is love been doing along the way? Consistent with the active, nonviolent love evident in Jesus Christ, God's interaction with the evolution of life on Earth should be of the same nature. God is actively inviting or wooing all of creation but never coerces even the smallest string, quark, or strand of DNA—the God who is nonviolent love cannot coerce. Yet at any time when a part of creation, from the smallest to the most complex aggregate (such as a human), submits to the wooing of God, then there is synergism between creator and creation, and the "will of God" is done on Earth (or anywhere in the multiverse). Although space does not permit a more thorough discussion of evolution, a brief discussion of the issue of predatory violence in the evolutionary process is possible. Predatory violence is a possibility in a world created by the loving, noncoercive God, but it does not reflect God's desires for the world. A world with the possibility of violence and coercion in the evolutionary process is the exact world that a noncoercive God could create, but the will and persuasion of that God points somewhere else—perhaps toward cooperation.

Joan Roughgarden's scientific work exemplified in *The Genial Gene: Deconstructing Darwinian Selfishness* illuminates how the methodological starting point of this chapter—the nonviolent, active love of Jesus—relates to evolution. Roughgarden, an evolutionary biologist at Stanford, challenges "the scientific accuracy of the philosophical world view that the phrase 'selfish gene' has come to represent." She does this by advancing social-selection theory and providing scientific evidence against sexual-selection theory, the theory that "portrays both the process and outcome of evolution as selfish, deceitful, and coercive. I have come to doubt that sexual-selection theory is correct."[18] Roughgarden's arguments are compelling but there is much disagreement regarding how evolution actually works and whether Herbert Spencer's phrase "survival of the fittest" and Tennyson's nature "red in tooth and claw" correctly characterize biological nature. If social-selection theory is correct, as Roughgarden argues persuasively, then conceptualizing Godly love as nonviolent and noncoercive not only makes sense theologically but also fits well with some of the best recent work in the field of evolutionary biology.

### Nonviolent Godly Love and Suffering

According to the Christian story, the true God is the murdered and resurrected God revealed in Jesus. The Christian claim is that incarnation trumps other God knowledges. Resurrection comes to the crucified God, but suffering continues. Stephen is tortured and murdered; Saul becomes a follower of Jesus(!); James is executed; Peter is released from jail(!); Peter is executed. The teachings of Jesus Christ about love and nonviolence, once allowed to inform our conceptualization of God and Godly love, make "sense" of the world as it is. However, the sense that Jesus Christ makes of this world is not the kind that makes sense in purely materialistic or reductionistic terms. The author of 1 Corinthians says that some call the way of Jesus Christ (the cross) stupid and foolish while others call it weak and ineffective, but those being redeemed call it the wisdom and power of God (1:18–31).

A God who is love, and for whom love necessarily includes not killing or coercing humans, could certainly be the creator of a world such as this. This world in which evil and suffering persist is the best world that a loving, nonviolent God could create. To desire another universe in which there is no evil and suffering is to desire a world not created by the God revealed in Jesus Christ, the God who is love and who is not violent.

One counter to the "God is love and cannot do violence" argument is that a God who loves by sometimes killing and doing violence—Godly violence—could also have created a world with evil and suffering such as this one. This conceptualization of Godly violent love or Godly killing love—God doing violence to people and creation as a God who is love—also makes "sense" of the world as it is. It means that there are occasions in history when God has in fact killed some people because he loved others, or killed specific people perhaps because he loved them. Yet this conceptualization of love does not correspond with the life, teachings, cross, and resurrection of Jesus Christ as the "image of the invisible God" who died rather than kill.

The question of whether God can do violence to God's creation becomes especially important to this discussion, although theologians have not reached a consensus. For example, Miroslav Volf is a fellow Christian committed to Christian nonviolence but who has argued that God can and will do violence (see the quote at the beginning of this chapter). Although there is much to like in *Exclusion and Embrace*, this author disagrees with Volf's assertion that God will be violent. Volf argues that the violence of the Rider on the white horse in Revelation (Jesus Christ) is the "symbolic portrayal of the final exclusion of everything that refuses to be redeemed by God's suffering love."[19] He offers a sustained argument that God's patience will end before every person is redeemed, so "God inflicts violence against the stubbornly violent to restore creation's original peace."[20] He says that those who would think that God will do no violence will have trouble explaining their theology in a war zone where "cities and villages have been first plundered, then burned and leveled to the ground, whose daughters and sisters have been raped, whose fathers and brothers have had their throats slit." Volf further claims that there is an inescapable choice between "either God's violence or human violence," and in the end Volf prefers God's violence because he thinks those are the only two choices. There is a third way—God's nonviolence and Christian nonviolence amid the violence of others, while working and waiting for the redemption of all. The third way is not an argument for a "nice" God, and the theology explored here can represent the Christian faith better in a war zone of rapes and murders than can a theology of a God who will someday avenge with violence. This is because of the ultimate victory of patient, self-giving, nonviolent, noncoercive, and active love—even if it takes billions of years, and even if humanity ceases to exist in the universe. Volf's view of history does not extend far enough into the future, and his patience understandably runs out (as does mine) before God's will. God's patience will not end until there is completion, until all of creation is reconciled to God, even if all humans eventually die and all the dead are redeemed.

Volf himself makes the point—"every postponement of vindication means letting insult accompany injury. . . . God's patience is costly, not simply for God, but for the innocent." And his quote of Revelation, read slightly differently, supports this case, for Christians are told "to rest a little longer, until the number would be complete." The "complete" number is "all," and the process may take billions of years.

This delaying of violence until the "end," as represented by Volf, is understandable, but it fails at several crucial points. First, God is guilty *now* of not stopping the rapes and slit throats on the battlefield if God can in fact be violent as a loving Father. Saying that God will someday avenge this violence by killing the evildoers does not really answer the question of suffering and evil amid the plundered and burned homes and bodies. One could argue that a God who is postponing a violent judgment that could be taking place now is culpable for every rape and murder until then. Second, when Volf claims that "divine violence is necessary," he reveals the common belief that violence is more trustworthy than nonviolence, that nonviolence was good for Jesus and good for us, but to really get the job done, someday God is going to have to kill some people.[21] As an alternative, Christians are to trust in God's nonviolent, patient love and realize that love cannot triumph with violence, for if it could, Jesus would have done it while in Palestine. We also should hear the insight of the Anabaptists, "a result gained by force is not the same result, however much it may resemble it superficially, as a result gained by free and intelligent cooperation."[22] The results or end that believers in a violent God hope for are not the same results or end that a nonviolent God will bring, for the *telos* to which we are heading "is an outcome that cannot be forced or seized with violence."[23]

But what about God's anger at injustice? It is possible to affirm that God is angry at injustice, but that violently ending injustice is not the loving way to act, for God does not do that—neither in our experience nor in the life of

Jesus Christ. Volf asserts that if God is not going to someday wield the sword and violently end violence, then God is not worthy of our worship. Some Christians would say that a God who could stop rape and murder but does not (but will someday!) is certainly not worthy of our worship. The "worthy of worship" criterion strengthens the case for a nonviolent loving God and undermines the theology of an eventually violent and loving God.

What about the wrath and judgment of God? There is no doubt that the Bible speaks of God's wrath and anger—at least a thousand times.[24] But the wrath and judgment of God is currently carried out and will continually be carried out through noncoercive, self-giving, and suffering love that does no violence. The sevenfold parenesis identified by Luise Schottroff in Romans 12 helps support this perspective.

Do not curse (12:14).

Repay no one evil for evil (12:17).

Never avenge yourselves (12:19).

Do not be overcome by evil, but overcome evil with good (12:21).

Leave it to the wrath of God (12:19).

Vengeance is mine, I will repay, says God (12:19).

If your enemy is hungry, feed him, . . . for by so doing you will heap
    burning coals upon his head (12:20).[25]

In other words, if we follow Jesus, we will seek to overcome evil with good by loving our enemies and, in so doing, demonstrate the way God judges "them" and shows his wrath to "them" (us?); it is certainly how God responded to God's enemies in Jesus. "God demonstrates his own love for us in this: while we were still sinners, Christ died for us . . . when we were God's enemies, we were reconciled to him . . ." (Romans 5:8–10).

Swartley states that "God's steadfast love and God's wrath are part of an integral whole in the divine nature." Extending this view, "wrath" is what we call the results of God's love necessarily allowing creation freely to reject God and selfishly seek its own way. Although many would find this proposal deeply disturbing, consider the possibility that the "wrath, judgment, and vengeance" of God could sometimes be carried out through prophetically critiquing our enemies out loud and in public, and also feeding, forgiving, and loving those same enemies in numerous ways. God's wrath does not have to be violent but is instead carried out in the real world as actions of peacemaking and reconciliation.

Perhaps the phrase "I'm going to hunt you down and forgive you" expresses this theology. Usually in popular movie parlance when the first part of this sentence is invoked ("I'm going to hunt you down. . . ."), it means that (1) there has been an offense or might possibly be an offense, (2) the offended person is committed to action in response to the offense, and (3) the rest of the sentence will usually end with a description of violent retaliation. But in Jesus we see that God has hunted down humanity and that, rather than responding violently, God judges us and forgives us through Jesus Christ. This allows us to see the nature of God more clearly in that (1) there have been and will continue to be offenses (rapes, murders), (2) the offended God is committed to action in response to these offenses, and (3) the action is always self-giving, suffering, forgiving love that never kills, and followers of this God who respond this way to the murder and rape of God's children can participate in the "heaping of burning coals."

So can God do violence?[26] Can God kill? If Jesus Christ, the *deus revelatus*, as fully human, could have killed yet did not, does this mean that God can kill but chooses not to? The Christian argument is that Jesus Christ lived the only way that a God who is love could have lived. God cannot not be loving; God *is* love. Jesus Christ is the clearest revelation of the character of God—the "exact representation of his being." So the nature of Godly love derives from Jesus Christ, and Jesus Christ's life of Godly love did not include killing and violence even in the midst of occupation, rape, murder, and torture. Jesus could not have killed and still been the carne of the God who is love; he would be a different God. And for Christians, who are monotheists, there is only one God—and when that God was shown clearly to the world, that God loved and was killed but did not love and kill.

How does this relate to divine action and evil today? God cannot coerce human action to stop suffering because to do so would be not to love, and God is nonviolent love who suffers with creation and who does not coerce creation. This is the sense that does not make sense, revealed in the narrative of Jesus Christ, the deus revelatus.

### Nonviolent Godly Love and Human Action for Justice

The Godly love exemplified in Jesus Christ should be inspiration for Christians and shape the creative, imaginative, and powerful ways they engage the world for justice and peace, for "the origin of action which accords with reality . . . is the incarnate God Jesus."[27] Nonviolence is not the same as passivity or inaction. The range of nonviolent loving actions, even aggressive ones, that people can engage in is probably limitless. If we learn anything from Jesus, we learn that speaking and acting—words and deeds—in opposition to injustice and sin while seeking to redeem the oppressors and enemies is powerful enough to bring violent opposition. Jesus never threatened with violence, yet his community-building friendships, table fellowship with outcasts, forgiveness outside the temple economic system, and myriad other subversive actions created alternative community to the oppressive status quos.

Sometimes when too strong of a correlation is perceived between the actions of humans and the actions of God, concerned theologians remind us that "humans are not God."[28] Humans are not God, yet Jesus's teaching does draw an important correlation between the actions of God and the actions of followers of Jesus.

> You have heard that it was said, "You shall love your neighbor and hate your enemy." But I say to you, love your enemies and pray for those who persecute you, *so that you may be children of your Parent who is in heaven; for God* causes the sun to rise on the evil and the good, and sends rain on the righteous and the unrighteous. For if you love those who love you, what reward do you have? Do not even the tax collectors do the same? If you greet only your brothers and sisters, what more are you doing than others? Do not even the Gentiles do the same? Therefore, *you are to be perfect, as your heavenly Parent is perfect* (Matthew 5:43–48).

Although much could be said about this passage, note the correlation between the hearer of these words and the nature of the "Parent" (this is the author's gender-neutral modification, it is "Father" in most traditional translations). Rather than hearing Jesus's teaching of love for enemies as a reductionist Christology in which only Jesus is involved, that leaves out God the Parent, the passage specifically names actions for the good of enemies as actions that God the Parent takes—loving enemies and sending rain and sunshine to both just *and* unjust/evil people. This allows us to hear Jesus regarding the nature and essence of God—we learn that, according to this passage, God is indeed what we see in Jesus; Jesus is truly the "image of the invisible God," and we are invited to live like God and be recognized as God's children. When children act like their parents, friends and family members are known to say, "I see your father in you when you do that" or "You're just like your mother." This is the correlation that Jesus is making between the God who loves enemies and God's children who do the same and are thus seen to be just like their Parent.

The word "perfect" (*teleiotos*) can be understood to mean "all the way to the end/completely." This renders Jesus's teaching as, "Love everybody, be all-inclusive in your love, love all the way to the ends of humanity, as your heavenly parent loves all the way to the ends of humanity and leaves no one out, not even unjust/evil people." "Be perfect" is not a call for moralistic perfectionism where one is expected to make no mistakes or never sin; it means that followers of Jesus are to love gratuitously just as he did. This does not mean that humans are God, but humans are invited to participate in a grace-filled life that is in concert with the loving and nonviolent ways that God has been acting in the world since before the big bang.

## Problems and Conclusion

The first problem with allowing Jesus Christ's complete nonviolence and nonkilling to shape our understanding of Godly love, to the extent that violence and killing are never ways that God loves or that God acts, is that the Hebrew Scriptures seem replete with references to God's violence, killing, and coercion. There are several methodological and hermeneutical moves that Christians have taken to address this and related issues; here we consider only two.[29]

First, some suggest that God progressively revealed Godself to humanity so that earlier revelation can be more greatly clarified by later revelation, or that humans apprehended God's revelation more clearly along the way. For instance, Torah calls for execution of children who curse their parents and execution of people who sacrifice to any god other than Yahweh (Exodus 21:17, 22:20), and Deuteronomy relates that God commanded Israel to annihilate their enemy without mercy (7:1–2), but some think that God later reveals that this is not the best way to live and/or not God's most perfect will. These views of progressive revelation see these earlier teachings about God and what God desired for people to do as accommodated to the people of the day, but then God changed what God was saying as humanity became better able to understand. Thus, the authors of Isaiah, Amos, and even Psalms sometimes claim that God does not truly desire animal sacrifices but would prefer to have people who live according to God's will and do justice (Isa. 1:11–17; Amos 5:21–24; Ps. 40:6–8). For Christians, they argue, this is most clarified in Jesus and the NT, so animal sacrifices, annihilation of enemies, and quite a list of other practices in the Hebrew Scriptures are discontinued. But this view of progressive revelation falls short for several reasons and is not able to provide a satisfactory explanation of God's violent history that is able to sustain the thesis of this chapter. For if God was able to both love and do violence just a few thousand years ago, then it is indeed possible to love through violence and killing. God could love children, adulterers, and the unfaithful while having followers kill them, or even love them while killing them Godself. If we maintain that God is and always has been love, then Godly love would have at one time involved violence and killing. It would have been Godly Killing Love. And that is inconsistent with the life and teachings of Jesus Christ.

Second, some suggest that portrayals of God's violence reflect historical perspectives of people at the times they were written. There are many communities and authors who contributed to the Hebrew Scriptures, and they had competing and diverse perspectives on many issues (kingship, sacrifices, wealth, violence, etc.). In these various views, one should naturally expect to find perspectives that are not in harmony with each other and that are not in harmony with what later communities would produce. Of course, some attribute all the content of the Bible to humans, with no influence from the divine at all, and this explains the existence of divine violence quite easily—it is human violence projected on the divine. But there is also the possibility that God does indeed exist, is not only a human projection, and that the Hebrew Scriptures and NT help us understand God. The Bible contains perspectives that are totally human with no influence from the divine, with clear revelations of the divine, and with all manner of variety in between.

A tentative theory of inspiration thus emerges from the thesis of this chapter: that God did not and could not control or coerce the writing of scripture. In this view, God lovingly influenced and spoke to women and men throughout history, inspiring them to write in ways that best promoted what we eventually see clearly in Jesus—love, peace, justice, reconciliation, truth, etc. But people do not have to do what God suggests; people are free to reject God's influence and humanity's historical rejections made their way into what we now call scripture. Humanity's clear-eyed and clear-eared heeding of God's influence also made it into what we now call scripture. A hermeneutical lens is necessary to help see what in scripture best reflects the nature of God, and that hermeneutical lens is the narrative of Jesus.

The second problem that arises is how to understand or explain divine action in relation to seemingly unexplained physical healings. John Milbank is helpful here, in that "understanding" and "explanation" are not the "only or primary modes of rationality" and that "narrative is a more basic category than either."[30] Yet the way many Christians narrate physical healings as divine acts seems to reflect an interventionist view of divine action. God does not intervene in coercive ways to bring about healings or miracles. It is better to adopt an immanentist approach whereby God is continually and always active with all of creation—always wooing, always persuading, always influencing toward the good, but never coercing. God is always acting for the best for all of creation. Regarding how this relates to physical healings that result sometimes from prayer and other rituals, a multilateral understanding might help answer some of these difficult questions. Oord suggests that "God initiates love and that creatures contribute responsibly . . . in these cases love involves multilateral causation."[31] So, God invites people to be healed, and some people cooperate to various degrees, but there are other influencing factors as well that can enhance or hinder both the believer and God. Even if God wants the healing, and the person praying wants the healing, there can be other issues that prevent it, and this leads to the diagnostic practices found in communities that believe in healings and miracles. So the "blame" for lack of healing need be directed neither at God nor at the believer, for there are multilateral causations. We should not be concerned about whom to blame for lack of healing. But since this theology of the loving, noncoercive God revealed in Jesus Christ is compatible with Christian prayers for healing and testimonies to the effectiveness of the same, then it should be addressed on the terms of those Christians who practice such prayers. In other words, we need not reject the reality of healings that occur independent of our ability to explain them according to our understandings of "natural causation." Not all people who claim that such events have happened to them or in their presence are deluded, misled, or projecting. These stories persist, in part at least, because the healings actually sometimes occur. They are not purely natural, and they are not coerced by God; they are results of the interaction between the creation and the noncoercive creator.

In conclusion, a Christomorphic approach to Godly love enables the claim that Godly love, at least as exemplified in and taught by Jesus, is always at a minimum nonviolent, while also actively engaged in redeeming and restoring. This conceptualization of Godly love implies that we should at least question, or perhaps reject, any claims that God encourages or supports human violence as loving action. This conceptualization of Godly love also suggests that studies of Godly love should deal with various theological variables; for instance, theological perspectives and traditions that are not committed to consistent nonviolence need to be factored into research, for they may produce quite disparate actions in the name of "love." Would social scientific research discern significant differences between those who perceive God as consistently nonviolent and never supportive of human violence and those who conceptualize God both as capable of violence and occasionally supportive of human violence? The perspective advanced here corresponds well to loving divine action from before the existence of the singularity, through the big bang, and through the evolution of life on Earth. This perspective also addresses the problem of suffering and evil in today's world, for Christ reveals that Godly love is essentially nonviolent—since God *is* love, God *cannot* act violently, or coercively, or kill murderers and rapists. We do not experience God acting violently for justice because the loving God cannot. Finally, perhaps conceptualizing Godly love as nonviolent action can encourage human nonviolent action for peace with justice, because when one acts, even sacrifices, for the good of others, one can know that such action corresponds to and is empowered by the very nature of the creator and sustainer of all universes.

## Notes

1. Miroslav Volf, *Exclusion and Embrace: A Theological Exploration of Identity, Otherness, and Reconciliation* (Nashville: Abingdon, 1996), 301, 299, 302–3, 285.

2. Victor Preller, *Divine Science and the Science of God: A Reformulation of Thomas Aquinas* (Princeton, NJ: Princeton University Press, 1967), 215. Also see Stanley Hauerwas, *With the Grain of the Universe: The Church's Witness and Natural Theology* (Grand Rapids, MI: Brazos, 2001), and "Connections Created and Contingent: Aquinas, Preller, Wittgenstein, and Hopkins," in *Performing the Faith: Bonhoeffer and the Practice of Nonviolence* (Grand Rapids, MI: Brazos, 2004), 111–34.

3. The theological arguments that all Christians should be nonviolent do not hinge on whether or not God does or does not do violence, or does or does not kill. Many Christians committed to consistent nonviolence accept that God has killed and/or commanded killing and/or will someday kill or do violence, but they argue for various reasons that followers of Jesus should not kill or do violence. A prime example of this is Miroslav Volf, *Exclusion and Embrace*, 275–306. The narratives of the life and teachings of Jesus remain normative for Christians, and therefore nonviolence should be a way of life for all Christians even if one believes that God can indeed be violent.

4. This is too much to explore adequately in one chapter; however, this chapter attempts at least a brief foray into the possibilities.

5. John Howard Yoder, *The Original Revolution* (Eugene, OR: Wipf & Stock, 1998), *The Politics of Jesus* (Grand Rapids, MI: Eerdmans, 1972), *The Priestly Kingdom* (Notre Dame, IN: University of Notre Dame Press, 1984), *For the Nations* (Grand Rapids, MI: Eerdmans, 1997), Stanley Hauerwas, *The Peaceable Kingdom* (Notre Dame, IN: University of Notre Dame Press, 1991), *The Hauerwas Reader* (Durham, NC: Duke University Press, 2001).

6. Yoder, *For the Nations*, 47.

7. Nancey Murphy, *Religion and Science: God, Evolution, and the Soul* (Kitchener, ON: Pandora Press/Scottdale, PA: Herald Press, 2002), 29, 41. Also see Nancey Murphy, *Theology in the Age of Scientific Reasoning* (Ithaca: Cornell University Press, 1990); Nancey Murphy and George F. R. Ellis, *On the Moral Nature of the Universe: Theology, Cosmology, and Ethics* (Minneapolis: Fortress, 1996).

8. Willard Swartley, *Covenant of Peace: The Missing Peace in New Testament Theology and Ethics* (Grand Rapids, MI: Eerdmans, 2006), 46. See also Richard Hays, *The Moral Vision of the New Testament* (San Francisco: HarperSanFrancisco, 1996); N. T. Wright, *Jesus and the Victory of God* (Minneapolis: Fortress, 1996).

9. Swartley, *Covenant of Peace*, 13.

10. Paul Ramsey, *The Just War: Force and Political Responsibility* (Lanham, MD: University Press of America, 1968), Lisa Sowle Cahill, *Love Your Enemies: Discipleship, Pacifism, and Just War Theory* (Minneapolis: Augsburg Fortress, 1994), and J. Daryl Charles, *Between Pacifism and Jihad: Just War and the Christian Tradition* (Downers Grove, IL: IVP Academic, 2005).

11. Walter Wink, *Engaging the Powers: Discernment and Resistance in a World of Domination* (Minneapolis: Fortress, 1992); Glen Stassen, *Just Peacemaking: Transforming Initiatives in the Sermon on the Mount* (Westminster/John Knox Press, 1992).

12. Thomas Yoder Neufeld, "Resistance and Nonresistance: The Two Legs of a Biblical Peace Stance," *Conrad Grebel Review* 21 (2003): 56–81.

13. Paul Keim, "Is God Nonviolent?" *Conrad Grebel Review* 21 (2003): 30–31.

14. John Milbank, *Theology and Social Theory: Beyond Secular Reason* (Oxford, UK: Basil Blackwell, 1990), 5. Volf, *Exclusion and Embrace*, 300.

15. Tom Oord, while arguing that "noncoercion is an *essential* feature of how God lovingly relates to creation" (with which this author agrees), further argues that *creatio ex nihilo* is a coercive act, so God "created our universe out of matter in chaos." He follows the Steinhard/Turok cosmology that there might be "an eternal succession of universes," rejects creatio ex nihilo, and suggests that God "fine-tuned" existing space/time/matter rather than created it out of nothing. He suggests that this allows us to "discard the idea that God has *ever* coerced or unilaterally determined others." However, God's noncoercive loving way of relating to creation can be explained well by *creatio ex nihilo* and that "fine tuning" existing matter out of chaos might be the kind of coercion that both Oord and this author seek to avoid in our theology proper. Also, trillions of years of multiple universes/big bangs/big crunches can still have a beginning point—it is just not necessarily at the beginning of our present universe. Thomas Jay Oord, *Science of Love* (Philadelphia: Templeton Foundation Press, 2004), 19–20. Also, "process theology rejects the notion of *creatio ex nihilo* [because it] is part and parcel of the doctrine of God as absolute controller." John Cobb Jr. and David Ray Griffin, *Process Theology* (Philadelphia: Westminster, 1976), 65. Again, creatio ex nihilo can correlate well with the author's understanding that God is love, not in absolute control, nonviolent, and noncoercive.

16. Murphy, *Religion and Science*, 36.

17. Ibid., 39.

18. Roughgarden doubts, based on her scientific work, that "selfishness and individuality [and competition], rather than kindness and cooperation, are basic to biological nature. Darwinism has come to be identified with selfishness and individuality. I criticize this evolutionary perspective by showing it misrepresents the facts of life as we now know them. I focus on social behavior related to sex, gender, and family where the reality of universal selfishness and sexual conflict is supposedly most evident. I show that the writings in the professional biological literature advocating a picture of universal selfishness . . . are mistaken. I present my laboratory's alternative evolutionary theories for social behavior that emphasize cooperation and teamwork and that rely on the mathematics of cooperative games." *The Genial Gene* (Berkeley and Los Angeles: University of California Press, 2009), 1.

19. Volf, *Exclusion and Embrace*, 299.

20. Ibid., 300.

21. Ibid., 299.

22. Murphy, *Religion and Science*, 41.

23. Ibid., 43.

24. Swartley, *Covenant of Peace*, 384.

25. Luise Schottroff, "'Give to Caesar What Belongs to Caesar and to God What Belongs to God': A Theological Response of the Early Christian Church to Its Social and Political Environment," in *Love of Enemy and Nonretaliation in the New Testament*, ed. Willard Swartley (Louisville: Westminster John Knox Press, 1992), 232–35. Cited in Swartley, *Covenant of Peace*, 392.

26. Willard Swartley writes that even talking about "violence" in relation to God is a "category fallacy" and a "misnomer," since violence is attributed to humans in Scripture, not to God. He suggests that "at this point in the debate speaking of God as violent or nonviolent is best avoided, for it appears to be a misconceived duality in relation to God." Swartley, *Covenant of Peace*, 395–96. Although this author agrees with and utilizes most of Swartley's work, on this point it is important to argue that God is not violent, for as Swartley himself says, "to attribute violence to God is to undermine the moral character of God. . . ."

27. Dietrich Bonhoeffer, *Ethics* (New York: Macmillan, 1962), 199.

28. Volf, *Exclusion and Embrace*, 301.

29. John Howard Yoder identified four common approaches to this issue. (1) "The New Dispensation" (dispensationalism) claims that Jesus simply set aside that which came before and introduced a novel way. He argues that this is insufficient because (a) Jesus does not say he is setting aside the Hebrew Scriptures, and (b) Jesus would have needed to say a lot more about what parts and how much needed to be abolished. (2) "Concession to Disobedience" claims that the change is because the concessions to human disobedience are now lifted and God's will never changed. (3) "The Pedagogical Concession" claims that God's concession was not "to a culpable hardness of heart but to an innocent primitive moral immaturity." In other words, those earlier humans could not comprehend the higher morality that came later, so God taught them as best they could handle. He argues this is insufficient because "one must look down on the ancient Israelites with a sense of moral superiority which is difficult to justify on objective grounds." (4) "The Division of Levels or Realms" claims that the Hebrew Scriptures were for the civil life of the Hebrew people and this still applies to the civil order today, and that nonviolence is only for Christians. This is not actually an answer to the issue with which we are dealing. John Howard Yoder, *The Original Revolution* (Scottdale, PA: Herald Press, 1971; Eugene, OR: Wipf Stock, 1998), 92–100.

30. John Milbank, *Theology and Social Theory: Beyond Secular Reason* (Oxford, UK: Basil Blackwell, 1990), 264; Hauerwas, *Performing the Faith*, 144.

31. Oord, *Science of Love*, 31.

# Five

# TESTING CREATURELY LOVE

# AND GOD'S CAUSAL ROLE

*THOMAS JAY OORD*

Two largely unanswered questions reside at the heart of theological and scientific research on love. The first—and more typically scientific—has to do with measuring love: how should love be measured? This chapter attempts to answer this question and offers general measuring domains scientists might use to pursue research on creaturely love. These three domains are essential to love itself: (1) intent/motives, (2) embodiment/environment, and (3) consequences/outcomes. Understanding these domains and their roles for measuring love proves essential for adequate love research.

The second question—which is theological in nature—pertains to divine activity: If God's love makes a difference, how should we measure it? This chapter proposes a method for measuring God's role in creaturely love, and calls it essential kenosis. In this theory, God acts as a loving causal agent in every event, but God never entirely determines any. God's influence oscillates and expresses diverse forms. Researchers justifiably make inferences with regard to the degree of divine love's effectiveness by observing creaturely action. Essential kenosis offers an overarching scheme to measure the influence of God's love.

## Measuring Creaturely Love

To some, the idea of measuring love is sheer foolishness. Love escapes any measuring mechanisms, in their opinion. Pressing them to identify how they know which action is loving and which is not, however, reveals quickly that they *do* adopt some measurement methods. The measurements they adopt are tacit or largely unconscious. Part of the scientist's task is to make explicit and robust our love assumptions currently implicit.

Crucial to measuring love—and yet a step so few researchers take seriously—is offering a clear and coherent definition of love. A good definition makes a huge difference. This chapter defines love in this way: *To love is to act intentionally, in sympathetic/empathetic response to others (including God), to promote overall well-being.* To put it differently, we love when we intentionally respond to others in the hope of doing good, especially increasing the common good. Details of this definition can be found in the author's *Defining Love.*[1] Here, however, are a few highlights of that definition.

To say that love entails acting intentionally means, first, that love involves proper motives. We should not regard as loving those actions done with motives for harm—even if those actions unintentionally result in positive outcomes. Motives matter. Furthermore, love entails a degree of freedom. We should not consider loving those actions entirely determined by one's environment, genes, or God. To say love entails acting intentionally means, finally, that love requires that the actor have some purpose in mind, even if that purpose has not been deeply contemplated. We can love in an instant; but sometimes love involves significant and sustained reflection. Whatever the time span, love is purposeful. These three factors are subsumed under the claim that lovers act intentionally.

Second, love involves relationships. Entirely isolated agents—if such existed—could not love. A lover's relationships may be with other humans, other creatures, one's environment, and even the members of one's own body. In our interrelated universe, relationships shape and constrain the freedom lovers have when choosing how to respond to others. The fact that love involves relations coheres well with the notion of cause and effect that science presupposes. However, the cause and effect of love is not deterministic. As noted in the previous paragraph, lovers retain some freedom as they respond to the various modes of causation influencing them.

Both "sympathetic" and "empathetic" in the preceding definition account for the notion that relationships genuinely affect the lover. To some degree, lovers "feel with" others. In philosophical circles, the word *sympathy* usually identifies this idea. However, psychologists often use *sympathy* to talk about pity and use the word *empathy* to describe the notion that others genuinely influence the one loving. Whichever word one prefers, the point is that lovers are internally influenced by others. A lover's relationships with others and various forces partially determine the lover.

Third, love promotes overall well-being. For this reason, consequences of actions matter. This does not mean that consequences alone determine whether an act is loving. It does mean that lovers are motivated to secure positive consequences. Lovers speculate prospectively about the good they might promote.

Insofar as actors purposely choose the good of one or a few at the obvious expense of the whole, they do not act to promote overall well-being. They act unjustly and injustice is antithetical to love. Fortunately, acting for the good of the few often enhances the good of the whole. In fact, self-love and love of kin are sometimes fitting expressions of love. However, sometimes love requires self-sacrifice. In addition, sometimes love involves acting primarily for the good of enemies instead of family or friends. In all of these cases, however, love involves what the Hebrew prophets called *shalom* and Jesus called "abundant life."

Promoting overall well-being can mean acting in many ways when do-ing good. It can mean meeting basic needs, such as providing food, water, air, and suitable living conditions. It can involve enhancing physical and mental dimensions. Promoting well-being may mean caring for others or establishing a sense of community. It can mean promoting diverse life-forms, opportunities, and cultural expressions. To do good by promot-ing overall well-being may mean securing in others a feeling of worth, providing medical soundness and physical fitness, fostering deep personal relationships, or cultivating social and political harmony. Promoting well-being often includes encouraging the development of virtues and charac-ter. To purposefully promote overall well-being is to act intentionally to do good in one, but often in many, of these ways.[2]

God's role in love has not yet been mentioned, even though there is a reference to God in our definition. God's role will be explained in the second portion of this essay. At this point, simply note that God plays a necessary but not sufficient role as one to whom lovers respond. This claim fits with a widespread religious belief that we can love because God first loves us (e.g., 1 John 4:19). In addition, it supports the idea many theologians affirm—especially Christian theologians—that God is the author of love.

### Three Domains of Scientific Research on Creaturely Love

With this definition in place, the three general domains of scientific re-search on love are explicated.

## 1—*The Actor's Presumed Intent or Motives*

If love requires intentionality, research on love may explore an agent's motives and intent. After all, motives matter. Of course, scientists cannot place motives under a microscope. In fact, we cannot perceive motives in themselves with sensory perception—sight, sound, touch, etc. This presents a problem for this aspect of research on love, because most scientists presuppose that sensory perception is the only perception possible.[3]

At best, we perceive or become directly aware of our own motives. Even then, we are not likely fully aware of all our motives. Research on love can overcome this problem at least partially, however, by concentrating on a subject's *primary* motive for any particular action. We all presuppose that at least sometimes one motive predominates when we choose to act in a particular way. In addition, most of the time, we can be accurate about discerning our primary motives.[4]

At least three general methods are available for researching primary motives as they pertain to love.

SELF-REPORT OF MOTIVES—The first method for research on the motives of love involves simply hearing from those who report their own motives. In particular, self-report-based research focuses on what subjects believe are their primary motives for intentionally acting in a particular way.[5]

Take the work of psychologists Susan S. Hendrick and Clyde Hendrick as an example. They used a self-report method to explore the relation of love to religious belief. The two scientists asked over five hundred participants in two separate studies to report on what kinds of love they express and to report on their religiosity. The self-report study focused on a forty-two-item love styles scale and addressed six types of love: *eros* (romantic), *ludus* (game-playing), *storge* (compassionate), *mania* (possessive), *pragma* (practical), and *agape* (selfless/religious).

The result of the Hendricks' research shows that participants who self-report as being very religious also self-report as expressing more storge, pragma, and agape love forms than do nonreligious participants. These same highly religious people, however, self-report expressing ludus love less than do nonreligious participants. The Hendricks conclude that "subjects who were more religious endorsed the more 'dependable' love styles of *storge* (compassionate), *pragma* (practical), and *agape* (selfless), while they relatively rejected *ludus* (game-playing)."[6]

Self-reports are advantageous, because they emerge from the witness of those who best know their primary motives: the subjects themselves.

The disadvantage of self-reports, however, is that those surveyed may not report their motives honestly. Exterior incentives may tempt them to characterize their primary motives as loving when they are not. For this reason, scientific research on love based on self-report is important but cannot lead to absolute certainty with regard to the research project goals. But absolute certainty is not possible for any scientific project and therefore does not disqualify self-report research methods.

INFERRING MOTIVES IN OTHERS—The second general way in which love research focuses on motives pertains to inferring a subject's motives based upon observations of that subject's actions. Researchers rightly infer some actions to be motivated primarily by the actor's intent to promote well-being. Observation and inference are bedrock activities in scientific research.

Admittedly, inferring another person's motives entails conjecture. Inference can result in misperception and never attains absolute certainty. But conjecture and failure to achieve certainty do not disqualify this research method. Other scientific methods based on observation—for example, scientific explanations for conflicts among Maasai lions or planetary research based on telescope observations—also rely on conjecture and cannot provide explanatory certainty. The fact that inferring the motives involves speculation grounded in observation should not discredit this approach as legitimate. However, it should prompt those who use this method to be modest and cautious when reporting their research results.

A scientist exploring love can increase the likelihood that he or she accurately infers a subject's motives. For instance, the researcher can reduce the likelihood that other factors influence a subject to exhibit nonloving primary motives. If researchers witness someone acting in various love-possible situations, they can draw reasonable inferences about the person's primary motives as loving or not loving.

For example, Daniel Batson's research sets up conditions to increase the likelihood of accurately inferring the motives of his subjects as loving or not loving.[7] In one experiment, Batson told undergraduates they would form teams of two participants. Each undergraduate would play a role in a stress experience. One student was randomly selected to undergo up to ten electric shocks. The second team member observed the first.[8] Batson told all participants they could withdraw from the experiment at any time.

Participants in this test did not know, however, that every undergraduate was "randomly" selected for the observer role. As assistants escorted each to an observation room, the undergraduate learned he or she would watch on closed-circuit television as a young woman named Elaine—the person they presumed was his or her randomly selected partner—received the series of electric shocks. The scene each student watched, however, had been prerecorded so that all participants watched the same experience.

By the end of the second "live" shock treatment, Elaine's reactions to the electrocution were so strong that the assistant administering the treatment "interrupted" the procedure. The assistant asked Elaine if she was feeling okay. A conversation ensued in which Elaine confessed that as a child, a horse threw her onto an electric fence. After the fence incident, a doctor told her that in the future she might react strongly to even mild shocks.

Hearing Elaine's (made-up) story, the assistant wondered aloud if the undergraduate participant watching in the adjacent room might take her place. With a mixture of reluctance and relief, Elaine consented to the assistant checking on this possibility.

After a brief moment, the assistant entered the room in which the student was watching the shock treatments on closed-circuit television. The assistant asked whether he or she would be willing to take Elaine's place. The assistant also gave the person the option to remain an observer.[9]

"If you decide to help Elaine by taking her place," the assistant concluded, "she'll come in here and observe you. You will go in and perform the recall trials while receiving the shocks. Once you have completed the trials, you'll be free to go. What would you like to do?"

Batson found that most observers who judged themselves dissimilar to Elaine (based upon previously completed questionnaires) opted out of taking the shocks in her place. However, those who judged themselves similar to Elaine—based on similarities evident in the questionnaires— were likely to take her place, even when they could easily escape the situation. Whereas only 18 percent of dissimilar observers helped Elaine when given an easy escape, 91 percent of highly similar observers helped Elaine when given an easy escape.[10] These results give reason to believe that the primary motive of some people in some situations is genuinely altruistic. They are willing to promote overall well-being by responding intentionally to relieve Elaine's stress.

Batson's experiments are powerful, in part, because he sets up controlled circumstances and introduces or eliminates various factors. This helps him increase the likelihood that he can correctly infer a subject's primary motives.

Batson is quick to say, however, that such studies do not prove irrefutably that the participants expressed altruistic love. After all, the possibility always exists that students such as those who took Elaine's place in the experiment acted with selfishness as their primary motive. It may be that some took Elaine's place, for instance, because they knew they would feel enormous guilt if they did not. Their primary motive was the selfish desire to avoid guilt.

In sum, scientific studies on motives to promote well-being are important. They cannot prove irrefutably that a subject acts lovingly, however. They play an important part in love research generally, because they examine the intentions of those who may have acted lovingly.

INTENTIONALLY ACTING ON CONVICTIONS—A final subdomain of research on intentions and motives explores how personal beliefs, convictions, and principles—when acted upon—influence a person's decision to love. This research also requires inferences based on observation of actions. But it relies upon observations of others over a long period of time rather than on a controlled experiment like the one Batson constructed.

In their book, *Some Do Care: Contemporary Lives of Moral Commitments*, developmental psychologists Anne Colby and William Damon look at 23 people who are moral examples of love.[11] Colby and Damon use both self-reports and their own inferences based on observation for their research.

The first moral exemplar Colby and Damon present in their book is Suzie Valadez, known as "Queen of the Dump." Valadez has spent her life handing out food to the poorest of the poor in the squalid conditions outside Ciudad Juárez, Mexico. Valadez worked for more than 30 years helping others, often sacrificing her own health and safety and that of her family members. Colby and Damon report that "she has become consumed by the work, fully and completely engaged. For Suzie, her work *is* her life. . . . As she sees it, the work with the poor of Juárez is what she is here for, what she most wants to do."[12]

Colby and Damon conclude that the moral exemplars they studied acted lovingly for others despite difficult circumstances. But all were motivated by unswerving commitment to principles.[13] These moral exemplars have "a common sense of faith in the human potential to realize its ideals," they report. Faith in the human potential to attain something better is "what made the center hold throughout all the decades of the exemplars' uniquely consequential lives."[14]

### 2—Relations with Others

If love involves sympathetic/empathetic responses to others, some research projects on love must explore the stimuli, conditions, and constraints others place on an actor's love. These relations exert causal influence on those who love. Science is best known for attempting to account for particular cause-and-effect relations in existence.

The kinds of relations and their causes vary widely. Some of the most interesting love research explores how these relations shape or hinder expressions of love. Three general types are noted: societal, interpersonal, and bodily.

First are *societal relations*. From ancient days, humans have believed that the wider social environment and broad communal relations influence our capacities and opportunities to promote well-being. Measuring this belief proves difficult. When the multiplicity of possible causes expands so widely as to include a whole society, researchers have difficulty identifying primary influences for or against love.

The notion that societies encourage altruism has been given special emphasis in the group selection theory of evolutionary sociobiology. In their book *Unto Others: The Evolution and Psychology of Unselfish Behavior*, biologist David Sloan Wilson and philosopher Elliott Sober argue that evidence shows groups of altruists can outcompete groups of egoists.

Group selection, say Wilson and Sober, "has been an important force in evolution."[15] "Altruism can evolve to the extent that altruists and non-altruists become concentrated in different groups," they report.[16] Groups of altruists can survive and thrive better than groups comprised of selfish types. The authors provide data in the biological and anthropological sciences to substantiate group-selection theory.[17] They conclude that "the concept of human groups as adaptive units may be supported not only by evolutionary theory but by the bulk of empirical information on human social groups in all cultures around the world."[18]

Others pursue research on the causal influence of society for love. Stacy L. Smith and Sandi W. Smith examined altruistically loving acts portrayed on television. They randomly selected and taped TV content for about three months, using a definition of altruism as "a voluntary intentional action—independent of motive—that benefits others beyond simple socio-ability or duties associated with a role."[19] The two primary actions deemed loving were helping and sharing.

Smith and Smith found that 72 percent of all programs they observed featured at least one instance of altruism. Most altruistic acts were toward friends (32%) and acquaintances (21%). The researchers concluded that some forms of altruism are important ingredients in the narrative structure of television programming. They believe their work is important, because "a social cognitive or socialization approach [to altruism] suggests that such portrayals may have a positive impact on viewer's propensity to help or share."[20]

The second type of relations that shape or hinder expressions of love is *interpersonal relations*. The kinds of relations we have with family, friends, and coworkers make a difference in our ability to love. These relations and their causal influence also affect the forms love takes. Intimate causal relations begin in the mother's womb and continue throughout a lifetime. Not surprisingly, the nature of interpersonal relations provides important scientific research data about a subject's capacity to love and the forms love takes.

A whole realm of psychology called "attachment theory" offers insights into the capacity for giving and receiving love based on interpersonal relations. John Bowlby and Mary Ainsworth were pioneers in empirical research suggesting that the relationship an infant enjoys with his or her mother (or significant caregiver) greatly influences that child's love for others.[21] A child's attachment system naturally elicits a positive mental representation of those who protect him or her. When the system functions well, individuals feel relaxed and confident and will more likely care for self and others.

Today, developmental psychologists employ attachment theory in their research on relationships at all stages of life. For example, Mario Mikulincer and Phillip Shaver find in their studies that those who feel a proper sense of attachment are more likely to act compassionately than those who do not have a secure attachment. "Our findings indicate," say Mikulincer and Shaver, "that the attachment behavior system affects the caregiving system, making it likely that heightening security will yield benefits in the realm of compassionate altruistic behavior."[22]

The research of Samuel and Pearl Oliner on the parental influence of those who rescued Jews during the period of Nazi rule illustrates well scientific work on how interpersonal relations influence love. Using interviews of rescuers and nonrescuers, the Oliners identified various factors influencing those who rescued Jews in Nazi Europe and those who did not. From these interviews, the Oliners constructed composite portraits of both types. They found that "close family relationships in which parents model caring behavior and communicate caring values" were typical of those who rescued Jews. Parents of rescuers set "high standards they expect their children to meet, particularly with regard to caring for others."[23]

George Vaillant's work serves as a final example of the causal role interpersonal relations might play for research on love. Vaillant followed the lives of 456 inner-city men whose lives had been characterized by extreme difficulty. He found that by the time the men reached their middle fifties, the nine men who led the most generative and self-giving lives said the greatest factor in their now positive lives was a loving marriage. This suggests that positive interpersonal relationships in marriage encourage men to promote well-being.[24]

Finally, *bodily relations and constraints* also shape or hinder expressions of love. Lovers are embodied beings. As such, their internal relations influence what kind of loving activity is possible. Bodies and the entities that comprise bodies provide both tools for loving and constraints to love. Research on this causal influence is important.

Nancy Eisenberg does research on prosocial behavior in children.[25] Eisenberg cites one study of six-month-olds that revealed about half of those examined responded to distressed peers with actions indicating empathy. This evidence suggests that even at an early age, humans are hardwired to respond to those in their environment. But the apparently involuntary response of children to others' distress decreases through childhood.[26] "Because preschool children are better able than younger children to take the perspective of others," says Eisenberg, "they are more motivated and better able to pinpoint the source of another's distress and to help in ways that are appropriate to the other's need."[27]

Much of the neuroscience research on love pertains to exploring the necessary neural requirements for complex forms of love. For instance, neurologists Antonio and Hanna Damasio document a number of contemporary cases in which the neocortical neurons necessary for empathy are destroyed or rendered dysfunctional from brain damage. In one research project, the team studied 13 adult patients who experienced prefrontal cortex damage. The wife of one patient with brain damage testifies that her husband was caring and affectionate prior to his brain alteration. After it, however, her husband reacted with indifference when she became upset or distressed. Despite the fact that his verbal and performance IQ scores ranked in the high 90th percentiles, the husband lacked empathy.

Adults in the study with damaged frontal lobes could not employ social and emotional facts to respond sympathetically. "Without the prefrontal cortex," Hanna Damasio says, "empathy, along with other adaptive social behaviors, becomes impaired."[28] Various regions of our brains may influence our capacity to empathize well with others, but these studies show that the neocortex is especially important for some forms of empathy.[29]

To conclude this section on love research on the domain of bodily and environmental relations and their causal influence, it is important to reiterate what was said in the above conclusion to studying the general domain motives and intentions. Just as explanatory certainty is not possible through research on motives, so explanatory certainty is not possible through studies of causal relations with others, whether those relations be social, interpersonal, or bodily. Scientists are rarely if ever capable of isolating causes sufficiently to know with absolute certainty that any particular cause played the primary role in producing a result. Furthermore, it seems unlikely that one cause is ever the full and sufficient cause for any result. For this reason, humility is required in scientific research. And yet scientists can argue for the greater plausibility of some explanations compared with others based on their research.

### 3—Consequences

Perhaps the most common way scientists engage in love research is to focus primarily on positive or negative consequences of various activities. This aspect is appropriate given the definition of love presented in this chapter, because love involves promoting overall well-being. Research on consequences typically assumes that actors can promote greater or lesser well-being. And it assumes we can measure well-being to some degree.

Admittedly, research on positive or negative consequences requires value judgments. Many have inaccurately believed science sets aside issues of value and have focused entirely upon the facts derived from observation. This view has been largely discredited in recent decades, however. Scientists bring to their work various values, and those values actually influence their observations. For this reason and others, making value judgments about the positive or negative consequences of various actions is a legitimate exercise in science.

The previous domains of love research implicitly or explicitly involve making value claims about consequences. So one may wonder why this third domain is even necessary as a separate general field of research. We may realize its importance, in part, when we note that some work on altruism attempts to eliminate any claims about creaturely intentions. For instance, sociobiological research on altruism is almost exclusively based on measuring consequences. Intentions play little or no role. The consequences biologists typically have in mind are very specific: survival, reproductive success, and/or the passing on of one's genetic heritage.

E. O. Wilson is perhaps the contemporary biologist best known for research on why some organisms and animals surrender "personal genetic fitness for the enhancement of personal genetic fitness in others."[30] Wilson's observations of ant self-sacrifice show that ants were more self-sacrificial toward those to whom they were most directly genetically related.[31] He extrapolates from ants (and other organisms) to suggest that these principles for altruism might also apply to humans.[32]

Richard Alexander explicitly argues that reproductive and genetic consequences are the hidden reasons why humans act for the good of others. While humans may believe their primary motives involve acting to benefit others at cost to themselves, they are self-deceived.[33] It is to their evolutionary advantage to become unconscious of the fact that they are ultimately self-interested.[34] "We gain by thinking we are right, and by convincing both our allies and our enemies," says Alexander.[35] In sum, "social learning has been all about becoming better at self-interest—indeed, about becoming so good at it that we will be regarded as honest, kind, fair, impartial, reliable, and altruistic not only by our social interactants but also by our own conscious selves."[36]

Alexander has many critics, and his research based on consequences undermines love research based on intentions. Furthermore, few would want to argue that we could reduce all aspects of what we mean by love promoting overall well-being to reproductive success and furthering genetic heritage. But biological research on altruism measured by consequences is legitimate, insofar as being reproductively successful or furthering one's genetic heritage *does* promote overall well-being. And for this reason, sociobiological research can contribute to love studies.

The most convincing love research involves more than one of the three general domains noted above. For instance, we are more convinced that a person acts lovingly when we see positive consequences from his or her actions and are also generally convinced that his or her motives were to promote such consequences. We are more convinced also that a person acts lovingly when that person must intentionally overcome relational obstacles—societal, interpersonal, or bodily—to promote well-being.

In sum, all three general domains encompass a very wide spectrum of possible specific research projects on love. Some very interesting work has been done. There is much yet to do.

## Measuring Godly Love

A perennially vexing question for the science and theology dialogue is how best to account for God's action. The question is difficult to answer for both methodological and metaphysical reasons. Some people assume that claims about divine causation are irrelevant to science and its methodologies. This view—often called methodological naturalism—is understandable for at least two reasons.

First, scientists are justifiably nervous when theists give supposedly sufficient theological explanations for events and things in nature. This nervousness is due, in large part, to the wide-ranging authority over science the church once maintained and the assumed sufficient nature of theological claims. Consequently, many scientists today resist theories that require or seem to imply that science should assume a subordinate position to the authoritative claims of theology and the church. And contemporary science resists the notion that theology gives sufficient explanations for events and things in the natural world.

The second reason divine activity has been assumed to reside outside the domain of science has, unfortunately, received much less attention. Theologians of various types—but especially Christian theologians—have affirmed Jesus's words that God's constitution is spiritual: "God is spirit, and we worship him in spirit and truth."[37] Insofar as spirits cannot be perceived through a human's five senses, it makes little sense to most people that an empirical method based upon sensory perception could identify divine activity. In turn, God's spiritual constitution suggests that science may be inadequate for describing God's action. Due mainly to these two assumptions, many scientists assume a form of methodological naturalism for their scientific work. Methodological naturalism allows scientists—scientists of theistic, atheistic, or agnostic persuasions—to ignore or set aside claims about divine action when doing research.

When asked about the ultimate explanation of things, however, scientists with Christian commitments are likely to refer to God. Some distinguish between the order of nature—which science can explain without reference to divine causation—and the order of grace—which requires an appeal to the mystery of faith. In this appeal, these Christians affirm methodological naturalism, while simultaneously affirming metaphysical supernaturalism. The dual affirmation of methodological naturalism and metaphysical supernaturalism intensifies the temptation to view science and theology as separate and autonomous domains.

A growing number of scholars, however, are right to criticize the view that science and theology can be neatly separated. Many Christians reject the view that theology is unconcerned about facts and the physical world, for instance. And it has become increasingly clear to most that science is value-laden and has important implications for morality. Reality cannot easily be divided into neat little compartments—some religious, spiritual, and moral, and others scientific, factual, and physical. Ian Barbour rightly says, "We cannot remain content with a plurality of unrelated languages if they are languages about the same world. If we seek a coherent interpretation of all experience, we cannot avoid the search for a unified world view."[38]

Many Christians also worry that methodological naturalism is de facto metaphysical naturalism. Assigning God no causal role in scientific explanations easily eliminates God from playing *any* explanatory role. The idea of God becomes an unnecessary addition to what can apparently be explained by natural causes alone. Or an appeal to God is simply an appeal to mystery, a kind of god-of-the-gaps argument. Matthew Lee and Margaret Poloma point out that research on human interaction—especially religious experience—is especially undermined when scientists assume methodological naturalism/atheism.[39] Methodological naturalism fails to answer our fundamental questions about God's activity, and it can easily be interpreted as providing complete answers to the phenomena of our world.

Christians who want scientific methodologies to include a legitimate place for divine causation—both methodologically and metaphysically— have a series of options from which to choose. Elsewhere, the author has noted eight such options and offered labels that describe briefly what is entailed: 1. incessant divine coercion, 2. frequent divine coercion, 3. accidental freewill theism, 4. essential freewill theism/essential kenosis, 5. steady state and uniform divine influence, 6. natural and/or supernatural action, 7. deism, 8. mysterious divine action.[40] Of the eight options for thinking about divine action, only four provide a basis for measuring divine activity with regard to love. And even among these four, only one provides a consistent measurement. That option is essential freewill theism, which is also known as essential kenosis. We could advance the dialogue between theology and social science, as well as interdisciplinary research on Godly love, by reflecting on essential freewill theism and explicitly adopting its approach in empirical studies.

## Essential Freewill Theism and Scientific Method

Essential freewill theism is the metaphysical hypothesis that God necessarily provides freedom and/or agency to creatures and seeks their cooperation. God's causal activity with creatures, however, oscillates and takes various forms.

Essential freewill theism provides a number of powerfully important theological advantages. It affirms love as God's supreme or reigning attribute, for instance. Noncoercive love is a necessary aspect of God's eternal and unchanging nature. Essential freewill theism denies that God ever coerces others and even denies that God is capable of such coercion.[41] It has the benefit of solving the theoretical aspect of the problem of evil, because it says God neither causes evil nor is culpable of failing to prevent evil. Essential freewill theism resolves the question of why a loving God would not see to the fair distribution of goods to the poor and needy. It solves the problem of why a loving God would allow an errant and ambiguous revelation of information this God apparently deems necessary for full salvation. Essential freewill theism solves the theoretical aspects of these problems and more by claiming that God cannot withdraw, override, or fail to offer freedom and/or agency to creatures.[42]

The point of this essay, however, is to argue that essential freewill theism provides a paradigm for thinking about divine action in relation to science. This paradigm, with its particular view of divine love, overcomes key metaphysical and methodological conflicts that arise in the science-and-theology dialogue. To support this argument, we must look more closely at five central features of essential freewill theism/essential kenosis.

### No Event Is Entirely Caused by God: God Cannot Coerce

Because God is never the sole or entire cause of any event or thing, divine causation should never be considered sufficient explanation for any particular event. This statement overcomes the fear that theology makes science superfluous. This rejection of methodological and metaphysical supernatural sufficiency means that science always plays an explanatory role in our attempts to make sense of existence in general and any event or thing in particular.

To say that God never unilaterally determines any event or thing also means that attempts to wed science and theology by selecting particular events as explainable only by divine design are unwarranted. For instance, essential freewill theism rejects intelligent design claims that the irreducible complexity of any particular molecular structure is best explained as the work of God *alone*. God never designs unilaterally, which means that all complex organisms emerge from both divine and creaturely causes. The argument that creatures or natural forces play no role in evolution in general or the emergence of any particular thing runs contrary to essential freewill theism.

### Creatures and/or Nondivine Forces Never Entirely Cause Events— Creatures Cannot Coerce

Because creatures or nondivine forces cannot unilaterally determine any event or thing, creaturely causation should never be considered sufficient explanation. Methodological and metaphysical naturalism is rejected. Any attempt to explain fully a particular event by reference to natural causes *alone* is inadequate. Creaturely causal closure does not exist. Instead, God also exerts causal influence on all existents.

To say that creatures never entirely cause any event or thing is also to deny metaphysical atheism. Any claim that science provides a full and sufficient explanation of any particular event without reference to divine action is unjustified. Contrary to the arguments of some well-known apologists for scientism, essential freewill theism argues that divine causation is necessary for every event or thing.

Every event or thing emerges through the causation of both divine and nondivine causes.[43] This combination of causes amounts to a type of uniformitarianism, in the sense that all events arise from both divine and creaturely causation. This consistency of causation overcomes the conceptual problems inherent in the other seven options mentioned above for how we might think of God's action. The other options either require or allow God to be the sole cause of some events. Or they allow for the possibility that creatures act as sole causes for some events. Essential freewill theism insists that God is a necessary but not sufficient cause in the evolution and continued existence of all things.

*Divine Causation Oscillates*

While every event has both divine and creaturely causes, essential freewill theism proposes that God's causal efficacy varies from event to event. Divine causation oscillates in the sense that God's will is more or less expressed as creatures respond well or poorly to God's freedom and/or agency-providing activity. God's activity is most clearly expressed when an event profoundly promotes overall well-being. God's activity is least clearly expressed when an event profoundly undercuts overall well-being. When well-being is undermined, God's purposes are not accomplished. And yet God exerts some causal influence on even those who do not respond well to God's calling.

It is important to note that the oscillation of divine causation is not a function of an arbitrary divine will. To say that divine causation oscillates does not mean that God arbitrarily chooses sometimes to be more influential and other times to remain relatively uninfluential. Instead, God's nature as love prompts God to exert the most influence possible in any situation. To use an engine metaphor: God always runs at full throttle. Divine oscillation occurs as creatures cooperate in greater or lesser degrees.

The claim that divine causation oscillates is particularly important for Christians doing research on love in the pentecostal tradition.[44] This tradition is known for its claims that God is the source of dramatic events, signs, and wonders. Pentecostals seek after and more often testify to divine healing, words of knowledge, and the miraculous. Essential freewill theism accounts for these dramatic events by claiming that God's causal activity is especially effective during those times. And yet the scheme does not claim that God is the sole cause of such events. God can do, and does, new things. And God's activity is profoundly revealed when creation conforms to the lure of divine love.

For example, Mother Teresa often cooperated with God's living action, and her life is a powerful witness to the power of God's love at work in the world. She used her freedom to conform to God's loving call, so God was not acting as a sufficient cause. But we rightly point to her life as an example of God's especially effective activity in the world.

### Divine Causation Is Diverse

Divine causation varies in form as God lovingly offers each creature opportunities to act relevant to that creature's situation and potential. How God loves a worm will be different from God's love for an eagle. God's love for bacteria differs from God's love for people. God's love for me as I type this essay differs in form from God's love for me yesterday, even if the forms do not differ dramatically. The form of God's causation varies depending on the diversity of the situations and opportunities.

The fact that God loves all creation is unwavering and uniform; God seeks overall well-being. But how God chooses to love each creature, in each situation, at each moment, varies. How God loves is pluriform. The diversity of the form of divine causation is possible in part because of God's omnipresence. But diverse divine causation also hinges upon the diversity of the creatures with which God relates. Diverse divine causation arises from God's own varying specific plans and desires. Divine causal diversity emerges from the diverse relations and communities that influence each creature. And God's diverse causation depends upon what possibilities for the future are genuinely available for instantiation in the present moment. The diversity of the divine vision and the diversity of creation shape the diversity of divine causation.

### Love Always Characterizes God's Causal Influence

Essential freewill theism understands divine love in a particular way. But this way conforms with the general definition of love provided at the outset of this chapter. Both God's love and creaturely love involve acting intentionally, in sympathetic/empathetic response to God and others, to promote overall well-being.

While both creatures and creators can express love, essential freewill theism claims that God necessarily or essentially expresses love. It affirms the Christian belief that God's nature is love. Pentecostal theologian Frank Macchia puts it this way: love "is at the very essence of God's nature as God."[45] Because of this, all divine acts have been, are, and will be acts of love. Divine causation always attempts to promote overall well-being.

Although love is God's essence, God freely chooses how best to love each creature in each situation.[46] God is free to decide how to love. God freely chooses some ways to love creation rather than other possible ways. God lovingly empowers and inspires others by providing them freedom/agency in relationship. Because God's nature is love, God cannot withdraw, fail to offer, or veto the freedom and/or agency God provides to all creatures capable of acting intentionally.

## Testing Divine Love

We are ready to conclude with what essential freewill theism means for testing God's love and informing research on Godly love as defined in the introductory chapter of this book. Because essential freewill theism necessarily requires both divine and creaturely causation for any event and acknowledges that God's causation oscillates and is diverse, it provides a consistent theory for testing divine action.

If, as the essential freewill theism option presupposes, God is a necessary cause in every event, scientific testing will not determine *if* God acts as a cause. God always plays a causal role. The scheme—or "research program," to use the language of Imre Lakatos—presupposes a particular view of divine causation that rejects the view that God is ever absent or inactive as a cause.[47] Testing cannot gauge whether God acts in the world. This scheme assumes that God acts.

The scheme does allow testing the degree to which divine causation is effective (see also the chapters by Poloma and Post in this volume, which discuss the concept of adequacy in the work of sociologist Pitirim Sorokin). In other words, divine causation is more effective in one or some events than in others. Testing this does not involve putting events or things under a microscope in the attempt to see more or less of God. As spirit, God's actions are not discernible by our five senses. Testing to gauge whether divine causation is more effective in some events compared to others requires a different measurement.

The general measurement proposed as most helpful for gauging divine action is the measurement of love. That is, divine causation is most evident in those events or things that express love, in the sense of promoting overall well-being. Divine causation is less effective, and therefore God's causal efficacy is less observable, in those events or things that undermine overall well-being. In short, testing divine action directly relates to the promotion of what the Hebrew prophets called *shalom* and Jesus called "abundant life." The extent to which an event promotes overall well-being reveals the extent to which God's causal activity is effective.

Several possible objections to love as the criterion for scientific testability are foreseeable. Answering these objections may render the plausibility and fecundity of this research program more obvious. While answering these objections, the contours of the proposed research program—with its methodology and metaphysics of love—should become clearer.

*First Possible Objection—*
*Essential Freewill Theism Assumes the Existence of God*

Some may object to the whole enterprise of testing divine action on the grounds that essential freewill theism assumes God exists and then promptly moves to test how God acts in the world. These critics would like proofs for God's existence before trying to test divine action. Yes, essential freewill theism assumes God exists. But all scientific research programs make assumptions. A number of strong arguments for God's existence suggest that it is more plausible that God exists than does not. But, perhaps more to the point of this argument, any adequate research program contains hard-core presuppositions that researchers accept up front as reasonable, although these are not capable of being proven with absolute certainty.

For instance, the vast majority of, if not all, scientific research programs assume some view of cause and effect. But proving cause and effect is, as David Hume pointed out, inherently difficult if not impossible. And the vast majority of, if not all, scientific research programs assume value-laden criteria to claim that some explanations are better than others (e.g., some explanations are more simple, more elegant, more comprehensive). Proving values and aesthetics is also inherently difficult if not impossible.

Those searching for the most adequate research program should compare the relative superiority of one program to another based upon how each accounts for what seem important facets and facts of existence. We are likely willing to accept one research program as superior if that program accounts well for what we know best.

The argument of this chapter is that essential freewill theism accounts for existence better than a naturalistic or an atheistic methodology. Among the advantages of the preceding proposal compared with nontheistic accounts is that it takes seriously the widespread accounts of religious experience, including claims about God's working in human lives and in creation. Claims about divine action based on religious experience are nonnegotiable to many Christians. Naturalistic methodology is less satisfactory because it cannot account well for religious experience. Furthermore, the proposed essential freewill theism/essential kenosis program does a better job than most for accounting for love in general and the view that love is not coercive in particular. Accordingly, this program seems potentially more fruitful for love research than others do.

## Second Possible Objection—Research Program Does Not Offer Certainty

Some may object to the criterion of love as the ultimate measurement for divine action, because the efficacy of divine love cannot be deduced with certainty from observed phenomena. "God" and "love" cannot be perceived by our five senses. But science does not offer certainty. Yes, the essential freewill theism research program does not provide absolute certainty. However, the assumption that any scientific explanation provides absolute certainty can also be rejected. Science—relying as it does on fallible sensory perception—does not provide grounds for absolute certainty. Science deals in the provisional, not the absolutely provable.

Furthermore, essential freewill theism does support scientific practices central to the scientific enterprise: induction and inference. It supports the scientific practice of moving from observed data to a hypothesis and then testing that hypothesis by further observation.

## Third Possible Objection—It Is Impossible to Measure Overall Well-Being

Some may object to the criterion of love as the ultimate measurement for testing divine action, because this criterion requires an assessment of nearly everything. That is, if love means promoting overall well-being, the critic might wonder how one could do this all-embracing measurement. "Overall" is . . . all-encompassing! Essential freewill theism does examine limited samples and makes generalizations to the whole. An all-inclusive measurement is obviously not possible by localized creatures. But this should not and does not prevent researchers from speculating about the whole based upon observations and experiments from a limited set. In fact, this general approach is a bedrock practice of science. Scientific researchers of all types examine the few and make provisional claims about what this means for the whole.

While love intends to promote overall well-being, it must assess what might be done to promote the global good when acting locally. Insofar as an intentional response to promote well-being is helpful to some and not an obvious detriment to the whole, it can provisionally be deemed an act of love.

*Fourth Possible Objection—*
*Testing Divine Action Requires Research on Creaturely Action*

Some may object to essential freewill theism as a basis for testing divine action because it requires appropriate responses from creatures to determine the degree of divine causation. This objection rightly sees that the essential freewill theism claims that the efficacy of divine causation directly relates to the love that nondivine beings express in response to God.

Response: In an interrelated universe of multiple causation, we must make inferences about which actors exert primary causation given what we have reason to believe about these actors. This objection reminds us that one agent is never entirely responsible for any particular event. All events and things in the world arise through the influence of multiple causes. Existence is interrelated. The scheme proposed in this chapter builds upon this interrelatedness and accepts a multiple-causation view of existence. But it also agrees with the widespread intuition that despite interrelatedness and multiple causation, we can plausibly attribute more causal responsibility to one agent than others. We can infer that some actors or causes are primary. Because of this, we can justifiably assert that God is more involved in some events than in others.

Let's look at an example of multiple and primary causes. What do we regard as the causal explanation when we say that a boy threw a ball through a window? Assuming that the boy actually threw the ball, we may simply attribute responsibility to the boy. We would be correct in doing this, so long as we do not claim that the boy is the sufficient cause of the event. After all, wind, gravity, the hardness of the ball, the thickness of the glass, and a host of other factors played contributory causal roles. When we say the boy is responsible, we are making a claim about a particular cause as playing the *primary* role. But we need not also claim that the boy's throwing was the full and sufficient role.

Saying that divine action is more prevalent in the world when creatures respond appropriately in love is compatible with saying that divine action is the primary cause of this love. This is especially true if one also has reason to believe that God is the source of all love.

*Fifth Possible Objection—*
*All Creatures Should be Equally Revelatory of Divine Action*

Some may object to love as the ultimate measurement for testing divine action, because it affords greater revelatory capacity to complex creatures—like dogs, dolphins, and humans—and less revelatory capacity to simpler entities—like atoms, cells, or microorganisms. This objection is based upon the view that all creatures are equally capable of revealing divine love. In response, note that complex creatures are potentially more revelatory of divine action, both because they exert greater and more varied freedom and diversity and because they are more similar to complex humans than simpler creatures. If divine causation is necessary for all events and things, nothing would be absolutely incapable of revealing God's activity. However, creatures that are more complex afford greater opportunities for testing divine action in the world based in part on the nature of human inquiry.

What we know best are our own complex experiences—although we still have much to learn. We are capable of more accurate inferences about creatures similar to ourselves than creatures less similar. We are more likely, for instance, rightly to attribute sadness to a dog after watching its listless behavior than we would sadness to a worm. Additionally, the degree to which atoms, cells, and microorganisms can respond appropriately or inappropriately seems impossible at present to gauge. Only metaphysical speculation is able to say that the smallest entities of existence—say, subatomic particles—have the capacity for responses.

But this does not mean that God is not active as a necessary and loving cause in the smallest entities of our universe. It only means that our ability to gauge divine activity at the micro-level is seriously hampered. Our ability to gauge divine activity increases among complex creatures in part because the diversity of their responses provides a wider range of possible actions we could assess as promoting or undermining overall well-being.

Christians have a strong precedent for claiming that organisms that are more complex can be more revelatory of divine love than the less complex. That precedent is Jesus Christ. Most Christians affirm that the highest revelation of divine love took human form. This suggests that our best scientific measurements for divine love are likely to be the more complex forms of existence. No strong argument or evidence is available that God has been incarnated among worms to the degree of complexity and diversity that God was incarnate in Jesus of Nazareth.

## Conclusion

This chapter has sought to answer two central questions for research on love. One has to do with testing love expressed by creatures. After offering a definition of love, three general domains for love research were noted, and examples of research in each were identified. These examples were by no means exhaustive. But perhaps the discussion provides a framework to account for research already completed and research yet to be pursued.

The task of measuring God's love has also been addressed through a scheme called essential freewill theism (or essential kenosis). The researcher who operates from the essential freewill theism research program can measure the effectiveness of God's love as seen in the actions of creatures. The more complex the organism, the more important reference to divine love becomes. The concept of Godly love, with its emphasis on benevolence and creaturely responsiveness, should be grounded in essential freewill theism. Doing so will help researchers evaluate the adequacy of benevolence and responsiveness in terms of a theological framework grounded in the promotion of overall well-being. Conversely, research purporting to offer a robust explanation of creaturely love without reference to God runs the risk of atheistic naturalism.

Essential freewill theism also provides a framework to help theists with language to refer to divine love. If the researcher believes in God and believes that God is the source of all love, explanations of creaturely love will be incomplete and less robust when divine action is not mentioned. Essential freewill theism provides a scheme to account scientifically for God's love in the world. Christians who believe in an active God that empowers and inspires love may be eager to accept a scientific methodology that not only accepts but also requires an explanatory role for divine action.

## Notes

1. Thomas Jay Oord, *Defining Love: A Philosophical, Scientific, and Theological Engagement* (Grand Rapids, MI: Brazos, 2010).

2. For strategies and research in promoting well-being in humans, see Margaret Schneider Jamner and Daniel Stokols, eds., *Promoting Human Well-Being: New Frontiers for Research, Practice, and Policy* (Berkeley and Los Angeles: University of California Press, 2000).

3. Some philosophers and theologians explicitly affirm nonsensory perception. This mode of perception is important for many reasons, not the least of which is that it provides an avenue to account for perception of God—a being usually regarded as an omnipresent Spirit incapable of detection by our five senses.

4. The issue of discerning motives and the role motives play in our decisions is complex. There exists no philosophical or scientific uniformity on the salient issues. The argument presented here requires only the claim that we have motives, that these motives influence our choices, and that we can be cognizant at least to some degree of what our primary motives might be.

5. See C. Daniel Batson's statements on primary and secondary motives in *The Altruism Question: Toward a Social-Psychological Answer* (Hillsdale, NJ: Lawrence Erlbaum Associates, 1991), chs. 1–2.

6. Susan S. Hendrick and Clyde Hendrick, "Love and Sex Attitudes and Religious Beliefs," *Journal of Social & Clinical Psychology* 5:3 (1987): 391–98.

7. Batson defines altruism as "a motivational state with the ultimate goal of increasing another's welfare" (*Altruism Question*, 6). Although this differs some from the definition of love proposed in this chapter, the differences do not affect the reasons for using Batson's work at this point.

8. Ibid., 113.

9. Ibid., 115.

10. Ibid., 116.

11. Anne Colby and William Damon, *Some Do Care: Contemporary Lives of Moral Commitment* (New York: Free Press, 1992).

12. Ibid., 64.

13. Ibid., 293ff.

14. Ibid., 311.

15. Elliott Sober and David Sloan Wilson, *Unto Others: The Evolution and Psychology of Unselfish Behavior* (Cambridge: Harvard University Press, 1998), 6.

16. Ibid., 26.

17. Ibid., chs. 3–5.

18. Ibid., 193.

19. Stacey L. Smith and Sandi W. Smith, "A Content Analysis of Altruistically Loving Acts on Television," in Compassionate Love Research Conference program (funded by Fetzer Institute, 2004), 22. Yet to be published elsewhere.

20. Ibid., 23.

21. See John Bowlby, *Attachment and Loss*, vol. 1, *Attachment* (New York: Basic Books, 1969).

22. Mario Mikulincer, Phillip R. Shaver, Omri Gillath, and Rachel A. Nitzberg, "Attachment, Caregiving, and Altruism: Boosting Attachment Security Increases Compassion and Helping," *Journal of Personality and Social Psychology* 89:5 (November 2005): 833.

23. Samuel P. Oliner and Pearl M. Oliner, *The Altruistic Personality: Rescuers of Jews in Nazi Europe* (New York: Free Press, 1988), 249–50.

24. George E. Vaillant, "Generativity: A Form of Unconditional Love," in *Altruism and Health: Perspectives from Empirical Research*, ed. Stephen G. Post, 219–29 (Oxford: Oxford University Press), 2007.

25. Among her many publications, see especially *Altruistic Emotion, Cognition, and Behavior* (Hillsdale, NJ: Lawrence Erlbaum Associates, 1986), *The Caring Child* (Cambridge: Harvard University Press, 1992), and (Eisenberg, ed.), *The Development of Prosocial Behavior* (New York: Academic Press, 1982).

26. C. Zahn-Waxler and M. Radke-Yarrow, "Development of Altruism: Alternative Research Strategies," in Eisenberg, ed., *The Development of Pro-Social Behavior*, 109–38.

27. Eisenberg, *Caring Child*, 13.

28. Hanna Damasio, "Impairment of Interpersonal Social Behavior Caused by Acquired Brain Damage," in *Altruism and Altruistic Love: Science, Philosophy, and Religion in Dialogue*, ed. Stephen G. Post et al. (Oxford: Oxford University Press, 2002), 281. Antonio Damasio's essay in the volume is "A Note on the Neurobiology of Emotions."

29. See James Van Slyke, "Theology in Mind: Reduction, Emergence, and Cognitive Science" (PhD diss., Fuller Theological Seminary, 2008).

30. Edward O. Wilson, *Sociobiology: The New Synthesis* (Cambridge: Harvard University Press, 1975), 106.

31. Ibid., 117–18.

32. E. O. Wilson, *On Human Nature: With a New Preface* (Cambridge: Harvard University Press, 2004 [1978]), 153.

33. Richard D. Alexander, *The Biology of Moral Systems* (New York: Aldine De Gruyter, 1987), 109–10.

34. Ibid., 121.

35. Ibid., 123.

36. Ibid., 139.

37. John 4:24.

38. Ian Barbour, *Religion in an Age of Science: The Gifford Lectures 1989–91*, vol. 1 (San Francisco: HarperSanFrancisco, 1990), 16.

39. See Matthew T. Lee and Margaret M. Poloma, *A Sociological Study of the Great Commandment in Pentecostalism: The Practice of Godly Love as Benevolent Service* (Lewiston, NY: Edwin Mellen Press, 2009).

40. See the particular description of each option in Oord, "Love as a Methodological and Metaphysical Source for Science and Theology," *Wesleyan Theological Journal* 45:1 (Spring 2010): 81–107.

41. I am not speaking of coercion in the psychological sense of bullying or meanness—although I also don't think God is mean or bullies. Rather, I refer to coercion in the causal sense. Causal coercion would involve the denial of freedom to the Other. Causal coercion entails unilateral determination. Divine causal coercion would mean that God withdraws, overrides, or fails to offer freedom and/or agency to others. These issues are explored more fully in Oord, *The Nature of Love: A Theology* (St. Louis: Chalice, 2010), and *Defining Love* (full citation noted above).

42. In the form that denies creation ex nihilo, essential freewill theism/essential kenosis has the benefit of affirming God's essential love for the world.

43. Lee and Poloma (*Sociological Study*, 7) make this point when they define Godly love as "the dynamic interaction between divine and human love that enlivens and expands benevolence."

44. See Amos Yong, *The Spirit of Creation: Modern Science and Divine Action in the Pentecostal-Charismatic Imagination* (Grand Rapids, MI: Eerdmans, 2011).

45. Frank D. Macchia, *Baptized in the Spirit* (Grand Rapids, MI: Zondervan, 2006), 259.

46. Macchia agrees (bid., 263).

47. A number of books address Imre Lakatos's work on research programs. One of the very best summaries of Lakatos's vision and the implications of that vision can be found in Joseph Bankard, "A New Defense of Universal Morality: Synthesizing the Natural and Social Sciences with Theism" (PhD diss., Claremont Graduate University, 2008).

# Part II

## Social Science and Godly Love

# METHODOLOGICAL AGNOSTICISM FOR

# THE SOCIAL SCIENCES?

## Lessons from Sorokin's and James's Allusions to

## Psychoanalysis, Mysticism, and Godly Love

### RALPH W. HOOD JR.

It remains an unsettled issue to what extent the term *science* applies to the domain of the social sciences. In a recent review of the psychology of religion, Emmons and Paloutzian called for a new *multilevel interdisciplinary paradigm*.[1] While the paradigm implies a natural-science approach, the call was accompanied by the assertion of the value of using data at multiple levels of analysis as well as the value of nonreductive assumptions regarding the nature of religious and spiritual phenomena. The call for this new paradigm is echoed again in Park and Paloutzian.[2] However, as we shall see, this call is not at all represented by contemporary research in psychology or sociology. Its absence in sociology forms the basis for Porpora's critical analysis of the sociology of religion, whose overarching assumption is the methodological atheism most forcefully championed by Peter Berger and best summarized by the claim that "every inquiry into religious matters that limits itself to the empirically available must necessarily be based on a 'methodological atheism.'"[3] While Berger speaks to sociologists, he echoes a sentiment of over a hundred years ago by the psychologist Theodore Flournoy, who argued for the methodical exclusion of the transcendent in the then-emerging empirical psychology of religion.[4]

Porpora's criticism of methodological atheism is based on the fact that insofar as one raises social constructionism to a methodological absolute, reality as empirically investigated is necessarily incapable of referring to anything outside of social constructs that may contribute to experience. Thus, insofar as social psychology is essentially a socially constructed psychology, ontological issues as to the nature of the "real" are not simply bracketed but ignored. This was not the case with the two great Harvard proponents of sociology (Pitirim Sorokin) and psychology (William James). They both argued for a transcendence of natural-science assumptions and of the methodological atheism inherent in reductive materialism. Porpora argues for a more epistemologically adequate methodological agnosticism. Part of Porpora's reasoning is based upon the limits of social constructionism recognized as incapable of being applied to the discipline of sociology even in Berger's coauthored defense of this methodological principle. Berger and Luckmann recognized that if the principle was reflexively applied to sociology, it would be like trying to push a bus from the inside.[5] Likewise, Collins and Yearly refuse to apply social constructionism to sociology in what has not so playfully been identified as the epistemological chicken-and-egg debate.[6] Bhaskar suggests his own neologism, "TINA" (there is no alternative), in what is a vain effort at ending philosophical reflection of the overarching assumption.[7]

If we return now to the call for a new paradigm noted above, an interdisciplinary paradigm offers possibilities that, while not denying the relevance of social constructionism, is not bound by its philosophically self-imposed limits. If we focus upon psychology, one of the earliest reviews of the social psychology of religion by Dittes identified four conceptual options available to those who study the psychology of religion and spirituality.[8]

Two of Dittes's options are reductionistic and implicitly subscribe to methodological atheism. The first is the claim that the only variables operating in religion are the same that operate in mainstream psychology. The psychology of religion need have no unique methodology, as its subject matter is not unique. The second option is that while the variables operating in religion are not unique, they may be more salient in religious contexts, and thus their effect is greater within than outside of religion. However, they remain purely psychological variables. Both of these options are consistent with methodological naturalism, which is inherently atheistic.

Dittes's other two conceptual options suggest that something is unique about religion, and thus that it may need methods that mainstream psychology ignores. They are implicitly methodologically agnostic. The least controversial of these is that established psychological variables uniquely interact in religious contexts and thus that there is a unique contribution that the interaction of psychological with religious variables makes to the total variance explained (option 3). This is consistent with Porpora's claim that transcendent realities may contribute to the totality of what is religiously experienced. Dittes's fourth option is that there are unique variables operating in religion that either do not operate in other contexts or are ignored by mainstream psychologists. Insofar as both of these options can give credence to ontological claims associated with religion, they can be identified as supporting a methodological agnosticism.

Hood has used Dittes's four options to suggest ways of studying religion and spirituality that are not limited by social constructionist assumptions.[9] Options three and four described above transcend social constructionist assumptions by noting that with respect to religious and spiritual experiences, the claim that something is an object or a source of the experience moves from a purely social constructionistic assumption to a social expressionism in which social and psychological mediators are efforts to express an experience that transcends its mere social construction.[10] Note that agnosticism here simply affirms that for the believer the object of experience has an ontological status that must enter into assessing relative interpretations offered by theories based upon methodological atheism or agnosticism. Porpora refers to this in general terms as "super-mundane objects of experience."[11] He also notes that psychology might be ahead of sociology in accepting such realities in an appeal to what Coon has identified as "physics envy."[12] Porpora notes: "Physicists at the moment are suggesting plenty of strange things: multiple other dimensions and universes; unidentified dark matter and repulsive forces; quantum action-at-a-distance. Why should sociology too not be open to what now only seems strange to distinctly modernist sensibilities?"[13]

Thus, it is scientifically legitimate to explore the possibility that part of the experience of God comes from God.[14] Porpora does not provide a description of the kind of science that is open to the ontological possibilities associated with taking seriously reports of religious and spiritual experiences. However, he suggests that psychology is ahead of sociology in acknowledging a transcendence that does not in Berger's own explicit concern provide anything more than a "quasiscientific legitimation of a secularized worldly view."[15] In the remainder of this chapter we will see how both Sorokin in sociology and James in psychology provided possibilities for the empirical exploration of transcendent or super-mundane realities. The author does this by emphasizing psychology rather than sociology, and James more than Sorokin. This is to confront Porpora's claim that psychology is ahead of sociology, a claim the author suggests is less than adequately descriptive of most contemporary psychology.

Our discussion focuses upon the psychoanalytic tradition that is at best on the margins of contemporary psychology and sociology of religion. This focus on psychoanalysis and the transition from classical Freudianism to object-relations views ironically demonstrates the obverse of both James's and Sorokin's treatment of religion. Both Sorokin and James included psychoanalysis in the treatment of religion. Both also rejected the reductive claims of Freud. However, they both would reject the move into object relations that characterizes contemporary psychoanalysis as an unwarranted commitment to methodological atheism that is simply a mask for progress that can be measured from a distance by the mature assumptions of both Sorokin's sociology and James's psychology. Freud denied methodological agnosticism, convinced that psychoanalysis had unlocked the empirical facts of religion's insight regarding super-mundane realities. Since as Sorokin anticipated, psychoanalysis is now at best on the defensive as a model for the social sciences and has virtually no place in modern American academic psychology, there is a lesson for both sociology and psychology of the risk of a premature exclusion of the transcendent demanded by methodological atheism. Thus, a research agenda on Godly love that is grounded in methodological agnosticism may avoid problems associated with the failure to learn this lesson.[16]

### Mysticism as a Common Mediator for Sorokin and James

Sorokin's insistence on the ontological status of love allowed him to postulate a supraconscious that he was not unwilling to call by several names, one of which was God.[17] While theologians are likely to be critical of Sorokin's linking of many equivalents to "God," such as truth, nature, or the Absolute, social scientists can appreciate that as a sociologist Sorokin is firmly entrenched in Dittes's two methodological agnostic options noted above. Sorokin bemoaned the empirical consequences that would follow from any attempt to develop a religion or a theory of altruism "devoid of the grace of the supraconscious."[18] Thus, altruism is *not* Godly love, simply because part of what is ontologically necessary (God) is ignored. The concept of Godly love prohibits the reductionism demanded by methodological atheism, however valid its explanations of mere altruism may be.[19]

Sorokin's appreciation of Freud was rather limited. While he accepted the reality of the unconscious, he deemed Freud's efforts to conceptualize it as "logical hash."[20] However, the crucial issue here is Sorokin's acceptance of the ontological status of an unconscious that will mirror a supraconscious that has an equal ontological status. Thus, Sorokin accepts God (supraconsciousness) and allows this concept to play a central role in his theory of love energy.

If we are to connect Sorokin and James via their reactions to Freud, we can add here Sorokin's appeal to mystical experience, perhaps necessary for the full practice of Godly love. Sorokin explores techniques for the altruistic transformation of both individuals and groups. With respect to the former he states, "*supreme love can hardly be achieved without direct participation of the supraconscious.*"[21] Such techniques of genuine altruistic transformation of the self can be empirically studied.[22] Furthermore, the effort to link such states with pathology fails. Sorokin notes that "the supreme goal of a monk is union with God."[23] Furthermore, he quotes Lao-Tzu to refute the claim that such mystical experiences of Godly love are pathological: "He who disciplines his soul and embraces unity cannot be deranged."[24] Techniques of transformation constitute the majority of Sorokin's text, but with cautionary warnings of the limits of methodological atheism. Sorokin acknowledges the usefulness of psychoanalytic techniques, however, only in monastic settings and often with reference to psychoanalysis in parentheses. Sorokin thought psychoanalysis to be "demoralizing ethically," its success due mainly to its congruity with the dominant disintegrating sensate culture of the West.[25] This argument could also be applied to the success of methodological atheism in general.

## James's Abandonment of Methodological Atheism

Social scientists who are familiar with James are likely to be so from James's *Varieties of Religious Experience* (1981, hereafter *VRE*), which is perhaps the one classic exemplar of methodological agnosticism in psychology and staunchly opposed to Flournoy's principle of the exclusion of the transcendent noted above. "James's presumption was that religious experients were genuinely experiencing something real; the question was what."[26] However, elsewhere the author has argued the *VRE* is best read as partly a response to issues that James alluded to in his monumentally influential *Principles of Psychology* (1890/1981, hereafter *PP*) but refused to address.[27] James's effort in *PP* was to restrict himself to the assumptions of natural science, explicitly excluding super-mundane realities inconsistent with a methodological atheism. However, scholars have noted that James failed in his attempt. The empirical data cited in *PP* quickly are embedded in philosophical and even metaphysical options.[28] Reading *PP*, one senses James's struggle to limit psychology so severely. In one of the earliest reviews of *PP*, Ladd noted its extensive engagement with metaphysical speculations. He titled his review, "Psychology as So-Called

'Natural Science.'"[29] In it he insisted that a psychology without metaphysical considerations is too constrictive. He astutely took James to task for attempting to admit only one metaphysical position (methodological atheism) as explanatory for psychology. Most empirical data cited are simply those of the correlation between thoughts and brain states. James and others quickly responded to Ladd's review. A debate was started that continues to trouble psychology today.[30]

James's efforts to ignore super-mundane realities in *PP* can be seen as an effort to show the limits of a natural science perspective, not to exclude psychological consideration of what is outside those limits.[31] In this sense, after *PP* James's oeuvre can be seen as an effort to start over, given the metaphysical limits that psychology must transcend if it is to appropriately confront the totality of experienced reality. As we shall see, residual issues left unexplained by the methodological atheism of the natural sciences could be reintroduced by a psychology in the *VRE* that is more sensitive to super-mundane realities (methodological agnosticism). The almost exclusive reliance upon reports of experience with super-mundane realities as the basic data in the *VRE* led Wundt to deny that it was a psychological work.[32] This amounted to simply acknowledging two psychologies: one, a natural science based upon methodological atheism, and the other, a human science based upon methodological agnosticism. The methodological exclusion of the transcendent that James tried in *PP* was abandoned in *VRE*.

The recognition of the relevance of James's discussion of philosophical and metaphysical issues in *PP* can be contrasted to the avoidance of philosophical commentary in contemporary psychology and sociology texts dealing with religion.[33] In James's abridgement of the *PP*, much of the reduction was accomplished by the exclusion of philosophical material. James concludes the greatly abridged *PP*, *Psychology: The Briefer Course*, as follows:

> at present psychology is in the condition of physics before Galileo and the laws of motion, of chemistry before Lavoiser and the notion that mass is preserved in all reactions. The Galileo and the Lavoisier of psychology will be famous men indeed when they come, as come they some day surely will, or past successes are no index to the future. When they do come, however, the necessities of the case will make them "metaphysical." Meanwhile the best way in which we can facilitate their advent is to understand how great is the darkness in which we grope, and never to forget that *the natural-science assumptions with which we started are provisional and revisable things.*[34]

## James's Turn to Methodological Agnosticism

James had much to say about being radically empirical as opposed to simply adopting natural science assumptions uncritically asserted to be empirical. James accepts empiricism, but one that is radical. Bernard notes that

James's empiricism is compatible with the assumption that the fundamental reality of nature may not at all be a "concatenation of impersonal forces."[35] Thus, *VRE* remains the empirical exemplar of what Miller has recently re-asserted: that a great majority of people worldwide accept the existence of nonmaterial realities viewed as sacred.[36] It is ironic that James's movement to methodological agnosticism in *VRE* is not accepted as empirical science by many psychologists. James's empiricism was intended to be a form of scientific positivism. However, as Perry has noted: "the positivism of James was almost the precise opposite of the doctrine which now passes by that name. Contemporary positivism closes all the doors but one, while James' positivism *opened all the doors* and kept them opened."[37]

Similarly, Perry notes that James responded in a letter to the positivist psychologist Ribot that the ordinary positivist "simply has a muddled metaphysic which he refuses to criticize or discuss."[38] With this we have come back to Belzen and Hood, who argue that psychologists must be sensitive to various philosophical assumptions (none of which are nonproblematic) that undergird various psychological methodologies.[39] Likewise, Dainton has noted that the phenomenological study of consciousness refuses to allow consciousness to be explained in terms of something else and thus requires that long-neglected metaphysical options be taken seriously once again.[40] Hence, methodological atheism cannot be mandated, as if what constitutes "science" has been settled once and for all.

## The Common Concern of Sorokin and James with Mysticism

If much of Sorokin's classic text on love is a discussion of techniques of altruistic transformation linked to union with the supraconscious, much of James's *VRE* is concerned with reports of spontaneous mystical experiences. Yet both of these giants of Harvard's earliest days of sociology and psychology adhered to a methodological agnosticism—allowing for the ontological reality of the experience of union that, as we shall see, is denied within the assumption of methodological atheism. Elsewhere, Hood has argued for reading James's treatment of mysticism as an example of the unity, or common core, thesis in mysticism.[41] The unity thesis is the view that both within and outside of the great faith traditions is an experience that is essentially identical, regardless of interpretation. This thesis is widely disputed and raises serious theological issues that are beyond the scope of this chapter. However, what is germane here is the ontological reality of the experience. James put the issue thusly:

> In Hinduism, in Neoplatonism, in Sufism, in Christian Mysticism, in Whitmanism, we find the same recurring note, so that there is about mystical utterances an eternal

unanimity which ought to make a critic stop and think, and which brings it about that the mystical classics have, as has been said, neither birthday nor native land. Perpetually telling of the unity of man with God, *their speech antedates language*, and they do not grow old.[42]

The two primary markers of mystical experience that James employs for his Gifford lectures are that these experiences are noetic and ineffable. His insistence on the noetic is crucial, especially when combined with the other primary marker of mysticism, ineffability. The noetic aspect of mysticism asserts that mystical experience provides knowledge about reality that is nevertheless incapable of being put into words. The appeal is thus to an ineffable knowledge that must be experienced to be fully appreciated. Here is the strongest claim to situate James within the common core or unity school of mysticism. Ironically, it is first expressed in a curious quote given James's intent to battle with monism: "In mystic states we both become one with the Absolute and we become aware of our oneness."[43] James's reference to the Absolute is partly sleight of hand, for he readily admits in the written lectures that his preference is for God since God is (a) a medium of communion and (b) a causal agent.[44] Regardless, the ontological reality of the Absolute or God is an integral part of both the description and the explanation of mystical experience. Hence, a methodology can neither adequately describe nor explain the mystical experience if it precludes a priori the possibility that part of the experience of God is from God. The role of language and culture in interpreting mysticism is not challenged, but the denial that there is no Absolute or God to be experienced is.

James relied upon F.W.H. Myer's subliminal consciousness rather than Freud's unconsciousness for several reasons, including Myer's belief in the survival of consciousness after bodily death.[45] Here we need but note that it is the structure by which James's methodological agnosticism can acknowledge the reality he simply identified as "MORE of the same quality."[46] He also notes, "It is when we treat of the experience of 'union' with it that their [mystics'] differences appear most clearly."[47] Thus, James can accept an aspect of the constructionist position that was articulated at the time of James's *VRE* by Rufus Jones: "The most refined mysticism, the most exalted spiritual experience is *partly* a product of the social and intellectual environment in which the personal life of the mystic has formed and matured."[48] Jones's emphasis is crucial, for it allows that portions of experience escape cultural influences. Stace notes that self-transcendence (James's "MORE") is part of the experience and *not* "of the interpretation of experience."[49] Methodological atheism denies the more of James as it does the supraconscious of Sorokin; however, the question is not a methodological declaration by fiat, but whether such a denial is adequate to either the description or experience of mystical Godly love—a term implicit in the claim that "the supreme goal of a monk is union with God, *through love of God and of neighbor.*"[50] However, the path of classical psychoanalysis and of its stepchild in various object relations schools would use methodological atheism to claim that if not the experience itself, the interpretation of the experience is either a delusion and hence pathological or an illusion and without ontological support from the social sciences, whose competency does not extend that far.

## Sorokin's and James's Reactions to Classical Psychoanalysis

We have already noted Sorokin's pejorative evaluation of psychoanalysis, a sister to sensate culture, and that both were moving in what he poetically referred as the "social sewers."[51] Somewhat surprising then is James's early appraisal of classical psychoanalysis. Of course, James did not have the hindsight of Sorokin and was only vaguely acquainted with psychoanalytic theory. He met Freud only once (at Clark University), where he is reported by Ernst Jones, one of Freud's earliest biographers, to have said, "The future of psychology is yours."[52] However, this is less likely correct in light of James's letter to Ms. Calkins of September 19, 1909, which records a more cautious appreciation of Freud and psychoanalysis: "I strongly suspect Freud, with his dream-theory, of being a regular *halluciné*. But I hope that he and his disciples will push it to its limits, as undoubtedly it covers some facts, and will add to our understanding of 'functional' psychology, which is the real psychology."[53]

Likewise, in *VRE* in a less thinly veiled reference to Freud, James echoed what has become a standard critique of classical Freudian theory—the refusal to abandon or limit the pansexual motivation *for* and explanation *of* the content of certain religious beliefs. James rejected the claim that religious belief was "perverted sexuality": "The plain truth is that to interpret religion one must in the end look at the immediate content of the religious consciousness. The moment one does this, one sees how wholly disconnected it is in the main from the content of the sexual consciousness."[54]

James's MORE noted above was not reductively sexual any more than was Sorokin's supraconsciousness. If James was suspicious of Freud's reductionist understanding of religious experience, his appreciation of the role of the subliminal was not far from Freud's. As Browning noted, "Since the subliminal for him [James] can also be a place of forgotten memories and obscurely motivated passions, it would have been only a small step for James to reach the classical Freudian position."[55] One cannot imagine

James endorsing Freud's phylogenetic theory as an answer to the origin of religion, but one can believe he would applaud Freud's persistence in asking the right question. If Freud's phylogenetic theory is not the proper answer, it awaits a better empirical alternative. The refutation of Freud's phylogenetic thesis must be empirical. James goes on to conclude, as he had in the abridgment of the *Principles*, that the real issue as to the natural science presumptions of Freud's pansexualism was metaphysical: "the whole theory has lost its point in evaporating into a vague general assertion of the dependence, *somehow*, of the mind upon the body."[56]

## Classical Psychoanalysis and the Freudian Theory of Religion

Freud's phylogenetic theory of religion is well known, and excellent summaries are readily available from both those committed to psychoanalysis and those uncommitted.[57] Our concern here is to address the courage of the Freudian theory of religion insofar as it (1) accepts the reality claims of religion or (2) provides a reductive explanation that (3) unmasks religion as pathology insofar as it is mass delusion. While we do not accept the theory, the logic of its claim and the empirical evidence for it must be met.

### Religion—Illusion or Delusion?

What James referred to as Freud's *halluciné* theory of religion acknowledged what Freud accepted, that knowledge of psychological motivation alone could not be used to refute religious truth claims. Religion as illusion simply means that (a) individuals more or less consciously know what they desire; (b) a religious *Weltanschauung* (worldview) offers solace that a natural-science *Weltanschauung* cannot. Freud stated this most succinctly in *New Introductory Lectures on Psychoanalysis*: "Religion is an attempt to master the sensory world in which we are situated by means of the wishful world which we have developed within us as a result of biological and psychological necessities. But religion cannot achieve this."[58] Desire and reality are orthogonal. An illusion may be true, but its truth must be tested by natural-science means. As a natural scientist Freud believed he could test the historical truth claims of the Judeo-Christian tradition and, further, that these claims were false. This phylogenetic interpretation of the origins of Judeo-Christian tradition has been nearly universally rejected both within and outside of psychoanalysis.[59] However, the crucial issue is that it can be rejected precisely because (a) it takes religious belief claims seriously, and (b) it purports to test these claims empirically.

In *Moses and Monotheism* Freud stated, "I have no hesitation that men have always known (in this special way) that they once possessed a primal father and killed him."[60] Freud's parenthetical reference is to a phylogenetic transmitted knowledge that apparently requires the inheritance of acquired characteristics. Grünbaum notes that the phylogenetic theory itself is intellectually comprehensible but weakly supported if it relies upon Lamarckian theory.[61] However, a reconsideration of Freud's phylogenetic speculation within the confines of Darwinian theory is possible and removes that critique.[62]

The psychological outcome of Freud's phylogenetic theory is embedded in the provocative thesis that there can be mass delusion in the sense of culturally shared religious beliefs that are nevertheless false. The beliefs may be adhered to as illusions, beliefs desired to be true, but if falsified, religious beliefs are delusions and falsifications of reality as understood by science. "If the development of civilization has such a far-reaching similarity to the development of the individual and if it employs the same methods, may we not be justified in reaching the diagnosis that, under the influence of cultural urges, some civilizations, or some epochs of civilization—possibly the whole of mankind—have become 'neurotic'?"[63]

The notion that the Oedipal drama individually experienced recapitulates an event in evolutionary history that resulted in humanization is the crucial claim by Freud for empirical evidence of the delusionary nature of religion.[64] Humankind killed its real biological father, not the God-man Jesus. This is the material truth distorted in various ways in the historical narratives of two of the Abrahamic faiths that Freud addressed. Christians, believers in the son-God, acknowledge the primal murder with Paul's doctrine of original sin, leaving modern Jews who believe in the father-God only to bear the burden of their denial that they murdered God.[65] With few exceptions, Freud's empirical and historical claims have been rejected.[66] However, the fact is that as historical and empirical claims they can be falsified. Thus, in this sense, Freud's personal illusion (atheism) may have motivated him to seek a refutation of religion, but to do so he had to take seriously the historical references in the content of religious faith.

*Freud's Phylogenetic Theory and the Limits of Social Constructionism*

The importance of Freud's phylogenetic view of religion is his claim that religion is a delusion and hence ultimately false, even though "no one, needless to say, who shares a delusion ever recognizes it as such."[67] Even if one accepts that religion is a cultural phenomenon, it is not protected from also being delusional. "In the case of delusions we emphasize as being essential their being in contradiction with reality."[68] The radical nature of Freud's phylogenetic theory of religion ought not to be under-estimated. It is one of the reasons for the rejection of classical Freudian theory by modern psychoanalysis and the almost universal rejection of Freud by contemporary American psychology. An example is the political correctness embedded in recent efforts to modify clinical understandings of those who adhere to delusionary beliefs, so that rather than being idio-syncratic individual neuroses, and hence a caricature of religion, they are mass delusions and a protective umbrella from the harsh reality of God's nonexistence—a clear ontological claim.[69]

It is this that Belzen suggests is the correct move precisely because cul-tural phenomena such as religion cannot be *psychologically* explained.[70] However, it is specifically the origin of religion that continues to intrigue psychologists and historians who take seriously the ontological claims of religion and offer a psychological explanation of religion's origin.[71]

Freud's suggestion that as a culturally shared delusion religion saves in-dividuals from creating their own idiosyncratic caricatures of religion easily identified as delusional is an empirical claim.[72] Two examples from opposite sides of the ontological argument can be briefly noted. LaBarre, a Freudian-influenced anthropologist, has a reductive view of the origin of religion. As such he stays within the confines of methodological atheism. He claims,

> Every religion in historic fact, began in one man's "revelation"—his dream or fugue or ecstatic trance. Indeed, the crisis cult is *characteristically* dereistic, autistic, and dreamlike precisely *because* it had its origins in the dream, trance, "spirit" posses-sion, epileptic "seizure," REM sleep, sensory deprivation, or other visionary state of the shaman–originator. All religions are necessarily "revealed" in this sense, inasmuch as they are certainly not revealed consensually in secular experience.[73]

LaBarre's view can be contrasted with William James's insight that the relationship between individual experience and collective shared experi-ence is empirically important and ontologically relevant to the reality of what we noted above as MORE, and is to be explored within the perspec-tive of a methodological agnosticism:

> A genuine first-hand religious experience . . . is bound to be a heterodoxy to its witnesses, the prophet appearing as a mere lonely madman. If his doctrine proves contagious enough to spread to any others, it becomes a definite and labeled heresy. But if it then still proves contagious enough to triumph over persecution, it becomes itself an orthodoxy; and when a religion has become an orthodoxy, its day of in-wardness is over: the spring is dry; the faithful live at second hand exclusively and stone the prophets in their turn.[74]

Empirically, processes by which individuals create idiosyncratic beliefs that are only caricatures of religion versus how individuals commit to religion whose existence is not simply cultural but historically true are important issues for both the psychology and the sociology of religion. However, they cannot be meaningfully addressed empirically if the content of culturally shared beliefs is immune from a critical assessment of their truth value.

## Mysticism, Godly Love, and Methodological Agnosticism

If both Sorokin and James would locate the possibility of a transcendence revealed in mystical experience, Freud's atheism precluded him from even accepting the possibility. Having established the illusory basis of much of the motivation for religious thought, he responded in *Civilization and Its Discontents* (1930) to the Nobel laureate Romain Rolland's critique that he had ignored mysticism, or what Rolland referred to as the "oceanic feeling," which Freud defined as "a feeling of an indissoluble bond of being one with the external world as a whole."[75] Freud accepted the reality of the experience but, in terms of his atheism, rejected that it could be of God. Instead it was interpreted as a repetition of or regression to a primary narcissism produced by a symbiosis with the mother prior to subject–object separation. Only later did this experience become linked with religion.

This author has criticized elsewhere Freud's general views of mysticism as a regressive phenomenon.[76] Scholars debate the nature of Freud's view of mysticism.[77] However, our concern here is simply that even in mysticism Freud's reductionism refuses to permit the possibility of an encounter with a reality that is both real and transformative, something Parsons argues is better acknowledged in Eastern forms of religion.[78] In their critique of this author's treatment of Freud and mysticism, Belzen and Uleyn note that Freud would not accept a reality sui generis for the object of religion and that they wished to "save" God from belonging to a realm that philosophy, psychoanalysis, or science can deal with.[79] This is precisely what methodological agnosticism denies. The social sciences can confront the possibility that super-mundane realities both are encountered and have real effects: that the object of experience is experienced as real is a necessary but not sufficient aspect of methodological agnosticism. It is empirically likely that empirical effects can be documented only to the extent that the object of experience is real.[80] In addition, however, the belief makes an ontological claim as well that methodological agnosticism needs to explore. Merkur has provided documentation from numerous psychoanalysts who on the basis of their own experience have accepted the ontological reality revealed in mystical experience and have fostered efforts to theoretically capture the nature of this reality.[81] Likewise, Hood and Byrom noted that ontological considerations can distinguish between narcissistic forms of mystical experience best expressed by the phrase "I am god," as opposed to a non-narcissistic mystical experience best expressed by "i am God."[82] The latter form is consistent with both Sorokin and James and the acknowledgment that the MORE revealed in mystical experience is a genuine encounter with what Hick simply refers to as the Real.[83]

In a response to the author's insistence on the relevance of theology for proposing psychological theories of religious experience,[84] Goldsmith has provided what is a fair option: "I believe that psychologists who do not like considering the kinds of ontological issues Hood calls for should not have to do so. But they should admit to a bias that rests on a deeply held value and tolerate with intellectual fairness those who consider ontological issues."[85]

Likewise, the author has noted in a commentary on Porpora's article that as a sociologist Porpora rightly chides his discipline for its uncritical methodological atheism but mistakenly applauds what he sees as psychology's openness to accepting more—citing as exemplary an edited text published by the APA.[86] The title, *Varieties of Anomalous Experience*, is an obvious reminder of *VRE*. The text explores a range of experiences that in each instance include ontological considerations. While Porpora is surely wrong to think this edited text and its openness to ontological considerations characterize mainstream psychology, the citation of this text is appropriate for illustrating the value of a methodological agnosticism, especially since the focus is on anomalous experiences that need not have religious framing. The range of experiences includes some that may seem absurd in terms of their ontological claims, for instance, alien abduction experiences. However, the point is that by including the ontological possibility that they may in fact occur (methodological agnosticism), the empirical evidence can be evaluated to suggest the merit of this possibility relative to other explanatory options. The crucial point for methodological agnosticism is that the conclusion is not made by an a priori reductive naturalism (methodological atheism) but by empirical means that are open to the possibility that experience may be veridical to realities contemporary science has failed to acknowledge.[87]

The issues raised by methodological agnosticism cannot be settled here, but the point is, as Porpora rightly notes, to raise the issues.[88] The author's use of Freud and the emergence of object relations theory was to select a tradition far from dominant in either modern psychology or sociology. However, the issues raised are suggestive of the fallacy of committing oneself to methodological atheism, where in allusion to James the only response is "less is more." To return briefly to the notion of Godly love rooted in Sorokin's mysticism, the acceptance of the possibility that one might have this experience and it might be transformative can be empirically studied. Two examples from the pentecostal tradition can be mentioned in closing. Poloma and Hood conducted a study of a Pentecostal emerging church whose charismatic leader claimed to practice Godly love and usher in the kingdom of God. From the data collected, the leader turned out on empirical grounds to have done neither.[89] Poloma and Hood allow readers to judge for themselves, based on considerable narratives, various ontological options. However, they do not simply accept the claim that narrative is all that sociologists and psychologists can study with respect to religious experience.[90] The veridicality of claims was assessed based upon Sorokin's criteria of the five dimensions of "Godly love." This group, known as Blood n Fire, was found deficient on several criteria and even though one of the primary investigators began the study open to the possibility that the charismatic leader was genuinely graced by the power of a supraconscious love, the empirical data could not sustain this interpretation.

On the other hand, in a 15-year study of the classical pentecostal serpent handlers of Appalachia, Hood and Williamson found that earlier studies based upon methodological atheism, such as LaBarre's Freudian-based anthropology, did not allow the genuine possibility of signs and wonders associated with this tradition to be appreciated.[91] While empirical data alone may not establish what is ontologically the case, methodological atheism simply asserts the denial a priori of what methodological agnosticism is open to consider. In this sense, as Porpora said of James (and this author says of Sorokin), they were unafraid to border on the theological.[92] To this the author simply adds that at this border one can hope that the call for a new multilevel interdisciplinary paradigm is not simply an illusion but will prove to be transformative for the social sciences and their investigation of realities that are not simply socially or psychologically constructed.

## Notes

1. Robert A. Emmons and Ray F. Paloutzian, "The Psychology of Religion," *Annual Review of Psychology* 54 (2003): 395.

2. Crystal L. Park and Ray F. Paloutzian, "One Step toward Integration and an Expansive Future," in *Handbook of Religion and Spirituality*, ed. Ray F. Paloutzian and Crystal L. Park (New York: Guilford, 2005), 550–64.

3. See Douglas V. Porpora, "Methodological Atheism, Methodological Agnosticism and Religious Experience," *Journal for the Theory of Social Behavior* 36 (2006): 57–75; cf. Peter Berger, *The Sacred Canopy: Elements of a Sociological Theory of Religion* (Garden City, NY: Doubleday, 1967), 100.

4. Theodore Flournoy, "Les Principes de la psychologie religieuse," *Archives de Psychologie* 2 (1903): 33–57.

5. Peter Berger and Thomas Luckmann, *The Social Construction of Reality: A Treatise in the Sociology of Knowledge* (Garden City, NY: Doubleday, 1967), 13.

6. Harry Collins and Steven Yearly, "Epistemological Chicken," in *Science as Practice and Culture*, ed. Andrew Pickering (Chicago: University of Chicago Press, 1992), 301–26.

7. Roy Bhaskar, *Plato Etc.: The Problems of Philosophy and Their Resolution* (New York: Verso, 1994), 10, 30.

8. James E. Dittes, "The Psychology of Religion," in *The Handbook of Social Psychology*, ed. Gardner Lindzey and Elliot Aronson (Reading, MA: Addison-Wesley, 1969), 5:602–59.

9. Ralph W. Hood Jr., "Ways of Studying Religion and Spirituality," in *International Handbook of Education for Spirituality, Care, and Wellbeing*, ed. Marian de Souza, Leslie J. Francis, James O'Higgins-Norman, and Daniel Scott (New York: Springer, 2009), 15–33.

10. Ralph W. Hood Jr., "A Jamesian Look at Self and Self Loss in Mystical Experience," *Journal of the Psychology of Religion* 1 (1992): 1–24; "The Soulful Self of William James," in *The Struggle for Life: A Companion to William James' The Varieties of Religious Experience*, ed. Donald Capps and Janet L. Jacobs (Newton, KS: Mennonite Press, 1995), 209–19; "The Mystical Self: Lost and Found," *International Journal for the Psychology of Religion* 12 (2002): 1–20; "The Common Core Thesis in the Study of Mysticism," in *Where God and Science Meet: How Brain and Evolutionary Studies Alter Our Understanding of Religion*, ed. Patrick McNamara (Westport, CT: Praeger, 2006), 3:119–38.

11. Porpora, "Methodological Atheism," 23.

12. Deborah J. Coon, "Testing the Limits of Sense and Science: American Experimental Psychologists Combat Spiritualism, 1880–1920," *American Psychologist* 47 (1992): 143.

13. Porpora, "Methodological Atheism," 73.

14. John Bowker, *The Sense of God: Sociological, Anthropological, and Psychological Approaches to the Origin of the Sense of God* (Oxford: Clarendon Press, 1973); Ralph W. Hood Jr., "The Relevance of Theologies for Religious Experiencing," *Journal of Psychology and Theology* 17 (1989): 336–42.

15. Peter Berger, "Some Second Thoughts on Substantive versus Functional Definitions of Religion," *Journal for the Scientific Study of Religion* 13 (1974): 128.

16. Matthew T. Lee and Margaret Poloma, *A Sociological Study of the Great Commandment in Pentecostalism: The Practice of Godly Love as Benevolent Service* (Lewiston, NY: Edwin Mellen Press, 2009).

17. Pitirim Sorokin, *The Ways and Power of Love: Type, Factors, and Techniques of Moral Transformation* (1954; reprint, Philadelphia: Templeton Foundation Press, 2002), 109–14.

18. Sorokin, *Ways and Power of Love*, 110.

19. C. R. Badcock, *The Problem of Altruism: Freudian-Darwinian Solutions* (Oxford: Basil Blackwell, 1986).

20. Sorokin, *Ways and Power of Love*, 86.

21. Ibid., 125, emphasis in original.

22. Ralph W. Hood Jr., "Self and Self Loss in Mystical Experience," in *Changing the Self*, ed. Thomas M. Brinthaupt and Richard P. Lika, 279–305 (Albany: State University of New York Press, 1994).

23. Sorokin, *Ways and Power of Love*, 387.

24. Ibid., 123.

25. Ibid., 87–88.

26. Porpora, "Methodological Atheism," 71.

27. William James, *Principles of Psychology* (1890; reprint, Cambridge: Harvard, 1981); cf. Ralph W. Hood Jr., "Theoretical Fruits from the Empirical Study of Mysticism: A Jamesian Perspective," *Journal für Psychologie* 16:3 (2008), http://www.journal-fuer-psychologie.de/jfp-3-2008-04.html.

28. John Daniel Wild, *The Radical Empiricism of William James* (New York: Doubleday-Anchor, 1969).

29. George T. Ladd, "Psychology as So-Called 'Natural Science,'" *Philosophical Review* 1 (1892): 24–53.

30. Jacob A. Belzen and Ralph W. Hood Jr., "Methodological Issues in the Psychology of Religion: Another Paradigm?" *Journal of Psychology* 140 (2006): 5–28; Amedeo Giorgi, "The Implications of James's Plea for Psychology as a Natural Science," in *Reflection on the Principles of Psychology*, ed. Michael G. Johnson and Tracy B. Henley, 63–75 (Hillsdale, NJ: Lawrence Erlbaum, 1990); David M. Wulff, "A Field in Crisis: Is It Time to Start Over?" in *One Hundred Years of the Psychology of Religion*, ed. Peter H. M. Roelofsma and Jacoba W. van Saane (Amsterdam: VU University Press, 2003), 11–32.

31. William Barnard, *Exploring Unseen Worlds: William James and the Philosophy of Mysticism* (Albany: State University of New York Press, 1997); Hood, "Theoretical Fruits from the Empirical Study of Mysticism," 3; and Charlene H. Seigfried, *Chaos and Context: A Study in William James* (Athens: Ohio University Press, 1978).

32. Jacob A. Belzen, "The Varieties of Functions of Religious Experience: James' *Varieties* Reconsidered," *Archives de Psychologie* 72 (2006): 49–66.

33. Belzen and Hood, "Methodological Issues in the Psychology of Religion," 11–12.

34. William James, *Psychology: The Briefer Course* (New York: Henry Holt, 1892), 468, emphasis mine.

35. Barnard, *Exploring Unseen Worlds*, 47.

36. Lisa Miller, "Watching for Light: Spiritual Psychology beyond Materialism," *Psychology of Religion and Spirituality* 2 (2010): 35–36.

37. Ralph Barton Perry, *In the Spirit of William James* (1938; reprint, Bloomington: Indiana University Press, 1958), 79, emphasis added.

38. Ibid., 58.

39. Belzen and Hood, "Methodological Issues in the Psychology of Religion," 11–12.

40. Barry Dainton, *Stream of Consciousness: Unity and Continuity in Conscious Experience* (London: Routledge, 2000), iv.

41. See Hood, "Common Core Thesis in the Study of Mysticism."

42. William James, *The Varieties of Religious Experience: A Study in Human Nature* (1902; reprint, Cambridge: Harvard University Press, 1985), 332, emphasis mine.

43. Ibid., 332.

44. Ibid., 402, n. 32.

45. Frederic W. H. Myers, *Human Personality and Its Survival of Bodily Death*, ed. Susy Smith (1903; reprint, New Hyde Park, NY: University Books, 1961).

46. James, *Varieties of Religious Experience*, 401, emphasis in original.

47. Ibid., 401.

48. Rufus Jones, *Studies in Mystical Religion* (New York: Russell and Russell, 1909), xxxiv, italics in original.

49. Waller T. Stace, *Mysticism and Philosophy* (Philadelphia: Lippincott, 1960), 153–54, emphasis added.

50. Sorokin, *Ways and Power of Love*, 387, emphasis added.

51. Ibid., 88.

52. See Robert D. Richardson, *William James: In the Maelstrom of American Modernism* (Boston: Houghton Mifflin, 2006), 514.

53. Cited in Ralph B. Perry, *The Thought and Character of William James*, 2 vols. (Boston: Little, Brown, 1935), 2:123.

54. James, *Varieties of Religious Experience*, 18–19.

55. Don S. Browning, *Pluralism and Personality: William James and Some Contemporary Cultures of Psychology* (Cranbury, NJ: Associated University Presses, 1980), 261.

56. James, *Varieties of Religious Experience*, 19, emphasis in original.

57. For overviews by the committed, see William W. Meissner, *Psychoanalysis and Religious Experience* (New Haven: Yale University Press, 1984), 23–133, and Edward P. Shafranske, "Freudian Theory and Religious Experience," in *Handbook of Religious Experience*, ed. Ralph W. Hood Jr. (Birmingham: Religious Education Press, 1995), 200–230. For discussions by the uncommitted, see Adolf Grünbaum, *The Foundations of Psychoanalysis: A Philosophical Critique* (Berkeley and Los Angeles: University of California Press, 1984), and "Psychoanalysis and Theism," *Monist* 70 (1987): 152–92; and Ralph W. Hood Jr., "Mysticism, Reality, Illusion and the Freudian Critique of Religion," *International Journal for the Psychology of Religion* 2 (1992): 141–59, and "Psychoanalysis and Fundamentalism: Lessons from a Feminist Critique of Freud," in *Religion, Society, and Psychoanalysis*, ed. Janet L. Jacobs and Donald Capps (Boulder, CO: Westview Press, 1997), 42–57.

58. Sigmund Freud, *The Standard Edition of the Complete Psychological Works of Sigmund Freud*, vol. 22, *New Introductory Lectures on Psychoanalysis* (London: Hogarth Press, 1933), 168.

59. See the following works referred to above: Meissner, *Psychoanalysis and Religious Experience;* Shafranske, "Freudian Theory and Religious Experience"; and Grünbaum, *Foundations of Psychoanalysis*.

60. Sigmund Freud, *The Standard Edition of the Complete Psychological Works of Sigmund Freud*, vol. 23, *Moses and Monotheism: Three Essays* (London: Hogarth Press, 1939), 101.

61. Grünbaum, "Psychoanalysis and Theism," 152–92.

62. C. R. Badcock, *The Psychoanalysis of Culture* (Oxford: Basil Blackwell, 1980).

63. Sigmund Freud, *The Standard Edition of the Complete Psychological Works of Sigmund Freud*, vol. 21, *Civilization and Its Discontents* (London: Hogarth Press, 1930), 144.

64. See Benjamin Beit-Hallahmi, ed., *Psychoanalysis and Theism: Critical Reflections on the Grünbaum Thesis* (Lanham, MD: Jason Aronson, 2010).

65. Freud, *Civilization and Its Discontents*, 132–37.

66. Badcock, *Psychoanalysis of Culture*, is one of the exceptions.

67. Freud, *Civilization and Its Discontents*, 81.

68. Sigmund Freud, *The Standard Edition of the Complete Psychological Works of Sigmund Freud*, vol. 21, *The Future of an Illusion* (London: Hogarth Press, 1927), 31.

69. Freud, *Civilization and Its Discontents*, 84–85.

70. Jacob A. Belzen, *Towards a Cultural Psychology of Religion: Principles, Approaches, and Applications* (New York: Springer, 2010).

71. Ralph W. Hood Jr., "Another Epistemic Evaluation of Freud," in B. Beit-Hallahmi, ed., *Psychoanalysis and Theism: Critical Reflections on the Grünbaum Thesis* (Lanham, MD: Jason Aronson, 2010), 135–54; Ann Taves, *Revelatory Events: Novel Experiences and the Emergence of New Religions* (New York: Oxford University Press, in press).

72. Sigmund Freud, *The Standard Edition of the Complete Psychological Works of Sigmund Freud*, vol. 9, *Obsessive Actions and Religious Practices* (London: Hogarth Press, 1907), 15–27.

73. Weston LaBarre, "Hallucinations and the Shamanic Origins of Religion," in Peter T. Furst, ed., *The Flesh of the Gods* (New York: Praeger, 1972), 265, emphasis in original.

74. James, *Varieties of Religious Experience*, 270, emphasis added.

75. Freud, *Civilization and Its Discontents*, 65.

76. Ralph W. Hood Jr., "Conceptual Criticisms of Regressive Explanations of Mysticism," *Review of Religious Research* 17 (1976): 179–88.

77. Besides Hood's work, see Jacob A. Belzen and Arnold J. R. Uleyn, "What Is Real? Speculations on Hood's Implicit Epistemology and Theology," *International Journal for the Psychology of Religion* 2 (1992): 165–69.

78. William B. Parsons, *The Enigma of the Oceanic Feeling: Revisioning the Psychoanalytic Theory of Mysticism* (New York: Oxford University Press, 1999).

79. Belzen and Uleyn, "What Is Real?" 168.

80. Porpora, "Methodological Atheism," 73.

81. Dan Merkur, *Explorations of the Psychoanalytic Mystics* (New York: Rodopi, 2010).

82. Ralph W. Hood Jr. and Greg N. Byrom, "Mysticism, Madness, and Mental Health," in *The Healing Power of Spirituality: How Faith Helps Humans Thrive*,

vol. 3, *Psychodynamics* (Santa Barbara, CA: Praeger, 2010), 176.

83. John Hick, *An Interpretation of Religion* (New Haven: Yale University Press, 1989).

84. Hood, "Relevance of Theologies for Religious Experiencing."

85. W. Mack Goldsmith, "Through a Glass Darkly, but Face to Face: Comments of Psychology and Theology Eyeing One Another," *Journal of Psychology and Theology* 17 (1989): 390.

86. See Ralph W. Hood Jr., "Commentary on "Methodological Atheism, Methodological Agnosticism, and Religious Experience," *Spirituality and Health International* 8 (2007): 161–63; and Etzel Cardeña, Steven J. Lynn, and Stanley Krippner, eds., *Varieties of Anomalous Experience* (Washington, DC: American Psychological Association, 2000).

87. Hood, "Commentary," 163; see also Ralph W. Hood Jr., Pete C. Hill, and Bernard Spilka, *The Psychology of Religion: An Empirical Approach*, 4th ed. (New York: Guilford, 2009), 295.

88. Porpora, "Methodological Atheism," 71.

89. Margaret Poloma and Ralph W. Hood Jr., *Blood and Fire: Godly Love in a Pentecostal Emerging Church* (New York: New York University Press, 2008).

90. David Yamane, "Narrative and Religious Experience," *Sociology of Religion* 61 (2000): 171–89.

91. See Ralph W. Hood Jr. and W. Paul Williamson, *Them That Believe: The Power and Meaning of the Christian Serpent-Handling Tradition* (Berkeley and Los Angeles: University of California Press, 2008); and Weston LaBarre, *They Shall Take up Serpents: Psychology of the Southern Snake-Handling Cult* (Prospect Heights, IL: Waveland Press, 1962).

92. Porpora, "Methodological Atheism," 72.

# Seven

# GODLY LOVE FROM THE

# PERSPECTIVE OF PSYCHOLOGY

*JULIE J. EXLINE*

The concept of Godly love suggests that love flows from a perceived God to people, who then pass that love to each other.[1] As shown in this volume, members of diverse disciplines have their own unique perspectives to contribute to this area of study. The aim of this chapter is to provide an overview of some concepts and methodology that would be relevant to the study of Godly love from a psychological perspective. The chapter begins with a discussion of whether psychology, given its scientific methods, is relevant to the study of Godly love—and also whether psychologists might benefit from considering Godly love as a research topic. From there, the discussion shifts to specific methods that psychologists might use to approach the study of Godly love.

## Are Psychological Perspectives Relevant to the Study of Godly Love?

Psychology is the scientific study of human thought, emotion, and behavior. Because psychology is a science, it focuses on things that are at least partly observable or measurable. As such, some might question whether a psychological perspective could be appropriately applied to the study of Godly love. Research on Godly love conducted to date has maintained an agnostic stance with regard to the existence of God.[2] At some level, however, the concept of Godly love seems most relevant for people who presuppose the existence of God and accept the notion that love flows from God to (and through) human beings. In addition, the Godly love concept makes assumptions about the nature of God: God is seen as a source of love, which is then passed on to people. Parts of the Flame of Love Project have gone a step further to focus specifically on pentecostalism,[3] a Christian movement that emphasizes the power of the Holy Spirit—power that is sometimes expressed in supernatural ways. These key ideas—that God exists, loves people, and is not bound by natural laws—are theologically based assumptions that do not lend themselves to evaluation based on the tools of empirical psychology.

What, then, might psychology have to offer to the study of Godly love? To conduct research on Godly love, must we necessarily step outside the traditional boundaries of psychology and into the misty and mysterious realms of parapsychology, the study of supernatural phenomena? Perhaps not. In a sociological study of Godly love, Lee and Poloma dealt with this issue by focusing on accounts of perceived interactions with God to demonstrate how these perceptions shaped benevolent actions.[4] Similarly, from the perspective of psychology, it is crucial to focus on constructs that we can at least attempt to measure, such as human belief, emotion, and behavior. Rather than trying to prove whether a miracle occurred, for example, a psychologist might attempt to assess relevant personal beliefs: "On a scale from 0 (not at all) to 10 (extremely), to what extent do you view this healing as a miracle?" Such assessments can provide useful information about people's beliefs without trying to answer the question of whether a miracle actually occurred. The same logic should apply to the idea of love flowing from God to a person (and from that person to others). Although psychologists might look at perceptions, emotions, behaviors, or even physiological activity that could suggest the presence of love, the aim would not be to directly evaluate whether acts of interpersonal kindness are ultimately caused by God's love.

On the face of it, it might seem that the psychological approach is a purely reductionistic one, one that attempts to explain away all supernatural phenomena and to eliminate faith. If so, such an endeavor could be seen as shallow, superficial, or misguided at best. At worst, it might be seen as a hostile attempt to strip away the deeper and richer layers of meaning associated with the Godly love concept. Yet a psychological approach need not assume a reductionist worldview. For example, consider a case in which a psychologist concludes the following: "When people believe that they have had a powerful experience of God's love, this belief predicts greater odds (statistically) that they will donate time or money to help others." Knowing that the belief in having experienced God's love predicts generous behavior does not imply that the belief is true, but neither does it imply that it is false. The psychologist's aim would simply be to understand the belief and its consequences. Even though research may identify naturalistic factors that feed into religious belief (e.g., socialization, personality, genetics, recent experiences) or identify the parts of the brain that are activated during spiritual experiences, the resulting findings would not address the issue of whether the beliefs are correct. Yet the psychological findings might provide useful insights in terms of understanding connections between religious/spiritual beliefs, emotion, and behavior.

On the flip side, the study of theologically grounded topics such as Godly love could represent an important new horizon for the field of psychology as well. Over the past two decades, psychologists have become increasingly sensitive to issues of diversity within the human community.[5] From a psychological perspective, it is important to start from a baseline of fundamental, shared aspects of human nature: how humans think and feel and what motivates them. Yet a deeper, more nuanced understanding of humanity may require that psychologists look beyond universal principles to consider specific beliefs and behaviors that characterize subgroups of people, which can vary based on factors such as culture, gender, sexual preference, age, socioeconomic status, and religion.

For many people, religious or spiritual beliefs are a foundational element of how they view and relate to the world.[6] Regardless of whether psychologists agree with the beliefs of a specific religious group, they might gain insights by closely examining the group's beliefs and practices. This includes taking seriously the particular theology of the group under study. They may be particularly interested in determining whether specific beliefs and practices have the power to affect other outcomes of broad interest within psychology, such as mental states (e.g., depression, happiness, psychotic symptoms) and socially consequential behaviors (e.g., aggression, generosity). Broadly speaking, then, if research were to show that seeing oneself as a conduit of God's love was a major predictor of generous or kind behavior toward others, such findings could pique the interest of psychologists (and perhaps other social scientists as well). The next section will focus on specific techniques that psychologists might use to examine this hypothesis.

## The Empirical Study of Godly Love— A Sample of Psychological Methods and Measures

In psychology, as with many of the other sciences, there are several common ways to learn about a phenomenon of interest: observe it directly, ask people questions about it, or try to manipulate it and note the effects. This section suggests some tools from psychology to consider how a psychologist might approach a basic question about Godly love: If people perceive themselves as experiencing God's love, will this perception make them more likely to show loving behavior toward others?

Note that the intent in this chapter is to focus on the concept of Godly love in broad terms. Although it stems from the Flame of Love Project, which focused initially on pentecostal Christians and will include some specialized material focused on this group, the discussion here is not intended to be limited to pentecostal Christians or to people seen as exemplars in terms of faith, leadership, or love. Instead, the chapter simply focuses on the notion that love might flow from God to an individual person (a *vertical dimension*) and between human beings (a *horizontal dimension*). It is conceivable, then, that the concept of Godly love as discussed here might be applicable within any theistic tradition. In fact, the Flame of Love Project anticipated this possibility and has already completed a national survey of American adults that is not limited to any specific religion, instead seeking to compare the benevolence of a variety of religious and nonreligious groups.

This chapter primarily emphasizes quantitative methods, in line with the author's primary training and experience. However, qualitative methods provide another vital set of tools for the researcher,[7] tools that may help to provide an in-depth understanding of how individuals conceptualize and experience Godly love. As in the exemplar interviews from the Flame of Love Project, a set of moderately structured questions might be developed to capture various facets of the Godly love concept. Some sample questions are listed below. The aim here would be for an interviewer to start with a set of basic questions while also having the freedom to follow the lead of the participant.

To capture the vertical dimension, questions such as these might be asked: When you think about God, what ideas or images come to mind? Do you think that God expresses love to people, and if so, how? Have you ever had a personal experience in which you felt deeply loved by God? If so, what was the nature of this experience? What thoughts and emotions come to mind when you reflect on this experience?

To capture the horizontal dimension, participants might be asked questions such as these: What types of thoughts or experiences make you want to do kind things for others? People often show kindness in their own unique ways. What are some ways that you typically show kindness to others? Some people think that God's love can actually flow between people. What are your thoughts about this idea? Have you ever sensed that God's love was flowing through you to other people? If so, can you tell me about one of these experiences?

In addition to giving participants considerable freedom in telling their stories, qualitative methods can help to identify common themes, develop hypotheses, and point out ideas that are not well tapped by existing quantitative measures. Use of qualitative methods might be especially fruitful when researchers want to examine ideas about Godly love in a population that has not previously been sampled, so that subsequent quantitative studies can most appropriately tap the beliefs, practices, and behaviors of that specific group. Studies that are primarily quantitative can also be enriched through the inclusion of open-ended questions or other elements that allow participants to share their personal experiences. Regardless of the exact format, the use of qualitative data can provide a contextualized, personal perspective that is often difficult to obtain using quantitative methods alone.

THIS SECTION will consider techniques that quantitatively oriented psychologists might use to examine hypotheses about Godly love. In quantitative studies, responses are usually combined across groups of individuals, with an attempt to search for associations, patterns, and/or group differences using statistical methods.[8] To approach the quantitative study of any topic, psychologists need to begin with questions about assessment: How can the different pieces of the research question be broken down into elements that are measurable (or at least partly measurable)?

This section begins with a focus on correlational studies and self-report measures before moving to experimental designs and behavioral measures. Note that the list of methodological ideas provided here is intended to be selective rather than exhaustive. Also note that the aim here is to describe methodological techniques, not to provide a review of all psychological research relevant to the Godly love concept; this goal would be far beyond the scope of this methodologically focused chapter.

ONE FAST and efficient way to address research questions about Godly love would be to use self-report methods. For example, topics related to Godly love could be tapped through a phone survey, an Internet-based questionnaire, or a set of paper-and-pencil measures. One downside of self-report methods is the risk of certain types of bias. For example, some participants tend to respond at the extremes of a scale (e.g., "never" or "always"), while others avoid the extremes and tend to cluster their responses toward the middle. Participants may also try to portray themselves in a favorable light, giving socially desirable responses.[9] Others may try to deceive the experimenter or may respond in random ways, perhaps due to fatigue or frustration. Yet despite their limitations, self-report instruments can be extremely useful tools for researchers who are interested in learning about people's thoughts and emotions.

A common research method in psychology involves giving self-report measures to large groups of participants (usually one hundred or more) and analyzing them using correlational methods. As described below, surveys containing multiple measures relevant to Godly love could be administered, and the resulting data could be analyzed using correlational analysis. In the simplest terms, correlations measure the extent to which two variables are associated along with the direction of the association. Correlations can range from –1.0 to +1.0, with 0 indicating that two variables are not at all associated. A correlation of .68, for example, would indicate a strong positive association, whereas a correlation of –.13 would indicate a weak negative association.

One thing to keep in mind when using correlational data is that correlations can provide information only about *associations* between variables—that is, how strongly they are linked together and in what direction. A researcher cannot infer, based on correlations alone, that one variable *causes* another—even though such inferences are often erroneously reported in the media (and sometimes in original research reports). It is particularly risky to make causal inferences when data have been collected at only one point in time. A better approach, while sometimes difficult in practical terms, is to do repeated assessments through a *longitudinal design*. Although still not precisely pinpointing cause and effect, longitudinal designs enable researchers to determine whether changes in one variable (e.g., feeling loved by God) coincide with subsequent changes in another variable (e.g., generous motives or behaviors).

Imagine that a psychologist was trying to develop a questionnaire-based study to examine whether there is a positive link between feeling loved by God and generous motives toward other people. What types of questions might be included in such a study? Where possible, it is best to use measures that have been carefully validated by other researchers. If an appropriate measure does not exist, the researcher may need to generate some new items or try to develop a new measure. This section outlines some types of measures that might be helpful to include, beginning with background questions, before moving to questions more directly linked to the Godly love concept.

*Background Questions—Demographics and Religious Beliefs*

In addition to testing their main hypotheses, most psychologists would want to collect some basic demographic information about participants. Psychological studies typically assess demographic variables such as age, gender, ethnicity, marital status, education, and income level. Also, unless a study is being conducted within only a single religious group, religious affiliation is another background variable crucial to assess. The author has found it helpful to provide several examples to participants while still keeping responses open-ended, so that participants from small or nontraditional religious groups do not feel excluded. For example, a prompt that the author has used in her own research is as follows,: "How would you describe your religious/spiritual tradition, if any? (for example, Catholic, Jewish, Baptist, Muslim, atheist, agnostic, spiritual but not religious, none . . .)." Answers can later be grouped into categories (e.g., Protestant, Eastern, nonreligious) based on criteria of interest to the researchers.

In virtually any study looking at religious/spiritual beliefs, it is important to examine a person's degree of overall religious or spiritual commitment. Although this aim might be accomplished in many ways,[10] the author has found it useful to include at least two measures: a brief measure of religious belief salience or commitment along with a measure of religious participation.[11] Although some studies simply record frequency of attendance at religious services, it may be helpful to supplement this information with items to tap the frequency of other religious activities, such as prayer or meditation, reading sacred texts or other religious materials, and talking and thinking about religious issues.[12] The measures of religious belief salience/commitment and those involving religious behavior tend to correlate quite highly with one another, and scores on these measures can be standardized and averaged together to provide a general measure of a person's religious or spiritual involvement.

For a study of Godly love, it will be important to assess beliefs about God's existence. Sometimes a single item will suffice: "On a scale from 0 (not at all) to 10 (totally), to what extent do you believe in the existence of God?" However, if the sample is likely to include people from diverse religious traditions (including people who identify as spiritual but not religious), it can be useful to include a few more questions. An open-ended question can allow participants to briefly describe the nuances of their beliefs. For example, "Please give a brief description of what the term *God* means to you." Specific questions might also be asked about belief in a single God versus multiple gods, whether God is seen as a personal being versus an impersonal force, and whether God directly intervenes in people's lives.[13]

Deciding whether and how to include participants with low levels of belief in God can be challenging. One might assume that deleting nonbelievers from the sample would be an obvious first step for research focusing on God. However, our research has revealed some interesting surprises with this group. For example, many people who claim current nonbelief in God (or considerable doubt about God's existence) may still have emotion focused on their residual images of God. Several of our studies have revealed, for example, that many atheists and agnostics report anger focused on God,[14] anger that may be focused on prior experiences and/or these residual images of God. Perhaps some nonbelievers might have positive feelings focused on these residual God images as well. For example, some agnostics might think, "I'm not sure whether God exists, but if so, then I believe that God is a source of love" or, perhaps, "I hope that a loving God exists, but I don't know if it's possible." Even among professed believers, doubts may arise about God's existence. As such, our own recent studies have included not only a question about belief in God but also one such as the following: "To what extent do you have doubts about whether God exists?"

Although not all studies will have room for extensive background measures, the inclusion of a few brief measures can be extremely helpful when the time comes to analyze the data. When it is not possible to include full measures, a subgroup of items might be chosen from existing measures. When this is done, the standard procedure is to ask for permission from the author of the original scale and to cite this original scale in the report of the study.

*Feeling Loved by God*

To tap the vertical dimension of the model (love flowing from God to a person), one possibility would be to examine a person's image or concept of God, perhaps assessing the extent to which God is seen as loving as opposed to severe or distant. Several measures could be used for this purpose.[15] Although God image measures can be informative, asking whether God is seen as loving is a rather abstract, conceptual question. It is not quite the same thing as asking whether an individual personally feels loved by God—a more emotional, experiential question. To assess a more personal sense of feeling loved by God, one might consider a measure of religious comfort[16] or positive religious coping.[17] Both types of measures also include items that tap spiritual struggles (e.g., feeling abandoned by God, anger toward God). Although not a primary emphasis of this chapter, the presence of spiritual struggles may be worth assessing, given the possibility that such struggles might be an impediment to the flow of Godly love.[18]

Several other useful measures related to God's love center on a specific idea: the notion that people can form relational attachments to God that are similar to those they share with parental figures or relationship partners. They might see their bond with God as a source of security, for example, or they might see God as an unreliable source of support. In addition to measures of attachment to God,[19] researchers might consider tools such as the Spiritual Assessment Inventory,[20] which also frames people's perceived bonds with God in relational terms—this time using an object relations perspective. Note that most of these measures have been validated primarily in Western samples, with Christians heavily represented in the studies. For the most part, their applicability to other cultural and religious groups has not yet been established.

LOVING BEHAVIOR. How would a researcher tap into the horizontal dimension of the Godly love model—a person's loving behavior toward others? One possibility would be to ask people to report on their own behaviors linked to generosity, such as the amount of volunteering that they do, the amount of money that they donate to charitable organizations, or the number of hours per week that they spend giving social support to other people. Because people often have trouble accurately recalling their behaviors, it may be wise to focus on activities from the recent past—the past week or month, for example, as opposed to the past year.

An important insight described by Post and Neimark is that people may give to others in a wide variety of ways.[21] Limiting one's assessment to a small range of actions such as volunteering or charitable giving may fail to capture the responses by people who give to others through the use of humor or courage, for example. Post and Neimark's book contains a survey that can help to identify a wide range of prosocial behaviors.

Rather than having people recall their past behaviors or reflect on their usual tendencies, researchers could also ask questions about in-the-moment motives to be generous toward others (e.g., friends, relatives, strangers, enemies). One problem with this technique, however, is that people often lack insight into their own motives. Furthermore, because people often are tempted to portray themselves in a favorable light, a measure of social desirability should be included so that its effects can be controlled statistically.[22] An additional problem is that attitudes are far from perfect predictors of behavior.[23] A good alternative might be to include measures of actual behavior as part of the study, as described below in the section on experimental designs.

CAVEAT—INTERCORRELATIONS. Before moving on, another methodological point should be mentioned: in groups that believe in a personal God, measures of feeling loved by God (or seeing God as loving) are likely to correlate highly with other measures of religious involvement. In other words, to the extent that people self-identify as highly religious, they also report feeling more loved by God.[24] Although these types of associations might make intuitive sense, they create challenges for researchers who are trying to disentangle the roles of unique variables. For example, if feeling loved by God was shown to be linked with generous motivations or behaviors, a researcher might want to see whether feeling loved by God predicted generosity even when other facets of religiosity were held constant. The larger the sample size, the easier it is to statistically distinguish between constructs that are likely to have high levels of overlap, such as religiosity and feeling loved by God.

## Experimental Approaches

Another approach that is commonly used in psychology is the controlled experiment. In an experiment, participants are randomly assigned to one of several conditions. Experimenters systematically alter aspects of the situation (e.g., prompts that participants read, tasks that they are asked to do), which are called *independent variables*. They then examine whether people respond differently, based on experimental conditions, on the outcome variables of interest, called *dependent variables*. Experiments are used when researchers are trying to make determinations about cause and effect. Because participants are randomly assigned to experimental groups, it is reasonable to conclude that differences between the groups are caused by differences in the independent variable.

### Possible Experimental Approaches to Godly Love

In an experiment on Godly love, a researcher might be curious about whether inducing a feeling of being loved by God would prompt generous behavior. She or he might thus want to create a task, prompt, or situation that would encourage members of one group to feel particularly loved by God "in the moment," whereas members of another condition (often called a *control condition*) would receive a neutral prompt or task that did not focus on God's love. The experimenter could then compare the two groups on a dependent variable related to generosity. This generosity measure might be one of the self-report measures described above. However, because of social desirability biases and the fact that attitudes do not always predict behavior, it is often helpful to use behavioral indicators of generosity. For example, a participant might be given an opportunity to donate money, help a stranger, or sign up for a volunteer opportunity as part of the experiment.

How might an experimenter induce a person to think about God's love—or to actually feel loved in the moment? There are many possibilities, some of which are quite direct. For example, participants might be asked to write a position paper clarifying why God should be seen as loving (versus not loving; or versus a control essay on another topic). If participants were all followers of a specific faith tradition, they might read a story or a set of scriptures from that tradition that focus on God's love (versus a control task). Another possibility would be to engage in a worship experience. Participants might also be asked to do an imagery exercise in which they imagine themselves having an intimate conversation with God—or perhaps receiving forgiveness, a hug, kind words, or some other sign of caring from God.

## Recalling Past Experiences of God's Love—A Risky Strategy?

Another option might be to ask people to recall a personal experience of God's love. However, one of the author's own experiments suggested that this technique might actually backfire in some cases. Study participants (198 shoppers in a mall) were each paid five dollars to participate. They were then randomly assigned to one of several experimental conditions: one in which they were asked to recall an experience in which they felt loved, encouraged, or cared for by God; one in which they were prompted to recall a time when they felt loved, encouraged, or cared for by another person; another in which they simply filled out a one-page questionnaire about their religious beliefs and behaviors; and a control condition with no additional questions or prompts. Participants were then given the option to donate part of their five-dollar study payment to charity.

It was expected that those who were prompted to recall an experience of God's love would be the most generous. After all, the author reasoned, members of this group should get a mood boost from reflecting on this positive experience; they would be primed with religious thoughts; and they would be primed with thoughts of God as a loving attachment figure. All of these effects should, it was thought, prompt greater generosity in comparison to the other groups.

The results revealed that the God's-love condition did not work as expected. Participants in the God's-love condition were no more generous than those in the other conditions. In fact, out of the 45 participants who were asked to recall an experience of God's love, 17 (40%) reported that they could not recall a time when they felt this way. Three of these participants did not believe in God, leaving fourteen participants who said that they believed in God but could not recall a time when they felt loved, encouraged, or cared for by God. Importantly, this subgroup of 14 participants ended up being the least generous group in the entire sample. In short, asking people to recall experiences of God's love seemed to be a risky strategy, because a good portion of people could not recall any such experiences—an outcome that, in turn, was associated with a tendency to withhold money.

*Caveats and Limitations of Experimental Designs*

Although experimental designs can provide good information about cause-and-effect relationships, they do have their limitations. Sometimes the situations created in experiments are highly constrained and may feel artificial to participants. Another thorny issue is that if the purpose of the study is too transparent, participants may either try to respond as they think the experimenter wants or may deliberately act in the opposite way. Although the use of subtle cues (e.g., a picture of a smiling Jesus on the wall; uncovering positive religious words in a word puzzle; brief flashes of religious words on a computer screen) can help to get around these problems, their effects are often small and hard to detect without a large number of participants.

To create powerful situations, social psychologists in particular have often devised scripted—and sometimes dramatic—cover stories to see how people react. Consider, for example, Darley and Batson's famous "Jerusalem to Jericho" experiment,[25] in which 40 seminary students were told that they needed to do a brief presentation in another building. Along the way, they passed a shabbily dressed person slumped by the side of the road. In terms of who stopped to help, it did not matter whether the students were expecting to give a talk on the Good Samaritan or on an irrelevant topic. Instead, the main predictor of helping was the amount of time available. Students who were told that they were late were much less likely to stop and help than those who thought they had plenty of time.

Although Darley and Batson's experiment clearly had dramatic flair and yielded important results, it raised the ethical issue of deceiving participants—a common issue in social psychology experiments. Ethical guidelines dictate that deception should be used only when it is essential to test the hypothesis in question. Furthermore, deception-based studies require in-depth debriefings of participants to explain the purposes of the study and the need for deception.

Another alternative, one that would not require deception, might be to have participants receive some act of kindness as part of the study (e.g., a gift, supportive listening) and then be experimentally prompted to attribute this kindness either to God or to the person giving the gift, or no such prompt. Of course, there is no guarantee that all participants will respond to the prompt in the expected way. But given careful pilot testing and a sufficiently large sample size, this type of design might warrant consideration.

## Conclusions—and Some Future Directions Likely to Interest Psychologists

This chapter describes several research methods relevant to the study of Godly love from a psychological perspective. As contributors to an interdisciplinary discussion on Godly love, psychologists can offer the use of empirical tools that may help to illuminate the thoughts, feelings, and behaviors associated with this phenomenon. Of course, psychologists will also have to take theology seriously if appropriate measures of religious beliefs are to be constructed. Because qualitative, correlational, and experimental studies all have their own strengths and weaknesses, a variety of techniques will undoubtedly be required to gain a deep understanding of the psychological aspects of the Godly love process.

At the close of this methodological chapter, it may be useful to look further into the future. Assume, for the moment, that across several carefully conducted studies (perhaps a mix of qualitative, correlational, and experimental designs), a clear link was identified: Feeling loved by God is indeed a strong predictor of generous behavior. What types of follow-up questions might be of special interest from a psychological perspective?

In general, psychologists are likely to be curious about the kinds of specific thoughts or emotional states that are prompting the generous behavior. They will also want to understand more about the consequences of generosity. For example:

* Could it be that simply being in a positive mood is enough to make a person more generous? If so, does a perception of feeling loved by God explain generosity over and above the effects of a positive mood?

* Several recent, high-profile experiments have demonstrated that simply prompting participants with religious ideas is enough to make them more generous.[26] Is there something specific about feeling loved by God that independently predicts generosity, or is it subsumed by this general religiosity effect?

* Is there something unique about attributing loving intentions to God

that makes people feel generous? Might the same generous response be obtained if people attribute loving intentions to another person— or if they are simply prompted with ideas about kindness?

* If feeling loved by God does lead to generous behaviors, are these behaviors motivated primarily by an internal desire to be generous versus other alternatives, such as a sense of obligation or a desire to follow religious rules? Do motives that are more internally driven lead to more positive emotions (after helping) than those that are driven by rules or obligation?

* Are perceptions of God's supernatural involvement important? For instance, are acts of love that are seen as miraculous more likely to lead to generosity than those that are not seen as miraculous?

* Are there certain types of people, at a personality level, who are more likely than others to feel loved by God and/or to be generous toward others?

* What are the consequences of Godly love for personal health and well-being? In general, helping others tends to lead to positive emotion and can promote good health outcomes. But is there anything unique about the Godly love process—as opposed to giving in general—that can affect mental or physical health?

## Notes

1. For more details, see Matthew T. Lee and Margaret M. Poloma, *A Sociological Study of the Great Commandment in Pentecostalism: The Practice of Godly Love as Benevolent Service* (Lewiston, NY: Edwin Mellen, 2009).

2. Margaret M. Poloma and Ralph W. Hood Jr., *Blood and Fire: Godly Love in a Pentecostal Emerging Church* (New York: New York University Press, 2008).

3. E.g., Amos Yong, *The Spirit Poured out on All flesh: Pentecostalism and the Possibility of Global Theology* (Grand Rapids, MI: Baker Academic, 2005).

4. Lee and Poloma, *Sociological Study of the Great Commandment.*

5. See Bruce E. Blaine, *Understanding the Psychology of Diversity* (Newbury Park, CA: Sage, 2007); Blaine J. Fowers and Frank C. Richardson, "Why Is Multiculturalism Good? *American Psychologist* 51 (1996): 609–21.

6. P. Scott Richards and Allen E. Bergin, *A Spiritual Strategy for Counseling and Psychotherapy*, 2nd ed. (Washington, DC: American Psychological Association, 2005)

7. See Jonathan A. Smith, ed., *Qualitative Psychology: A Practical Guide to Research Methods* (Newbury Park, CA: Sage, 2008), for a review.

8. For a recent review, see Roger E. Millsap and Alberto Maydeu-Olivares, eds., *The Sage Handbook of Quantitative Methods in Psychology* (Newbury Park, CA: Sage, 2009).

9. William M. Reynolds, "Development of Reliable and Valid Short Forms of the Marlowe-Crowne Social Desirability Scale," *Journal of Clinical Psychology* 38 (1982): 119–25.

10. For reviews, see Peter C. Hill and Ralph W. Hood Jr., eds., *Measures of Religiosity* (Birmingham: Religious Education Press, 1999); and Peter C. Hill and Kenneth I. Pargament, "Advances in the Conceptualization and Measurement of Religion and Spirituality: Implications for Physical and Mental Health Research," *American Psychologist* 58 (2003): 64–74.

11. E.g., Bruce Blaine and Jennifer Crocker, "Religiousness, Race, and Psychological Well-being: Exploring Social Psychological Mediators," *Personality and Social Psychology Bulletin* 21 (1995): 1031–41; Everett L. Worthington Jr., Nathaniel T. Wade, Terry L. Hight, Jennifer S. Ripley, Michael E. McCullough, Jack W. Berry, Michelle M. Schmitt, James T. Berry, Kevin H. Bursley, and Lynn O'Connor, "The Religious Commitment Inventory—10: Development, Refinement, and Validation of a Brief Scale for Research and Counseling," *Journal of Counseling Psychology* 50 (2003): 84–96.

12. See Julie J. Exline, Ann M. Yali, and William C. Sanderson, "Guilt, Discord, and Alienation: The Role of Religious Strain in Depression and Suicidality," *Journal of Clinical Psychology* 56 (2000): 1481–96; and shorter adaptation in Julie J. Exline, Crystal L. Park, Joshua M. Smyth, and Michael P. Carey, "Anger toward God: Social-Cognitive Predictors, Prevalence, and Links with Adjustment to Bereavement and Cancer," *Journal of Personality and Social Psychology* 100:1 (2011): 129–48.

13. Douglas Degelman and Donna Lynn, "The Development and Preliminary Validation of the Belief in Divine Intervention Scale," *Journal of Psychology and Theology* 23 (1995): 37–44.

14. E.g., Exline et al., "Anger toward God."

15. See Glendon L. Moriarty and Louis Hoffman, eds., *God Image Handbook for Spiritual Counseling and Psychotherapy: Research, Theory, and Practice* (Philadelphia: Haworth Press, 2007).

16. Exline, Yali, and Sanderson, "Guilt, Discord, and Alienation"; Benjamin T. Wood, Everett L. Worthington Jr., Julie J. Exline, Ann M. Yali, Jamie D. Aten, and Mark R. McMinn, "Development, Refinement, and Psychometric Properties of the Attitudes toward God Scale (ATGS-9)," *Psychology of Religion and Spirituality* 2:3 (2010): 148–67.

17. Kenneth I. Pargament, Harold G. Koenig, and Lisa M. Perez, "The Many Methods of Religious Coping: Development and Initial Validation of the RCOPE," *Journal of Clinical Psychology* 56 (2000): 519–43.

18. For reviews of the spiritual-struggle literature, see Julie J. Exline and Ephraim Rose, "Religious and Spiritual Struggles," in Raymond F. Paloutzian and Crystal L. Park, eds., *Handbook of the Psychology of Religion* (New York: Guilford, 2005), 315–30; Kenneth I. Pargament, Nicole Murray-Swank, Gina M. Magyar, and Gene G. Ano, "Spiritual Struggle: A Phenomenon of Interest to Psychology and Religion," in William R. Miller and Harold Delaney, eds., *Judeo-Christian Perspectives on Psychology: Human Nature, Motivation, and*

*Change* (Washington, DC: APA Books, 2004), 245–68.

19. E.g., Richard Beck and Angie McDonald, "Attachment to God: The Attachment to God Inventory, Tests of Working Model Correspondence, and an Exploration of Faith Group Differences," *Journal of Psychology and Theology* 32 (2004): 92–103; Wade C. Rowatt and Lee A. Kirkpatrick, "Two Dimensions of Attachment to God and Their Relation to Affect, Religiosity, and Personality Constructs," *Journal for the Scientific Study of Religion* 41 (2002): 637–51.

20. Todd W. Hall and Keith J. Edwards, "The Initial Development and Factor Analysis of the Spiritual Assessment Inventory," *Journal of Psychology and Theology* 24 (1996): 233–46, and "The Spiritual Assessment Inventory: A Theistic Model and Measure for Assessing Spiritual Development," *Journal for the Scientific Study of Religion* 41 (2002): 341–57.

21. Stephen G. Post and Jill Neimark, *Why Good Things Happen to Good People: The Exciting New Research That Proves the Link between Doing Good and Living a Longer, Healthier, Happier Life* (New York: Broadway, 2007).

22. E.g., Reynolds, "Development of Reliable and Valid Short Forms."

23. E.g., Icek Ajzen and Martin Fishbein, "Attitude–Behavior Relations: A Theoretical Analysis and Review of Empirical Research," *Psychological Bulletin* 84 (1977): 888–918.

24. E.g., Exline, Yali, and Sanderson, "Guilt, Discord, and Alienation," and Wood et al., "Development."

25. John M. Darley and C. Daniel Batson, "From Jerusalem to Jericho: A Study of Situational and Dispositional Variables in Helping Behavior," *Journal of Personality and Social Psychology* 27 (1973): 100–108.

26. Azim F. Shariff and Ara Norenzayan, "God Is Watching You: Priming God Concepts Increases Prosocial Behavior in an Anonymous Economic Game," *Psychological Science* 18:9 (2007): 803–9.

# Eight

# SOCIOLOGY, PHILOSOPHY,

# AND THE EMPIRICAL STUDY

# OF GODLY LOVE

## MARGARET M. POLOMA

"In the triangle of love between ourselves, God and other people, is found the secret of existence, and the best foretaste, I suspect, that we can have on earth of what heaven will probably be like."

—Samuel M. Shoemaker[1]

The question may be asked, "What does "God" or "love" have to do with sociology?" The epigraph by Samuel M. Shoemaker, an Episcopal priest and leader of the Oxford Group, whose spiritual principles were built into Alcoholics Anonymous (AA), provides one illustration that casts light on this question. Bill Wilson, who together with Dr. Bob Smith founded AA, described Shoemaker as another "co-founder" of what has become a worldwide movement. Wilson wrote: "Dr. Silkworth gave us the needed knowledge of our illness, but Sam Shoemaker had given us the concrete knowledge of what we could do about it, he passed on the spiritual keys by which we were liberated. The early AA got its ideas of self-examination, acknowledgment of character defects, restitution for harm done, and working with others straight from the Oxford Group and directly from Sam Shoemaker, their former leader in America, and from nowhere else."[2] Many social scientists have researched and written about AA, but the emphasis has been on the lower triangle of the Diamond Model of Godly love that deals with human action and its effects.[3] The top half of the model that incorporates the relationship between God and humans has been seemingly off-limits for social scientific research. Yet the partnership between God and human actors may well hold an important key to unlocking the success of a social institution like AA. It could be argued that Alcoholics Anonymous began with a "triangle of love" between God, divinely led founders, and other people, reflecting Shoemaker's suggestion that at least some social movements reflect a bit of heaven on earth.

Sociology has been reluctant to talk about God, love, or heaven—even after research polls have demonstrated time and again that such concepts are meaningful to most Americans. If the reader is unfamiliar with the parameters of the discipline of sociology, a quick inquiry from Ask.com (accessed April 15, 2010) provides a handy description of this field of study. Sociology is defined as "1. The study of human social behavior, especially the study of the origins, organization, institutions, and development of human society. 2. Analysis of a social institution or society segment as a self-contained entity or in relation to society as a whole." With roots in mid-nineteenth-century philosophy, sociology—particularly European sociology in the mid-nineteenth and early twentieth century—asked "big questions" about human society. Pitirim Sorokin, whose classic sociological works are foundational to a sociology of Godly love, wrote in the tradition of classical European sociology in the middle of the twentieth century when empirical sociology (in an extreme form known as "positivism") was on the rise in the United States. It was a period described by the contemporary sociologist-critic C. Wright Mills as "dustbowl empiricism" within a discipline that he claimed had lost its "sociological imagination."[4] American sociology had slowly moved away from its European philosophical roots in favor of a more focused naturalistic approach that favored quantification over philosophy. It arguably had lost its mooring and its interest in the "big questions" that were central to the writings of the early masters.

It is thus not surprising that much of mid-twentieth-century sociology would ignore Sorokin's masterpiece, *The Ways and Power of Love: Types, Factors, and Techniques of Moral Transformation*.[5] What was retained from its early philosophical roots was a "methodological atheism" that incorporated early sociology's bias against premodern societies where religion once played a significant role. In the postmodern world in which we now live, however, there has been a slow return to the recognition that spiritual forces and material factors may be different entities, but they continue to coexist. Replacing the mid-twentieth-century thinking that the rise of science would spell the death of religion, postmodern thought makes room for dialogue between religion and science. Such exchange may well mark a significant departure from the bifurcation of ideas and the segregation of disciplines that characterized modernity. Reality is not simply black or white, but shaded with gray and alive with hues of color reflected in differing perspectives.

The interdisciplinary approach of the Flame of Love Project to the study of Godly love is but one attempt to use what C. Wright Mills called a "sociological imagination" to study this newly defined topic that takes nonmaterial reality seriously. The Flame Project also serves as an example of the return to a study of "big questions" that, like Godly love, are too complex for a single discipline to unravel. The study of Godly love requires (as we see in chapters found throughout this edited volume) interdisciplinary scholarship. For sociology, especially a sociology that takes God and love seriously, this journey includes going back to its philosophical roots.

## The Three Faces of Love

> From even this preliminary investigation, it is apparent that love is a complex and rather awkward concept. . . . One of the objectives of the present study is to show that, however complex and mysterious love may be, the concept is coherent and open to philosophical analysis. Moreover, any theory of love that does not take account of the three principal forms of love, and the linkages between them, will be seriously incomplete.[6]

Rather than attempt to describe what love "*really* is," philosopher Rolf Johnson identifies the "central concern" of his work as "the less ambitious matter of what the word 'love' means."[7] His typology consists of three components—union-love, care-love, and appreciation-love—a classification that he describes as "more analytic than historical and springs from the wish to dig deeper than the distinctions already embedded in the language."[8] The "three faces of love" reflect three primary senses of a coherent concept that have been found to be invaluable in researching and interpreting the findings that have developed and tested the theory of Godly love.

The word *love* is commonly "misused" or intended to be taken metaphorically rather than literally (e.g., "I love chocolate") or used euphemistically ("as a polite or socially acceptable way of referring to sex") and other ways "in which its range of meaning is extended beyond primary to more peripheral applications."[9] In his attempt to "explore what is implied or presupposed by the more legitimate, central uses of the concept," Johnson contends there are some universal features of love "on which nearly everyone would agree." These include that (1) there is a subject (lover) and an object (the beloved); (2) there is a sense of "value or the process of valuation" in that what is loved is judged to be valuable; (3) the lover is drawn or inclined toward the love object; and (4) "love must have an affective component." While recognizing that it is possible that the affective component in which "the lover must feel something for or with the loved" may be questioned by some, Johnson insists that it is "widely agreed upon, if not absolutely noncontroversial," particularly in the modern Western world.[10] With the "universal features of love" in place, Johnson then puts forth his primary thesis regarding "what kinds of relations between a subject and an object, and what kinds of inclination or action tendencies regarding it, enable us to identify a relation as love."[11] He succinctly states:

> A central thesis of the present work is that, if we allow ourselves to be guided by ordinary English usage and also by the history of love theory, there is no single correct answer to this question. Instead there are three different answers and, thus, three distinguishable phenomena we call "love." The names we will use for these phenomena are "care-love," "union-love," and "appreciation-love." They differ from each other principally in how the lover is inclined toward the loved and, thus in their respective action tendencies. Each love has a different objective, though not necessarily a different object.[12]

*Care-love* provides one way in which we "relate to an object we love," namely, to "simply care for or about it." According to Johnson, "care-love embraces all forms of concern for the well-being of the loved. Its objective is simply the good of the love object."[13] Affect or feelings associated with it are commonly care, concern, and compassion.

While *care-love* is about relationships that involve concern for the loved, *union-love* is about joining together the lover and the loved. Union-love tends to be more passionate than care-love, with "action tendencies hav[ing] to do with efforts to effect, preserve, or deepen the valued union."[14] Mystical love and romantic love are both examples, suggesting that the lovers and the loved ones may be either divine or human persons.

*Appreciation-love* is commonly both more abstract and more passive than are the other two faces of love. Johnson notes, "Instead of reaching out to care for or striving to unite with, these lovers merely behold what they love, appreciating it for being what it is (or is taken to be)."[15] While appreciation for a person is usually mixed with the other two loves, appreciation-love embraces a wider range of phenomena (e.g., ideals, principles, visions, a sense of calling) where valuing the loved entity is central.

## Faces of Love at Blood n Fire

The concept of *Godly love* was first introduced by sociologist Margaret Poloma and psychologist Ralph Hood in their presentation of an ethnographic case study of Blood n Fire (BnF), a neo-pentecostal ministry to the poor in downtown Atlanta.[16] Although they had yet to read *The Three Faces of Love* when they began their work, the original research proposal did include two of Johnson's designated love types. Care-love was clearly at the core of the ministry's work with the homeless, the poor, and drug addicts, but they also hypothesized that a love relationship with God (union-love) seemed to be empowering the selfless service of the young people who devoted their lives to working with Atlanta's poor. Thus, a primary thesis was that the neo-pentecostal experiences of the Holy Spirit were an important source of the loving family-like relationships observed at BnF—a thesis that would later find support in a survey conducted with both the poor and their providers. An unanticipated development that surfaced during the first year of this four-year project forced Paloma and Hood to think beyond their original thesis. Love seemed to run amok. BnF, whose goal it was to usher in the kingdom of God (first to Atlanta and then to the world), was imploding before our very eyes.

When Poloma and Hood discovered Rolf Johnson's work, they found a significant key for a better understanding of Godly love as studied at BnF. They had collected both qualitative and quantitative data that provided thick descriptions of the union-love experienced by BnF leaders, followers, benefactors, and beneficiaries. This observation fit well with Poloma's research, especially her findings from research on pentecostal revivals that had swept across the country in the 1990s, as presented in *Main Street Mystics*.[17] Her ongoing research on religious experience suggests that mystics who walk and talk with God may be living next door and that mystical experiences may well lead to greater benevolence or care-love.[18] By the end of the first year of the study the breakdown in care-love relationships within BnF was notable and the future of the ministry in serious doubt.

In time it became clear that many of the difficulties leading to the fatal schism stemmed from the ever-changing visions of the charismatic leader that paradoxically prophesied an ushering in of a kingdom of God (once firmly anchored in demonstrating love to the poor and the broken) while at the same time allowing for practices in which both love and prophecies seemed to have failed. The community meltdown thus can be partially described as a breakdown in union-love and illustrated in breaches of care-love, but there still seemed to be another factor that played into the research drama.

Poloma and Hood's original plans for data collection and analysis went beyond what is common for studying interaction in social groups in their decision to include God as a perceived actor, their collection of data on religious experience that reflected what the community described as "walking in the supernatural," and using both survey and interview data to establish a relationship between experiences of the divine (union-love) and acts of benevolence (care-love). Had they stopped there, however, the analysis would have fallen short of explaining the demise of this unique and once-promising ministry. Johnson's philosophical thesis on the three forms of love suggested the need to take a closer look at the appreciation-love held by the leader and his faithful followers for BnF's vision. The deep appreciation-love of many community members for the leader's ever-changing and expanding vision seemed to be a factor that impeded care-love within the Atlanta community.

Johnson's thesis furthermore suggests a need to explore the relationship among the different types of love. The three faces of love may at times seem to melt together, but a closer examination reveals that one form dominates a particular interaction process. When Poloma and Hood began studying BnF, the focus was primarily on care-love and on demonstrating the efficacy of the ministry. They recognized that the BnF story could not be told without sharing the account of the role that the divine was believed to play in individual lives and in the birth of this social ministry. Clearly, union-love was reflected in the narratives shared by interviewees that repeatedly included perceptions of encounters of the divine that provided a "call" to ministry and the "grace" to live out the open and embracing family-like relations that seemed to permeate BnF. As the BnF story unfolded, it was apparent that appreciation-love for the founder and his vision, and by the founder for his own vision, had cast a particular reflection on Godly love that affected union-love and most certainly impacted care-love within the community.

### Pitirim Sorokin's Dimensions of Love

Throughout Johnson's discussion of the different types of love relationships, he does note that there are differences in intensity and duration. Love may be fleeting in a compassionate encounter between two strangers, or it may last a lifetime between two lovers. Johnson also acknowledges that love may be intensely passionate, a special characteristic of union-love (both romance and mysticism) or relatively nonemotional. Although he takes great care not to judge love, Johnson is still forced to recognize that some expressions of love are better than others. This line of thinking, however, is not well developed by Johnson. Pitirim Sorokin's thesis on a "five-dimensional universe of psychosocial love" raises sociological issues that complement Johnson's philosophical insights.

Of particular relevance to the model of Godly love is that both Johnson and Sorokin do make room for divine love in their theses. As we have seen, Johnson regards mystical love as a prime illustration of union-love. Sorokin in conceptualizing love as "one of the highest energies known,"[19] does acknowledge the "probable hypothesis" that "an inflow of love comes from an intangible, little-studied, possibly supra-empirical source called 'God,' 'the Godhead,' the Soul of the Universe,' 'the Heavenly father,' 'Truth,' and so on."[20] While Johnson presents a model that identifies the forms of love, Sorokin has developed a model that seeks to measure (albeit imprecisely) the energy flowing through psychosocial interaction. In more contemporary sociological terms, love energy can be conceptualized as "emotional energy" generated by "interaction rituals" within Johnson's three conceptually distinct forms of love.[21]

Sorokin's first dimension of love is *intensity*. Low-intensity love makes possible minor acts of care-love, such as giving a few pennies to the destitute or relinquishing a bus seat for another's comfort; at high intensity, much that is of value to the agent (time, energy, resources) is freely given. There is no reason that degrees of intensity cannot be used to describe union- and appreciation-loves. Union-love, almost by definition, would tend to be highly intense, while appreciation-love would probably demonstrate a much wider range of intensities (similar to that of care-love). Sorokin does not fully develop the different potential degrees of intensity, but his point remains clear. The range of intensity is not scalar—that is, research cannot indicate "how many times greater a given intensity is than another," but it is often possible to see "which intensity is really high and which low, and sometimes to even measure it."[22]

Sorokin's second dimension of love is *extensivity*: "The extensivity of love ranges from the zero point of love of oneself only, up to the love of all mankind, all living creatures, and the whole universe. Between the minimal and maximal degrees lies a vast scale of extensivities: love of one's own family, or a few friends, or love of the groups one belongs to—one's own clan, tribe, nationality, nation, religious, occupational, political and other groups and associations."[23] Within the list provided by Sorokin we find examples of objects of care-love (family members, friends) and those perhaps better classified as objects of appreciation-love (nationality, religion, political party). It would appear that the extensivity range for union-love would be much more restricted than for care- and appreciation-love. The interface of the forms of love, however, is reflected in Sorokin's questioning how one might balance love for family and friends (the nearest and dearest) with love for the very neediest of all humanity. As an example of extensivity he offers St. Francis, who seemed to have a love of "the whole universe (and of God)."[24] It may well be that through union-love (mysticism) care-love can be stretched to the maximum, embracing a wide range of love objects.

Sorokin next added the dimension of *duration*, which "may range from the shortest possible moment to years or throughout the whole life of an individual or of a group."[25] For example, the soldier who saves a comrade in a moment of heroism but may then revert to selfishness can be contrasted to the mother who cares for a sick child over many years. This dimension would appear to apply to all three faces of love. Differences in the duration found in union-love can be demonstrated by the comparison of lifelong mystics, those who occasionally enjoy mystical experiences, and those who have never experienced mysticism. A similar observation can be made for appreciation-love as illustrated by a sense of life vision, purpose, or calling. A sense of life purpose may be as short as a dream that quickly fades from memory, or it may take the form of an unseen force that supports a long purpose-driven life.

The fourth dimension of love is *purity*. Here, Sorokin wrote that pure love is characterized as affection for another that is free of egoistic motivation. By contrast, acting out of a desire for pleasure, personal advantage, or profit is a sign of a love that is in some way "spoiled." According to Sorokin (and subject to much debate), pure love—that is, love that is truly disinterested and asks for no return—represents the highest form of emotion.

In contrast with *purity*, a dimension that rests on questionable assumptions about the appropriate role of reciprocity in human behavior and assumptions about the meaning of purity, *adequacy* arguably is at the core of sociological analysis. It represents a complexity in human life that considers both the causes and potential effects of love interactions as they shape human society. Love, according to Sorokin, can be judged to be adequate in that it produces positive effects or inadequate insofar as its effects are undesirable. It is possible to pamper and spoil the child with love, in which case love has a consequence opposite of the love goal. Inadequate love is devoid of practical wisdom; adequate love achieves ennobling purpose and is, therefore, anything but blind or unwise. According to Sorokin, love can be judged inadequate in yet another way. It is possible that a person may have no loving intentions yet generate a consequence that is beneficial to others. For love to be judged adequate, loving intent and beneficial consequences must be in alignment.

Sorokin's five dimensions of love allow us to ask empirical questions about strength or weakness in different dimensions and how such differences vary with other dimensions. How intense, extensive, enduring, unselfish, and wise is any particular manifestation of love—and, to extend Sorokin's line of questioning to include that of Johnson's, what forms do these love manifestations take within care-love, union-love, and appreciation-love? In seriously pondering and seeking answers to such questions, sociology and philosophy can be integrated to inform research projects, particularly those integrating religio-spirituality components within its design, with results that have implications for both social science and theology.

## Godly Love in a Pentecostal Denomination

While it was Poloma and Hood's ethnographic study of a downtown Atlanta neo-pentecostal ministry to the poor that gave birth to the construct of Godly love, it was Poloma and political scientist John Green's study of a major religious denomination that put the model to its first major statistical test.[26] With survey data collected from the Assemblies of God (AoG; the ninth-largest American denomination) involving nearly 350 pastors and two thousand congregants, Poloma and Green used the Diamond Model of Godly love to guide their analysis of the relationships found among the different forms and dimensions of love in this pentecostal denomination.[27] Their statistical analysis of the AoG data further demonstrated the importance of positioning God as an actor in the chain of human interaction that facilitated benevolent attitudes and actions. Using their statistical findings, Poloma and Green also demonstrate the differing effects that appreciation-love potentially has on different measures of care-love and union-love. They note that appreciation-love

is not a categorical definition of love, but rather an effort to describe an abstract form of "interpersonal love relationships." *Appreciation-love* can be theoretically regarded as a complement to *union love* (vertical relationship with God) and *care-love* (horizontal relationship with others). In our analysis of the congregational data, we have conceptualized the "object" (to use Johnson's terms) of *union-love* as "being one with God"; the object of *care-love* as to "seek to benefit" another; and the object of *appreciation-love* as "ideals, principles, or abstract qualities."[28]

Appreciation-love seems to be present throughout in the diamond-shaped model of Godly love, permeating it somewhat like a computer operating system working behind the scenes to activate the other software. Its reflection is found throughout the Diamond Model, albeit in different intensities, affecting the interpersonal interactions that are the substance of Godly love and reflecting the culture and structures in which Godly love is embedded. Of special significance for describing appreciation-love in the AoG is the application of the sociologist Philip Rieff's thesis on charisma and interdicts.

In a posthumously published work, Philip Rieff, a critic and theorist of culture, addresses the issue of charisma and traces how "the gift of grace" has become a casualty of modern/postmodern culture.[29] At the heart of the dynamic charismatic process is a dialectical dance between faith and guilt once held fast by interdicts, divinely given cultural mores that impose limits on behavior and demand unqualified obedience. For Rieff the modern therapeutic culture, the conceptual thesis for which he is best known, is synonymous with unbelief.[30] It is a destroyer of genuine charisma, because it undermines divine authority and substitutes a moral relativism that allows individuals to make virtually unlimited life choices guided only by what they believe will contribute to their "self-actualization." Rieff's interdicts or divinely ordained rules can be regarded as a concrete "object" of appreciation-love, rules that had been vigorously enforced in early pentecostalism but in recent decades have been softened by forces of modernity. For example, no longer are pentecostal women forbidden to wear jewelry or to cut their hair, nor are adherents forbidden to go to movies or sporting events. Despite the greater acceptance of modern norms and values, vestiges of earlier legalism remain throughout the denomination. Traditional beliefs (e.g., about divorce, homosexuality, and gambling) and practices (e.g., tithing, glossolalia, and other pentecostal rituals) as measured in the AoG survey are reflected in a scale Poloma and Green call "traditional Pentecostal values," a measure that provides an empirical face for traditionalism and its interdicts.

Poloma and Green (together with Matthew Lee) in the concluding chapter of *The Assemblies of God* revisit their major findings on the AoG—findings that point to the importance of the social structure in which the interaction takes place for understanding the process of Godly love. Using data from the pastors' surveys to compare the AoG judicatory and its contractual social structure with data collected from the congregations where covenantal relations and care-love are the norm, they were able to describe different forms and dimensions of love as found within the judicatories and congregations. Although networks of care-love can and probably do coexist as secondary forces within the AoG judicatory, the primary object of love for the judicatory rests on an appreciation of the denomination—its principles and values, its well-run organization and structure, and ultimately its size and its influence. Poloma and Green conclude: "In sum, divine–human love energy can and probably does infiltrate religious contractual models through a leader's private devotional life but it is difficult (and perhaps unwise from a management perspective) to integrate experience of the divine into the contractual relations themselves. General Councils are not times of revival; board meetings are not spent praying for supernatural discernment; leaders are not elected for their piety."[31]

In contrast, care-love is the dominant form of love within congregational structures. For the most part, respondents expect their congregations to be family-like and report experiences of familial care-love love from other members of their church. In congregations care-love tends to dominate, while contractual concerns are seemingly secondary in importance. Of AoG congregations, Poloma and Green note:

It is within this covenant of believers that congregants live out their pentecostal identity that commonly includes alternate spiritual ways of viewing reality. It is here that many experience Spirit baptism, see miracles, learn to pray in tongues, give and receive prophesies, and pray for healing. It is within highly affective revival services that many pentecostals first felt the ecstatic and palpable presence of God. Although some of the qualitative interviews with AoG adherents have provided examples where the church family may have been spiritually dysfunctional, there are even more examples in which the congregation has played a significant role in developing and affirming the powerful love relationship between the respondent and God. Union-love, as we have examined it experientially within the model of Godly Love, is a significant factor in enhancing benevolence, especially evangelism, healing, and compassion.[32]

The illustrations used thus far to provide empirical support for the Godly love model have come from research conducted in the pentecostal (broadly defined) religious traditions. Both the ethnographic research conducted at Blood n Fire that gave rise to the model and the largely quantitative survey data collected on a large Protestant denomination to statistically test the model found positive relationships between experiencing God's love and benevolence. The findings suggest that spiritual experiences may often include "hearing" a divine call that elicits a human response in the form of benevolent action. These early findings do raise questions, however, about the viability of the model for non-pentecostals, especially those belonging to religious organizations birthed before the modern era. To explore Godly love and the role religious experience can play in benevolent activities outside the Protestant pentecostal tradition, we selected a case study from Roman Catholicism, a denomination that differs from both the neo-pentecostalism of BnF and the traditional pentecostalism of the AoG in its organizational structure and the strength of its interdicts. In fact, Rieff contended that Catholicism, especially during the era between the two Vatican Church Councils (1870–1970), had been less susceptible to the "therapeutic culture" that he alleges has permeated Protestantism.

The case study selected to further explore the role of interdicts and, in the process, of Godly love is that of Mother Teresa of Calcutta (Kolkata). Mother Teresa remains an iconic figure in death as she was in life—a saint of love, whose international fame has transcended her Roman Catholic Christian roots. Her lived-out faith within global Catholicism (where many interdicts, particularly those governing Catholic religious communities, remain strong in developing nations) provides a social context different from the AoG discussed earlier, with its reticulate weblike organization (where old pentecostal interdicts lacked the institutional foothold and continue to wane) and from BnF (where interdicts were unevenly enforced in this loosely structured but short-lived community).

## Mother Teresa and Godly Love

Born Agnes Gonxha Bojaxhiu (1910–1997), Mother Teresa, an Albanian nun who became a citizen of India, founded the Roman Catholic religious community known as Missionaries of Charity (MC) in the slums of Calcutta in 1948. This religious community of women took a fourth vow in addition to the customary three vows of poverty, chastity, and obedience—to give wholehearted and free service to the poorest of the poor. The religious order was approved by the pope in 1950, expanded to include both a community for brothers and one for ordained priests, and eventually would spread to over a hundred countries outside India. Non-Catholics and lay Catholics can participate in the MC through the Co-Workers of Mother Teresa, the Sick and Suffering Co-Workers, and the Lay Missionaries of Charity. In the 1970s Mother Teresa became an internationally known figure, brought to renown in part due to British journalist and author Malcolm Muggeridge's film (1969) and book (1971), both with the title *Something Beautiful for God*.[33] Among the many honors Mother Teresa received during her long life were the first Templeton Prize for Progress in Religion, in 1973, the Nobel Prize for Peace in 1979, and India's highest civilian honor, the Bharat Ratna, in 1980, granted for her humanitarian work. During her lifetime she became an icon of charity and compassion for Catholics and non-Catholics alike; following her death she was beatified by Pope John II, given the title Blessed Teresa of Calcutta.[34]

Although it is safe to contend that the work of Mother Teresa has always had more supporters than detractors, it is not the task of social science to render judgments in support of her hagiographers or her critics. Sociology, however, does provide a unique lens through which more complex assessments can be made. Guided by the Godly love model, sociology makes it possible to place the paradox found between the positive assessments and the negative critique within psychosocial, situational, and cultural context, leaving the final judgment to the reader. As in the presentation of the two earlier case studies (of the AoG and BnF), Mother Teresa's story is told here using Johnson's typology on the faces of love in tandem with Sorokin's psychosocial measures of love. The analysis begins with union-love and an examination of the generation of "love energy" that empowered her life and ministry.

## Union-Love

In his first encyclical, *Deus Caritas Est* ("God is love"), Pope Benedict XVI mentions Mother Teresa three times, using her life to clarify one of the main points of his encyclical that fits well into our basic thesis on Godly love, namely, that God is love and divine love empowers selfless service toward others. Benedict XVI writes, "In the example of Blessed Teresa of Calcutta we have a clear illustration of the fact that time devoted to God in prayer not only does not detract from effective and loving service to our neighbour but is in fact the inexhaustible source of that service."[35] The papal descriptive of Mother Teresa's "time devoted to God in prayer," however, is a general and illusive reflection of union-love that calls for some clarification, which is found in Mother Teresa's personal accounts and in the reports of her biographers. There is a seeming dissonance between what Mother Teresa taught publicly about prayer and the inner void she wrote about in letters to her spiritual directors that raises questions. What was the relationship between a prayerful union with God and the faithful observation of prayer rituals that allegedly energized her tireless ministry? What exactly was the spiritual darkness that she claimed blanketed her spiritual life? And how did the light of prayer function together with the dark night of the soul as Mother Teresa sought to live out a life of love?

On the occasion of Mother Teresa's beatification, a step that precedes the Roman Catholic proclamation of sainthood, Benedict XVI's predecessor, Pope John Paul II asked, "Where did Mother Teresa find the strength and perseverance to place herself completely at the service of others?"[36] Like his predecessor, Benedict XVI credited prayer for Mother Teresa's strength—meditative prayer that was integrated with prescribed ritual. The ambiguity of both John Paul II's and Benedict XVI's papal descriptions on prayer reflect Mother Teresa's own reticence to share accounts of her prayer experiences with anyone except her personal spiritual directors (made public by the church after her death). Even details of the "call within a call" (used by Teresa to demarcate the specific "call" she received as a teenager to become a nun from the "call" she received in 1946 to work with the "poorest of the poor") were not shared by Mother Teresa for decades.

The Catholicism prior to the Second Vatican Council in which Mother Teresa was raised and matured to adulthood had given mixed messages about religious experience. The author remembers growing up in this religious subculture where children were told stories about the mystical experiences of canonized saints, but their world of visions and prophecies was seemingly impossible for most mortals to access. Personal experiences of God were reserved for the very holy—the relatively few and long-dead saints of old. The world of most pre–Vatican II Catholics was one that centered on Catholic ritual, not on religious experiences—attending Mass, regular reception of the church sacraments, rites of benediction and adoration that venerated the reserved Blessed Sacrament, saying the rosary, making prayerful novenas, or taking pilgrimages to holy sites, to name the most common. Religious experiences, if they were to come, were generally expected in the context of approved rituals, especially the Mass and the reception of the sacraments, through which God's grace was said to come whether or not the recipient felt anything. (In the 1970s the Catholic priest, popular novelist, and sociologist Andrew Greeley, after discovering that Catholics were significantly less likely than Protestants to report having religious experiences, quipped during an interview published in the now-defunct *Transaction* magazine: "If you have papal infallibility, who needs religious experience?") Intense religious experiences that occurred outside the sacramental parameters (even those of men and women who would later be raised to sainthood) were officially regarded with some degree of suspicion. In this cultural context it might have been best for a young mystic like Mother Teresa to keep her unusual encounter with God that directed her to launch the Missionaries of Charity a matter between her and her God.

Silence about her personal spiritual life was a lifelong stance of Mother Teresa. One illustration can be found in what her biographer (and founder of an order of priests affiliated with the MC) Joseph Langford described as "the key to understanding Mother Teresa."[37] This "key," writes Langford, "lay in the two simple words she placed on the wall of her chapels around the world—Jesus' words from the cross: 'I thirst' (Jn. 19:28)." The story behind the key is a mystical experience that remained unknown even to the sisters in her religious order for decades.

Langford notes that in each of the chapels of the MC that he visited, the words "I thirst" appeared beneath a cross, whether "carved in wood, painted on plaster, or cut from paper."[38] He concluded that these two words "spoke silently of some great truth that had apparently been Mother Teresa's anchor and inspiration." Although he knew that Mother Teresa had received an "extraordinary grace" during a train ride in India in 1946, he also knew that she described this experience "as simply God's call to leave her convent and to work in the slums." There were no further details given. It would take years after Langford met Mother Teresa and collaborated with her in the MC before she would confide further details about her "inspiration" and the meaning of "I thirst." Langford says of her experience that it was one "of such intense 'light and love,' as she would later describe it, that by the time her train pulled into the station at Darjeeling, she was no longer the same."[39] He continues: "Within eight short days, the grace of this moment would carry her and her newfound inner fire back down the same mountainside, and into a new life. From the heights of the Himalayas she would bring a profoundly new sense of her God back into the sweltering, pestilent slums of Calcutta—and onto a world stage, bearing in her heart a light and love beyond her, and our, imagining."[40] This experience that Mother Teresa would call "Inspiration Day" was one "she considered so intimate and ineffable that she resisted speaking of it, save in the most general terms. Her silence would prevail until the last few years of her life, when she at last was moved to lift the veil concerning this sacred moment."[41]

Although Langford acknowledges that he does not know with certainty what it was that prompted Mother Teresa to begin to share more details about "Inspiration Day" and its message, he suggests that it was a Lenten letter written to the church by John Paul II: "For the first time, the thirst of Jesus had been mentioned in a Church document, and in Mother Teresa's same terms and language."[42] Within weeks after the letter was issued—a letter that she regarded as an affirmation of the message she had received decades earlier—Mother Teresa began to talk about the divine encounter and its context. She told Langford that it was Jesus's thirst—"that he longs for us, 'thirsts' for us, with all the intensity of his divine heart, no matter who we are or what we have done"—that had been the center of her train experience in 1946.[43] Jesus's thirst points to God—"what Mother Teresa describes as 'the depths of God's infinite longing to love and to be loved.'" The deep union-love that Mother Teresa seemingly experienced during the early years of her work with the poor would dry into a spiritual desert of longing and interior anguish for much of her remaining long life. Three months before she received the Nobel Peace Prize in December 1979, she wrote a letter to a spiritual confidant, the Rev. Michael van der Peet, which was not made public until 2007. In it she assured van der Peet of Jesus's "special love" for him, and then continued, "as for me, the silence and the emptiness is so great, that I look and do not see,—Listen and do not hear—the tongue moves [in prayer] but does not speak. . . . I want you to pray for me—that I let Him have [a] free hand."[44] In fact, rather than being an isolated incident, this desolation brought on by the seeming absence of God is now known to have been the state of Mother Teresa's spiritual condition for much of her life.

In another of her letters published in *Come Be My Light: The Private Writings of the "Saint of Calcutta,"* Mother Teresa writes the following to one of her spiritual directors:

> Now Father—since [19]49 or [19]50 this terrible sense of loss—this untold darkness—this loneliness—this continual longing for God—which gives me that pain deep down in my heart—Darkness is such that I really do not see—neither with my mind nor with my reason—the place of God in my soul is blank—There is no God in me—when the pain of longing is so great—I just long & long for God—and then it is that I feel—He does not want me—He is not there— . . . God does not want me—Sometimes—I just hear my own heart cry out—"my God" and nothing else comes—The torture and pain I can't explain.[45]

The depth and length of suffering brought on by this spiritual darkness made known only after her death took even those who thought they knew Mother Teresa by surprise. Critic and avowed atheist Christopher Hitchens, framing this revelation with his own presuppositions, would say: "She was no more exempt from the realization that religion is a human fabrication than any other person, and that her attempted cure was more and more professions of faith could only have deepened the pit that she had dug for herself."[46] Brian Kolodiejckuk, a priest who joined the MC in 1984 and who edited and wrote commentary on Mother Teresa's letters, offers another explanation that fits better with a sociocultural assessment that acknowledges the importance of a particular Catholic worldview for her spiritual formation. Kolodiejckuk recognizes that the experience of darkness caused her great pain after having enjoyed such great intimacy with God. He then adds:

With the help of her spiritual directors, she progressively came to grasp that her painful inner experience was an essential part of living out her mission. It was a sharing in the Passion of Christ on the Cross—with a particular emphasis on the *thirst* of Jesus as the mystery of His longing for the love and salvation of every human person. Eventually she recognized her mysterious suffering as an imprint of Christ's Passion on her soul. She was living the mystery of Calvary—the Calvary of Jesus and the Calvary of the poor.[47]

## Union-Love through a Psycho-Social Prism

Based on this brief description of Mother Teresa's experience of union-love, Sorokin's dimensions of love can be used to put these experiences into a larger social context. Mother Teresa undoubtedly had highly *intense* mystical experiences beginning in 1946 that generated (to use Sorokin's term) "love energy."[48] Through it she was empowered to respond to her "call within a call" to serve the "poorest of the poor." The intense experiences of union-love, however, proved to be of short *duration*, thus supporting Sorokin's thesis concerning the inverse relationship that commonly exists between the intensity of love and its duration.[49] We have only Mother Teresa's letters (letters she never wanted made public) to describe the depth of her personal sense of divine abandonment when, after four or so years, she ceased having intense experiences of union-love. In reading books about her ministry, it would appear that signs of divine presence and energy were all around her, as reported time and again by others who witnessed "miracles" in response to her intercession or her instructions to intercede for some specific need.[50] Although it was through the lens of a culturally specific faith that Mother Teresa recognized God's acts of providence, she seemed unable to internalize them in a way that would assure her of a divine light and love burning within her. Mother Teresa's unique mystical experiences of the late 1940s appear to have been much deeper than the main-street mysticism described by the research findings of priest-sociologist Andrew Greeley and possibly of less duration than the revival mysticism described by Poloma.[51] According to most accounts from strangers and coworkers alike, Mother Teresa radiated the faith, joy, and peace that main-street mystics seem to enjoy, but her personal letters speak of darkness and void. Perhaps she continued to have union-love experiences in which her deep love for God was reciprocated. If so, these experiences of union-love must have paled into darkness when compared with her experiences of Jesus during the "call within a call."

Union-love, seemingly by definition, is not *extensive;* it focuses on the beloved with whom the lover desires union. In the case of Mother Teresa (and perhaps all mystics, great and small), there lies a paradox. Although she pledged herself to the jealous Divine Lover in accord with the command to love God above all, through union with him she was driven and empowered to live out the second commandment to love everyone as God loved her (see Matt. 22:36–40). Whether holding the dying, dressing the wounds of the leper, or feeding a starving child, Mother Teresa purported to see Jesus in those she served. Yet, according to her letters, it appears this "seeing of Jesus" was a matter of faith rather than feeling. It may well be that a culturally shaped pre–Vatican II faith in Catholicism and its interdicts served to energize Mother Teresa during the many decades when spiritual feelings were still.

Love's *purity* is often difficult to determine—perhaps because human love is so often soiled by self-centered concerns. Despite Sorokin's discussion of *purity* as a dimension of love, purity (like beauty) may lie more in the eye of the beholder than be something directly amenable to sociological assessment. Having acknowledged a methodological problem, it is safe to say that Mother Teresa's supporters would regard the message of love derived from her experience and lived out by her and her disciples as evidence of a level of purity that is extraordinary and worthy of canonization to Catholic sainthood. [As the author will demonstrate, however, critics (especially the British journalist Christopher Hitchens) would disagree.]

The *adequacy* of love is perhaps the most important single sociological measure raised in Sorokin's discussion of the dimensions of love. In relating the dimensions to the Diamond Model of Godly love, adequacy is generally best evaluated by sociological analysis through assessing the direct effects of union-love and/or appreciation-love on care-love and then considering the adequacy of the care-love itself in terms of the benevolent acts it may have generated. Thus, adequacy is an issue that is best explored by studying benevolence or care-love, because union-love or appreciation-love may only indirectly result in overt behaviors that may benefit others through the pathway of inspiring care-love.

### Appreciation-Love as Love Energy

There is another face of love coloring divine–human as well as interhuman relations in the model of Godly love, as discovered in the study of BnF discussed earlier, namely, appreciation-love. In the case of Mother Teresa, it can be argued that the culture of the Catholic Church (specifically the pre–Vatican II church, together with its rituals and interdicts) illustrates appreciation-love, described by Johnson as "an abstract form of interpersonal love relationships."[52] Mother Teresa loved her church with its theology, which taught that it is the bride of Christ and the representative of God upon the earth. It is a church, particularly in its pre–Vatican II form, that stressed the role that suffering and self-denial played in any authentic spirituality. Based on growing up and being educated in Catholic schools for sixteen years, it is the author's sense that the pre–Vatican II church focused more on the bloodied body of a crucified Jesus than on the victorious Christ of the resurrection—a sense supported by the corpus found on the Catholic crucifix (in contrast to the Protestant bodyless cross). Although she respected and served the needy in all religions, there is no doubt that Mother Teresa's allegiance was to Catholicism and to those she believed were God's special representatives on earth, especially the pope. It is highly unlikely, for example, that Mother Teresa would have heeded her "call within a call" as she did had she not received the necessary permission from Rome to do so. Papal approval or disapproval probably would have trumped her private revelation.

It is within appreciation-love that we find Philip Rieff's "interdicts" or rules that were discussed earlier, interdicts that can themselves become love objectives (i.e., "loving of law"). Pre–Vatican II Catholicism was rife with interdicts, most of which have been softened in subsequent decades. The Catholic Church in which the author was raised (and in which Mother Teresa began the MC during the 1950s and '60s) threatened members with eternal damnation for willfully missing Mass on Sunday, eating meat on Friday, getting remarried after an unwanted divorce, using birth control, and, of course, abandoning the "true church." Catholic sisters of that day all wore "religious habits" (commonly consisting of long dark tunics and a veil that covered them from head to toe), were generally not permitted to visit local homes or eat meals outside their convents, were cautioned from developing "special friendships" with sisters inside their community as well as with friends outside, were transferred at will from place to place by their superiors, and for the most part were not permitted normal relations with their families (e.g., letters and phone calls were limited and visiting often prohibited, even in the case of family funerals). Not surprisingly, these interdicts and others were also found in Mother Teresa's religious community for women (and reportedly were maintained after many other religious orders modified to adapt to modern culture). A former member of her community provided the following succinct description: "The archetypal Missionary of Charity was not a questioner. She was submissive, obedient, and trusting. She maintained a veneer of cheerfulness and surrendered her life without reserve."[53] Of the penitential practices, including wearing spiked chains around their waists during prayer and self-flagellation with knotted ropes on bare thighs, former MC sister

Colette Livermore reports that sisters were told they "were meant to help us share in the suffering of Christ and the poor and to help us become better people."[54] Not surprising is that this conservative Catholic identity was core to the ministry and sometimes spilled over into the public sphere. Some critics have questioned Mother Teresa's integrity when she publicly supported "political" interdicts of Catholicism (as when she proclaimed that abortion was the greatest threat to world peace in her acceptance speech for the Nobel Peace Prize or her condemnation of artificial methods of birth control in countries where overpopulation has dire consequences).[55]

It is conceivable that appreciation-love for the Catholic Church and its interdictive rituals, rules, and doctrines was actually a source of empowerment for Mother Teresa, providing her with a lifeline to hold fast to the difficult call on her life as her Divine Lover seemingly abandoned her. This is the faith that never seemed to waver. *Note that this author does not claim that Mother Teresa was devoted to the personalities that occupied church offices, but rather that she was committed to what the church represented. While she professed a faith in God alone, it is the church that was said to represent God on earth.* The intense love energy propelled by a two-way experience of union-love (knowing her deep love for God and experiencing in return God's deep love for her) seemingly served to energize her early work as founder of the MC. As these experiences diminished, it may well have been her faith in God—a God who operated through the structural charisma of the Roman Catholic Church (with its sacramental theology of grace and ritual prayer)—that energized her during her long decades of spiritual darkness when union-love seemed to flow as a deep human cry for God. In other words, it was *faith in God and in the church* (rather than intense personal religious experiences) that played a significant role in her interactive process of Godly love. An example of this process can be found in one of Mother Teresa's letters cited earlier as the popular Catholic theology of suffering allegedly helped Mother Teresa to work through her sense of divine abandonment.

The relationship between care-love and self-denial and suffering is yet to be more fully explored. There may well be a positive link, as suggested by the long history in Catholicism of establishing schools, hospitals, and other works of benevolence by Catholic religious orders. In Mother Teresa's case, the "faith" that critic Christopher Hitchens berates (including the seemingly strange interdicts) may have been precisely what sustained and empowered her care-love through her long dark night of the soul. Her appreciation-love for God as incarnated in the church was of lifelong duration, a safety net when personal experience of a reciprocal union-love with God had been muted or was perhaps totally absent.

*Care-Love*

The discussion of a relationship between union-love and appreciation-love has been somewhat detailed in part due to the scant attention given to the potentially social effects of mysticism in social science. Union-love plays a significant role in the top portion of the Diamond Model of Godly love (see Introduction, fig. 1) that has customarily not been the subject matter of sociology. On the other hand, care-love, which "embraces all forms of concern for the well-being of the loved—[and] . . . simply the good of the love object,"[56] is well within the province of the social sciences, which have tended to focus on the bottom triangle of the Diamond Model. Other terms commonly used to refer to care-love are *care, concern,* and *compassion.* Mother Teresa's remarkable care-love unfolded over the course of a lifetime of committed service, but her frequent admonition to her followers was a simple "do small things with great love."

Few would disagree, as already noted, that Mother Teresa's care-love was exemplary. It was of long *duration,* with the best-known work beginning in 1948 when she went to the slums of Calcutta, and continued until she died in 1997. Reading about her works of love and hearing her instructions to others, it is apparent her care-love was *extensive,* touching homeless lepers and beggars as well as presidents and world leaders. Despite the parochial nature of the pre–Vatican Council II Catholicism that promoted itself as the "true religion" (a view she undoubtedly shared), Mother Teresa respected and served the poor of many different religious traditions, including Hindus, Buddhists, and Muslims. Purity and intensity dimensions are less amenable to quick assessment. It is probably safe to say that most would judge Mother Teresa's care-love to the poor as being very *intensive,* since she was willing to sacrifice personal comfort and amenities to provide more resources for the poor. She and her sisters enjoyed minimal possessions and physical comforts, striving to live as close as possible to those to whom they offered simple food and shelter. Many are the accounts of their bringing the dying from the gutters of Calcutta to a place where they could die with dignity. A few vocal critics of the MC have insisted that things could have been done very differently, such as providing more formal education for the sisters, setting up hospitals, doing more to discern the curable from the incurable patients, and producing an audit (the MC had no budget) to assure benefactors that their vast donations were being spent appropriately.

Perhaps no critic is better known for his acrimonious attacks on Mother Teresa's purity of motives and adequacy of lived-out mission than journalist Christopher Hitchens, who struck her and her ministry with the full brunt of militant atheism.[57] Hitchens argued that her intention was not to help people: "It was by talking to her that I discovered, and she assured me, that she wasn't working to alleviate poverty."[58] She was working to expand the number of Catholics. She said, 'I'm not a social worker. I don't do it for this reason. I do it for Christ. I do it for the church.'" He goes on to say:

> MT was not a friend of the poor. She was a friend of *poverty*. She said suffering was a gift from God. She spent her life opposing the only known cure for poverty, which is the empowerment of women and the emancipation of them from a livestock version of compulsory reproduction. And she was a friend to the worst of the rich, taking misappropriated money from the atrocious Duvalier family in Haiti (whose rule she praised in return) and from Charles Keating of the Lincoln Savings and Loan [financial scandal].[59]

It can be argued that this war between Mother Teresa and her critics has been less a matter of the adequacy of her care-love than one of irreconcilable differences in appreciation-love. Mother Teresa's faith in God as nurtured in her Catholic tradition is at odds with her critics whose stance is one of modern rationalism rooted deep in the soil of secular atheism. Her devotion to the pre–Vatican II Catholic Church has already been noted. Her love for poverty as embraced by the MC was modeled by a favorite saint, the twelfth-century Francis of Assisi; suffering with Jesus was modeled by another favorite, Theresa of Lisieux, a young nineteenth-century contemplative nun who offered up her suffering and sacrifices to God for missionaries and their potential converts. Mother Teresa was socialized into a Catholicism where early twentieth-century Pope Pius X's condemnation of the "modernist heresy" permeated Catholic culture. Catholics were instructed to submit their intellect and their will to the teaching authority of the Catholic Church and not to the whims of secular society. Her community was in part a product of that culture. It is likely that the practice of care-love within the community was at times overshadowed by the interdicts of appreciation-love. With daily life tightly regimented, there were few opportunities for intimacy among community members or with those outside the community, which perhaps blocked important channels for the flow of care-love and a generation of love energy. For example, although sisters commonly traveled with partners rather than alone, they were encouraged to use the travel time to engage in ritual prayer rather than idle talk. Relationships with beneficiaries reflected caring and concern, but they too were guided by interdicts, seemingly to prevent them from becoming a source of affect and satisfaction. In the last analysis, however, the committed service of Mother Teresa and her followers has won the praise and support of people of all walks of life throughout much of the globe, with her mission and message perpetuated by her followers in the Missionaries of Charity.

## Conclusion

Human love is inevitably flawed, and it is always possible to continue to question its adequacy. As we have seen, even Mother Teresa's exceptional love for the poor falls short when taken outside its cultural context of pre–Vatican II Catholicism. It would appear that the interdicts within the MC at times reflected more a "love of law" than a "law of love," and the negative effects inevitably spilled over into the ministry itself. However, the narratives and anecdotal reports of Mother Teresa's work with the poor by and large reveal a woman who had mastered the "law of love" for the poorest of the poor she felt called to serve. With her charismatic personality and example, she successfully challenged thousands of others to do the same, especially through the Missionaries of Charity. What began as a small community with twelve members in Calcutta in 1950 today has over 4,500 nuns running orphanages, AIDS hospices, and charity centers worldwide, and caring for refugees, the blind, the disabled, the aged, alcoholics, the poor and homeless, and victims of floods, epidemics, and famine in Asia, Africa, Latin America, North America, Europe, and Australia.[60]

Tightly knit religious communities such as Mother Teresa's and Blood n Fire present instructional cases for the study of Godly love in which appreciation-love plays a significant role with mixed results. In BnF, for example, the founder's love for his lofty vision took precedence over the living out of the care-love espoused in the vision. It was a distorted appreciation-love that became an important factor in the community's demise. It seems likely that experiences of union-love, although varying in intensity and duration, generated loving and empowering energy for care-love, as did Mother Teresa's "call within a call." But mystical experiences occur within cultural contexts, and they are interpreted and lived out within them, much as Mother Teresa lived out hers within a particular Catholic culture commonly found in the first seventy years of the twentieth century. Appreciation-love for Catholicism and its interdicts may have provided an inner strength for Mother Teresa, but it also at times worked against living out care-love, as Colette Livermore has illustrated.[61]

The final test of the adequacy of Godly love, however, is not found in the warts and wrinkles that are certain to be part of any attempt to live out a life of love. Nor is it in assessing the real ministry against some ideal that was not the intent of the founder. Mother Teresa's "call within a call" was not the Herculean task of changing social structures that created poverty, nor was it to usher the Catholic Church into the new millennium. As she saw it, her call was simply to serve God and to proclaim his coming kingdom by doing "little things with great love" for the poorest of the poor. It is unlikely that any life devoted to love will be judged adequate in all ways for all persons or in all situations. Benevolence takes place in differing social contexts between giver and recipients with multilayered intents and goals. Any model used to assess adequacy should be an interdisciplinary one that allows for differences in cultural norms and interdicts as well as complex interactions found in the proffered care-love and the multifaceted needs of the recipients.

## Notes

1. Samuel M. Shoemaker, cited in Frank S. Mead, *12,000 Inspirational Quotations* (Springfield, MA: Federal Street Press, 1965), 285.
2. Cited in Wikipedia (accessed April 19, 2010).
3. See the introductory chapter for a discussion of the Diamond Model.
4. C. Wright Mills, *The Sociological Imagination* (New York: Oxford University Press, 1959).
5. Pitirim A. Sorokin, *The Ways and Power of Love: Types, Factors, and Techniques of Moral Transformation* (1954; reprint, Radnor, PA: Templeton Foundation Press, 2002).
6. Rolf M. Johnson, *Three Faces of Love* (DeKalb: Northern Illinois University Press, 2001), 26.
7. Ibid., 3.
8. Ibid., 4–5.
9. Ibid., 19.
10. Ibid., 14.
11. Ibid., 24.
12. Ibid.
13. Ibid.
14. Ibid., 25.
15. Ibid.
16. See Margaret M. Poloma and Ralph W. Hood Jr., *Blood and Fire: Godly Love in a Pentecostal Emerging Church* (New York: New York University Press, 2008).
17. Margaret M. Poloma, *Main Street Mystics: The Toronto Blessing and Reviving Pentecostalism* (Walnut Creek, CA: AltaMira Press, 2003).
18. See Margaret M. Poloma, "Inspecting the Fruit of the 'Toronto Blessing': A Sociological Assessment," *Pneuma: The Journal for the Society for Pentecostal Studies* 20 (1998): 43–70, and other Poloma publications referenced above.
19. Sorokin, *Ways and Power of Love*, 36.
20. Ibid., 26.
21. See Randall Collins, *Interaction Ritual Chains* (Princeton, NJ: Princeton

University Press, 2004).

22. Sorokin, *Ways and Power of Love*, 15–16.

23. Ibid., 15.

24. Ibid.

25. Ibid., 16.

26. Margaret M. Poloma and John C. Green, *The Assemblies of God: Godly Love and the Revitalization of American Pentecostalism* (New York: New York University Press, 2010).

27. See chapter 1; also Matthew T. Lee and Margaret M. Poloma, *A Sociological Study of the Great Commandment in Pentecostalism: The Practice of Godly Love as Benevolent Service* (New York: Mellen Press, 2009).

28. Poloma and Green, *Assemblies of God*, 168.

29. Philip Rieff, *Charisma: The Gift of Grace, and How It Has Been Taken Away from Us* (New York: Vintage Books, 2007); see also Philip Rieff, *The Triumph of the Therapeutic: Uses of Faith after Freud* (New York: Harper and Row, 1968).

30. Rieff, *Charisma*.

31. Poloma and Green, *Assemblies of God*, 197.

32. Ibid., 198–99.

33. Malcolm Muggeridge, *Something Beautiful for God: Mother Teresa of Calcutta* (New York: Harper & Row, 1971).

34. Kathryn Spink, *The Miracle of Love: Mother Teresa of Calcutta, Her Missionaries of Charity, and Her Co-Workers* (San Francisco: Harper & Row, 1981); Joseph Langford, *Mother Teresa's Secret Fire: The Encounter That Changed Her Life and How It Can Transform Your Own* (Huntington, IN: Our Sunday Visitor, 2008).

35. Benedict XVI, Pope, *Deus Caritas Est* (2005), §36 (available at: www.vatican.va/holy_father/benedict_xvi_encyclicals).

36. Wikipedia.org/wiki/Mother_Teresa (accessed April 23, 2010); John Paul II (20 October 2003). "Address of John Paul II to the Pilgrims Who Had Come to Rome for the Beatification of Mother Teresa." *Vatican.va*. http://www.vatican.va/holy_father/john_paul_ii/speeches/2003/october/documents/hf_jp-ii_spe_20031020_pilgrims-mother-teresa_en.html (accessed March 13, 2007).

37. Langford, *Mother Teresa's Secret Fire*, 39.

38. Ibid.

39. Ibid., 44.

40. Ibid.

41. Ibid.

42. Ibid., 53.

43. Ibid., 51.

44. Quoted in David Van Biema, "Mother Teresa's Crisis of Faith," *Time*, August 23, 2007 (http://www.time.com;accessed August 6, 2010).

45. Mother Teresa, *Come Be My Light: The Private Writings of the "Saint of Calcutta,"* ed. Brian Kolodiejckuk (New York: Doubleday, 2007), 3–4.

46. Quoted in Van Biema, "Mother Teresa's Crisis of Faith," n.p.

47. Kolodiejckuk, in Mother Teresa, *Come Be My Light*, 3–4.

48. Sorokin, *Ways and Power of Love*, ch. 3.

49. Ibid.

50. Cf. Edward LeJoly and Jaya Chaliha, *Mother Teresa's Reaching Out in Love: Stories Told by Mother Teresa* (New York: Barnes and Noble Books, 1998).

51. Andrew Greeley, *The Sociology of the Paranormal: A Reconnaissance.* Sage Research Papers in the Social Sciences (Beverly Hills: Sage, 1975); Margaret M. Poloma, *Main Street Mystics: Toronto Blessing and Reviving Pentecostalism* (Walnut Creek, CA: AltaMira Press, 2003).

52. Johnson, *Three Faces of Love*, 25.

53. Colette Livermore, *Hope Endures: Leaving Mother Teresa, Losing Faith, and Searching for Meaning* (New York: Free Press, 2008), 45.

54. Ibid., 33.

55. Christopher Hitchens, *The Missionary Position: Mother Teresa in Theory and Practice* (London: Verso, 1995), and "Mommie Dearest: The Pope Beatifies Mother Teresa, a Fanatic, a Fundamentalist, and a Fraud," http://www.slate.com/ articles/news_and_politics/fighting_words/2003/10/mommie_dearest.html (2003) (accessed May 1, 2010).

56. Johnson, *Three Faces of Love*, 24.

57. Hitchens, *Missionary Position*, "Mommie Dearest," and *God Is Not Great: How Religion Poisons Everything* (New York: Twelve, 2007).

58. Hitchens, "Mommie Dearest."

59. Ibid.

60. http://en.wikipedia.org/wiki/Missionaries_of_Charity (last accessed May 1, 2010).

61. Livermore, *Hope Endures.*

# SOCIALIZATION, EMPIRICAL STUDIES,

# AND GODLY LOVE

## A Case Study in Survey Research

### MARK J. CARTLEDGE

This chapter is situated at the interface of theology and social science. It is written by a theologian who uses empirical research methods within the discourse of theology, but who also uses social science theory to inform that discourse. In other words, while the overall approach is driven by the desire to offer a theological account of religious life, nevertheless it takes seriously the contribution that social science makes to this endeavor. In the course of this approach, social science theories are considered and instruments developed in the same manner as a sociologist or social psychologist might develop them in order to establish valid and reliable measures of beliefs, attitudes, and practices. This is the approach associated with the International Society for Empirical Research in Theology, of which the author is a member, and the *Journal of Empirical Theology* (Brill), which disseminates research from this sector. The society encourages scientifically informed empirical research in theology, but also theologically informed empirical research in social science. This means that it provides a context in which theologians and social scientists are able to dialogue about ways in which qualitative and quantitative research methods can be used to explore and test various theoretical perspectives among religious groups. The key person associated with this scholarly tradition in recent times is Johannes A. van der Ven from Nijmegen in the Netherlands.[1] He has pioneered this approach and firmly established it in the field of practical theology.[2] The author's own perspective has built upon this tradition and extended it by connecting it to the field of pentecostal and charismatic studies.[3] It is therefore from within this scholarly tradition that the chapter is written, even if its focus for the purpose of this volume is the social scientific dimension, particularly its implications for the newly emerging study of Godly love.

This study considers one theory, namely socialization, and charts how the author has developed a measure to test the influence of this theory on the acquisition of specific theological understandings of glossolalia and the nature of God, before considering its impact on the acquisition of experiences of Godly love. In this way the author's disciplinary perspective of empirical theology and his experience of researching socialization in relation to theological themes are used to research Godly love as a distinct field of inquiry. The chapter outlines socialization theory before considering the way in which aspects of the theory were tested among charismatic Christians and theology students. From these studies an instrument was developed to test socialization factors with respect to experiencing a relationship of love with God among pentecostals. Finally, the author offers some reflection upon this instrument and outlines some preliminary findings that suggest further analysis and future research.

## Socialization Theory and Factors

Socialization refers to the process whereby individuals become members of a particular social group and adopt certain roles and behavior, in other words, become actors or agents in the various scenarios of life in particular cultures. It is a process that usually begins within a family context (referred to as primary socialization) and continues throughout the life-span of individuals as they move through formal education and on into the world of work (referred to as secondary socialization). Standard sociological textbooks normally outline a number of theoretical perspectives, for example, role theory, associated with the structural-functionalist tradition, symbolic interactionism, and psychoanalytic theory.[4] Sociologists of religion are usually concerned with the ways in which beliefs, values, attitudes, and behavior are transmitted, either generationally or as individuals join new religious groups, thus moving from the outside to the inside.[5] The process enables a particular religious subculture to be maintained as the person adapts to the new culture and fits into its ethos.[6]

It is through a set of ongoing relationships within the group that shared attitudes and accepted roles can be maintained and indeed owned by the newcomer.[7] It is in this process of integration that beliefs owned by the group also become beliefs owned by the individual such that they become internalized. As Berger states: "He draws them (meanings) into himself and makes them *his* meanings. He becomes not only one who possesses these meanings, but one who represents and expresses them."[8] For the person to remain part of a religious group, these beliefs must continue to be both represented and expressed in his or her life by means of specific religious practices and experiences. This is especially pertinent to the study of experiential forms of religion, such as pentecostalism.

There are a number of key factors associated with socialization theory that influence the ways in which individuals are raised within religious groups or are brought into religious groups from outside and retained. The first is a group of peers often called a "reference group."[9] It can be quite small or quite large, for example, a church congregation, and it encourages and supports the acquisition and maintenance of new beliefs, values, and practices. The reference group mediates the existing beliefs and values of the religious culture that it represents. It is this mediation that allows individuals coming from outside to be more easily integrated into the existing social structures and to internalize the religious values of the group. And it is the integration of individuals that functions as a mechanism of retention. The greater the integration of the individual within the group, the greater is the likelihood of retention. A reference group maintains shared meaning among its members and enables that shared meaning to be "taken for granted."[10] It has been called the chorus group that routinely affirms one's place in the general scheme of things.[11] In today's pluralistic network, culture reference groups are chosen for a variety of reasons, and even religiously affiliated individuals can find themselves engaging with a number of different kinds of competing reference groups.

Second, all social groups have individuals who stand out and who represent in a public manner the beliefs and values of the group; they are "significant others." These people provide role models for the rest of the group, and indeed for wider society. They also, along with the reference group, contribute to the plausibility of the religious identity they represent.[12] Therefore plausibility is an important dimension of socialization. A significant other epitomizes the beliefs and values of the religious tradition and contributes to the maintenance of the religious "reality." This means that there is always an important relationship between the significant others and the reference group. They are guardians of the religious tradition and hand it on to the next generation.[13] Significant others may be officially sanctioned as authorized church leaders, or they may in fact be gifted lay leaders, who nevertheless command the respect and allegiance of others. Their influence can be considerable, and they usually police the boundaries of the group ideologically and socially, including the management of group expectations and social discipline where necessary.[14] Therefore, the relationship between the reference group and the significant other is important. Conflict between them can lead to fractures in the meaning system that is taken for granted by its members, leading to a loss of group membership or worse.

Third, religious groups express their beliefs and values in cultural artifacts, such as literature of one kind or another; media in a broader sense, including radio, TV, and the Internet; and buildings or places of worship. Pentecostal Christians from the earliest days produced statements of faith, magazines, and tracts, all of which mediated their beliefs and values to others and importantly to themselves. Over the course of the twentieth century they embraced new electronic media, such as radio and TV, and it is now relatively easy to find out about certain groups via cyberspace. There is a huge market in popular books, music CDs, and DVDs of worship and Christian teaching, all of which assist in the wider socialization of individuals and groups into pentecostalism more generally. They have tended to construct functional worship spaces rather than grand cathedrals, suggesting that God is immediate and active rather than transcendent and remote. It is the combination of all of these factors that contributes to the construction of a worldview embodying and supporting particular beliefs and values, enabling individuals to acquire the appropriate language to use and to engage in meaningful social discourse.[15] The power and ubiquity of these media are culturally sanctioned and religiously endorsed by different kinds of groups.[16]

Fourth, it is important to consider the role that personal agency plays in the process of socialization; otherwise it could be construed as an entirely deterministic process. Clearly, the very different ways in which religious groups emerge, develop, transmute, and disintegrate suggests that personal agency factors play a significant role in these processes. Individuals enter and position themselves in relationship to a religious culture with differing degrees of commitment. Some individuals become so committed to the values of the group that the self becomes a tough taskmaster with high expectations of success and conformity. Highly socialized individuals can be anxious about the limits of what might be considered acceptable behavior, while less socialized persons ignore convention and can be considered unreasonable or selfish. Indeed, self-identity is never purely an individual affair, because it is developed in constant interaction with others, be they the reference group or the significant other, or via media and broader society and culture. Nevertheless, in the ebb and flow of human relations in all their complexity, there is always the dimension of personal human agency.

## Survey Instrument Development

To test attitudes toward these theoretical factors among pentecostal and charismatic Christians, a socialization instrument was developed.[17] It was subsequently tested via a congregational survey in the United Kingdom, retested through a survey of theology students in the United Kingdom, and then redesigned and tested among pentecostals in the United States. This section explains the research context in which the instrument was designed and offers a brief exploration of its significance for the study of Godly love through the means of survey research.

### Socialization and Glossolalia

Socialization emerged as a significant theoretical perspective from which to understand glossolalia in the work of Samarin.[18] He used it to understand and explain how individuals within the pentecostal and charismatic movements acquired glossolalia, or tongues speech. Glossolalia has been defined variously, but the definition of Poythress is worth using as a starting point.[19]

> *Free vocalization* (glossolalia) occurs when (1) a human being produces a connected sequence of speech sounds, (2) he cannot identify the sound-sequence as belonging to any natural language that he already knows how to speak, (3) he cannot identify and give the meaning of words or morphemes (minimal lexical units), (4) in the case of utterances of more than a few syllables, he typically cannot repeat the same sound-sequence on demand, (5) a naive listener might suppose that it was an unknown language.[20]

This definition, although useful, needs at least three qualifications. First, there is an ongoing debate surrounding the linguistic nature of tongues speech, and in terms of semantics the matter is unresolved. Second, a practiced tongues speaker probably could offer a fairly lengthy set of speech on demand, although he or she might be reluctant to do so for the sake of observation. Third, the most recent research on the subject based on speech act theory suggests that the performance of tongues speech in certain kinds of settings influences not only its "meaning" but its effects.[21]

However, despite these caveats, the definition orients the reader to understand what it is that is being explained in terms of socialization theory.

Samarin's research suggested that the social context provides clues as to why people speak in tongues, even if the act of tongues speech might be regarded as a "jump in the dark."[22] He conducted a survey of members of the Full Gospel Business Men's Fellowship drawn from different countries, including Canada, Germany, England, the Netherlands, and the Unites States of America (N = 84). In this survey he explored the socialization question by inviting respondents to comment on their desire to speak in tongues, their proximity to family and friends who speak in tongues, and any encouragement or guidance as to how to begin to speak in tongues, together with the difficulties that might be encountered. In addition, he was interested in the first experience of speaking in tongues and how the practice improved as time passed. He discovered that tongues speech could not be said to be learned in the same manner as one might learn a regular human language. Rather, each speech was more or less unique to the individual, but it was also associated with becoming a member of a group. The key to being able to speak in tongues was the desire of the individual to become and remain a member of the tongues-speaking group as part of a personal search for spiritual fulfillment. Therefore the language of instruction was often couched in language suggesting relaxation and submission to God. Sometimes explicit linguistic instructions were given, such as being told to speak out whatever comes to mind or to make sounds of some kind, or perhaps to repeat a phrase such as "Praise Jesus." An atmosphere of expectancy, with the use of silence and hushed voices, as well as the laying on of hands, gave an immediate context to this practice.[23] However, no clear model of glossolalia was given to them. Instead, they were merely taught that whatever they said would be regarded as "real words from a real language unknown to themselves."[24] He suggests that it is more likely that phonetic patterns of glossolalia are imitated informally as people hear tongues speech around them in the context of worship and prayer meetings, which in turn assists individuals to improve their own speech.[25]

Initially, Samarin's use of socialization theory was explored via a qualitative study.[26] Findings suggested that all of those interviewed (N = 13) had desired to experience some greater spiritual fulfillment by engaging in tongues speech. Most had been encouraged to speak in tongues by someone they already knew or had met. Three appeared to have received explicit instructions on how to speak in tongues from those attempting to initiate the person into the practice. These instructions included verbalizing any sounds that came into the mind or to start speaking without thinking about what is being vocalized, which the person interpreted as saying a single word repeatedly until fluency was achieved. Almost all of the interviewees had wider knowledge of pentecostal or charismatic Christianity from other contexts than their present church and thus brought with them a greater knowledge and experience, which also had an impact on their understanding and expectation. From the perspective of socialization, this movement represents a broader reference group, with the particular church community offering a localized expression of it. Significant others play a key role in the acquisition process for some people but not for others, and this must be set in the context of the wider communal and social context.

These findings informed the basis for the development of an instrument to test the nature of socialization in relation to the understanding of glossolalia among independent charismatic Christians in the UK.[27] The instrument devised was a seven-point Likert question that asked how much the following items had helped the respondent to understand speaking in tongues (1 = very little, 7 = very much): famous preachers, church leaders, friends, conferences, books, magazines, audiotapes, videotapes, and personal Bible study.[28] These items were developed into a nine-item scale (see table 1).[29] The findings demonstrated that all the key aspects associated with glossolalic speech, namely, the symbolic representation of beauty, awe, power, intimacy, faith building, and vulnerability, were statistically associated with socialization. Regression analysis demonstrated that socialization was a significant predictor of all of these symbolic qualities. This meant that glossolalia as a learned experience had considerable support empirically.[30] In other words, individuals learned how to appreciate glossolalia in these terms via specific socialization factors. A causal path was suggested, running from Eysenck personality dimensions via charismatic experience to socialization and from socialization to the glossolalia symbols.[31] It demonstrated that socialization was itself predicted in terms of the frequency of certain practices, such as using tongues speech as a form of self-edification, prayer generally, and prophecy. It was also predicted directly by the Eysenck personality dimensions of extraversion (positively) and psychoticism (negatively), suggesting that those scoring high on the extraversion scale associate more with charismatic socialization, while those scoring high on the psychoticism scale (indicating greater tough-mindedness and independence) dissociate themselves from it. In other words, they are less likely to allow themselves to be socialized into speaking in tongues, which is entirely what one might expect.[32]

TABLE 1—The Socialization of Understanding Glossolalia Scale
*Inter-item Correlations*

|                      | r   |
| -------------------- | --- |
| famous preachers     | .56 |
| church leaders       | .45 |
| friends              | .32 |
| conferences          | .63 |
| books                | .59 |
| magazines            | .55 |
| audiotapes           | .64 |
| videotapes           | .53 |
| personal bible study | .36 |
| Alpha                | .81 |

Further analysis of these data subsequently allowed each of the nine items in the scale to be examined in more detail.[33] This study revealed that the frequency of tongues speech is positively associated with all of the socialization factors, apart from friends, with personal Bible study displaying the strongest association (r = .256, p .01). The data also demonstrated that the frequency of tongues speech for the purpose of prayer, prophecy, worship, and spiritual battle was positively associated with all of the socialization factors, with personal Bible study scoring high, especially for the frequency of tongues speech for prayer (r = .395, p .01), worship (r = .340, p .01), and spiritual battle (r = .268, p .01). What emerges from these data is a question mark against the role that friends play in the acquisition and support of this key religious practice. Personal Bible study emerges as a key indicator of personal agency within charismatic spirituality, as well as the role of sacred texts to inform theological understanding.

### Socialization and Understanding the Nature of God

To test the role of socialization more widely, it was used as a measure of the ways in which theology students (N = 244) understood the nature of God.[34] The measure was not substantially altered, because of its previous reliability score, but was retested in relation to a completely different subject. However, the range of scores was contracted to be from 1 = very little, to 5 = very much. This time the scale gave a Cronbach alpha reliability score of .76, reinforcing the earlier reliability of the measure (see table 2). The items showing the strongest inter-item correlations were famous preachers (r = .47), magazines (r = .50), audiotapes (r = .55), and videotapes (r = .50). As in the previous study, it was deemed worth exploring these factors in a fine-grained manner by considering each item separately.

TABLE 2—The Socialization of Understanding God Scale
*Inter-item Correlations*

|  | r |
|---|---|
| famous preachers | .47 |
| church leaders | .39 |
| friends | .30 |
| conferences | .42 |
| books | .44 |
| magazines | .50 |
| audiotapes | .55 |
| videotapes | .50 |
| personal bible study | .37 |
| **Alpha** | .76 |

The findings indicate that there is a statistically significant difference between women and men, with women socialized more by friends and conferences and men by famous preachers. This suggests that the under-standing of God is socialized more relationally for women via the reference group, rather than the significant other of the preacher, as for men. It also suggests a more active and participatory involvement in socialization. Younger people are socialized more by church leaders, friends, conferences, and videotapes than are older people. The less-educated person is socialized more by church leaders, friends, conferences, magazines, audio- and videotapes, and personal Bible study. The different educational contexts of the students (Adventist, ecumenical, evangelical, and pentecostal) also proved important. Famous preachers, church leaders, and conferences are generally associated positively for all the contexts, but especially for pentecostals. Personal Bible study is generally very strongly supported by all the contexts, but again especially so for pentecostals and also for Adventists. Thus, gender, age, education, and religious educational context are significant factors in how socialization is played out among these Christians and influence which factors are given greater weight in the overall process. In general terms, the most socialized individuals would tend to be younger, less-educated pentecostal women who nevertheless exhibit strong personal agency through the individual interpretation of the Bible.

This study gave an opportunity for the instrument to be reflected upon methodologically and critically evaluated.[35] In this reflection it was observed that although the instrument was now ten years old, having been shaped by the social science literature on glossolalia, it was now rather dated (even if statistically reliable). It was suggested that the reference group could be enhanced by testing specific subgroups within a congregational setting, such as youth groups, men's and women's groups, study groups, and house groups. It was noted that significant others as a factor was limited and could be improved as a measure by offering a wider variety of roles, such as clergy, lay leaders, youth workers, schoolteachers, worship leaders, musicians, spiritual directors, and prayer partners. Famous preachers and church leaders were simply too restricted to capture all the subtleties of the different kinds of leadership influence. The media items also needed to be updated with the change in technology, so CDs and DVDs needed to replace audio- and videotapes, and new items were required, such as the Internet. Nothing in the instrument related to the phyVsical environment, so it was suggested that an item relating to the church building be added. It was also suggested that personal Bible study was the only item reflecting personal agency, and this would need to be supplemented in light of its significance statistically.

*Socialization and Godly Love*

The opportunity for revising the instrument came when the Flame of Love Project accepted an application to study the socialization of Godly love among Church of God (Cleveland, Tennessee) pentecostals in the United States. In the overall project, Godly love was defined as the dynamic interaction between divine love and human love that enlivens benevolence, which allows for "remarkable self-forgetfulness in the agent."[36] It is an expression of the love of God and the love of neighbor as oneself. Furthermore, it is a love energy produced through a two-way exchange of loving and being loved by God. Margaret Poloma and Ralph W. Hood define Godly love as the "dynamic interaction between human responses to the operation of perceived divine love and the impact this experience has on personal lives, relationships with others, and emergent communities."[37] The main theory of love energy is drawn from the work of Pitirim Sorokin.[38] For Sorokin love energy is constantly being produced through the process of human interaction and is embedded within culture, including religious cultural values. Sorokin acknowledges the possible hypothesis that the inflow of love can originate in a transcendental reality, although it is recognized that this reality is beyond empirical measurement. Nevertheless, inferences may be drawn from the perception, experience, and behavior of individuals and groups engaged in benevolent action.

This understanding resonates with the work of Werner G. Jeanrond, who has given the most up-to-date treatment of the theology of love and in doing so has reminded us of the key thinkers who have contributed to this subject over the centuries. He answers the question "What is love?" by stating:

> Love seeks the other. Love desires to relate to the other, to get to know the other, to admire the other, to experience the other's life, to spend time with the other. Nobody else can love in my place. There is no vicarious love. Love requires a concrete agent, a loving subject. Love can be accompanied by much joy and much pain; it can give rise to great emotional turmoil and heavenly bliss. Hence, love always includes emotion, yet it is more than emotion. It has the potential to affect the entire fabric of our human relationships.[39]

For Jeanrond, love is fundamentally a praxis, which includes an encounter with the other but also some form of reflection on that encounter.[40] He suggests that love always has a social location, is embodied, is gendered, and includes eroticism. It is expressed via larger networks of relationships and is composed of attitudinal, emotional, and relational features. This means that love is a complex reality.

Jeanrond addresses the focus of this present inquiry, namely, the way in which love is acquired. He advances the view that:

> Love can be learned. At various stages of our life we subject ourselves to new learning experiences in the vast field of love. Love is not instinctual behaviour, but a praxis resulting from cultural processes in which each human being passively and actively participates. While only few visit specialized schools of love, all women, men and children can be said to be emerging disciples of love in the different "schools of life." Unlike sex, politics, household management, etc., love is not a subject on the school curriculum, yet it relates to all aspects of our lives and it requires learning.[41]

Jeanrond argues that the family is the primary institution of love, as children grow up into familial love, even if at times this fails. Love always has a social and conventional side to it, even if these conventions are adapted by subjective agents. In this context we learn to recognize forms and expressions of love, which can be built upon and refined later in life. Other social institutions from school, to marriage, to church, to clubs can assist in the praxis of love via inherited patterns of expression. There are two institutions that are especially relevant to this study, namely, the family and the church. In the New Testament the invitation to become a disciple of Christ relativized the existing household structure to the lordship of Christ and opened up the boundaries of the family (Luke 11:27–28; 14:25–26; 18:28–30). Thus, there is an obvious link between the family and the church, which is the community seeking to love God, neighbor, and the whole of creation through the power of the Holy Spirit.[42] The implications of this learned love are stated by Jeanrond:

> Human love for God is a wonderful gift from God. However, it is . . . a gift that always draws us more deeply into the entire network of loving relations. Whenever we love God, we are at the same time directed towards God's creative and reconciling project, we are directed to the larger body of love which in Christian experience is desired as the body of Christ. Even the most intense experience and expression of our love of God thus involves the entire love story between God and God's creation.[43]

This enables us to consider an important conceptualization of this interaction between divine and human love that leads to benevolent praxis in the world: Godly love. It is this experience of a relationship of love with God that provides the impetus for redesigning the socialization instrument.

As part of the project, "Learning to Love and Loving to Serve: A Study of the Socialization of Godly Love and Its Influence on Vocation," designed by Alexander and Cartledge, with the support of Bowers, the previous research instrument by Cartledge was redesigned in the light of new theoretical considerations. This study is a survey of 127 congregations affiliated with the Church of God (Cleveland, Tennessee) in the United States from which 52 churches participated (41%) and returned 1,522 usable questionnaires. Two batteries were included in the questionnaire; the first comprised 15 items, and the second 18 items. Both these batteries were introduced with the question: "How much have the following helped you to *experience* a relationship of love with God?" and gave a five-point Likert answer option (1 = very little, to 5 = very much). In this instrument the emphasis (hence the italics) was placed upon experiencing a relationship of love with God, rather than a cognitive understanding of Godly love. (1) The reference group is measured by: close friends, women's group, men's group, small group, church holidays, youth group, and camp meetings. (2) Significant others is measured by: youth pastors, father, mother, other family members, pastors, evangelists, mentors, prayer partners, and worship leaders. The item of spouse was excluded in order to improve the reliability score. (3) The Christian media is measured by: Christian teaching on DVDs, church music, Christian music on CDs, Christian news articles and features, sermon recordings, and Christian literature. (4) The secular media is measured by: general radio, the Internet, and general media. (5) The church environment is measured by: church buildings. (6) Personal agency is measured by: individual decision, deliberate choice, step of faith, and personal Bible study. (7) The perception of direct divine agency is measured by: direct encounter with God. The scales representing the theoretical dimensions of (1), (2), (3), (4), and (6) are shown in table 3. All of them, except (4), display good reliability scores as measured by a Cronbach alpha score of .7. Therefore, all except (4) can be used in further analysis.

TABLE 3—The Socialization of Experience of Love Scales
*Inter-item Correlations*

| Reference group | r | Secular media | r |
|---|---|---|---|
| camp meetings | .42 | general radio | .35 |
| church holidays | .46 | Internet | .28 |
| close friends | .42 | general media | .26 |
| men's group | .29* | **Alpha** | .47 |
| women's group | .42 | | |
| small group | .48 | | |
| youth group | .43 | | |
| **Alpha** | .71 | | |

| Significant others | r | Personal agency | r |
|---|---|---|---|
| evangelists | .39 | individual decision | .51 |
| father | .39 | deliberate choice | .52 |
| mentors | .48 | step of faith | .58 |
| mother | .40 | personal Bible study | .45 |
| other family members | .54 | **Alpha** | .73 |
| pastors | .48 | | |
| prayer partners | .52 | *Christian media* | r |
| spouse (excluded) | – | Christian teaching on DVDs | .54 |
| worship leaders | .46 | church music | .46 |
| youth pastors | .33 | Christian music on CDs | .57 |
| **Alpha** | .76 | Christian media | .60 |
| | | sermon recordings | .56 |
| | | Christian literature | .59 |
| | | **Alpha** | .80 |

* This is a borderline score. Normally scores of >.30 are retained; however, when this item is removed the alpha score is weakened,and therefore it has been retained.

TABLE 4—Individual Socialization Factors
*Experience of a Relationship of Love (valid %)*

| Reference group | Agreement | Secular media | Agreement |
|---|---|---|---|
| camp meetings | 25.9 | general radio | 25.1 |
| church holidays | 32.9 | Internet | 10.4 |
| close friends | 51.7 | general media | 11.4 |
| men's group | 16.9 | | |
| women's group | 27.5 | **Church environment** | **Agreement** |
| small group | 32.2 | church buildings | 22.6 |
| youth group | 23.7 | | |

| Significant others | Agreement | Personal agency | Agreement |
|---|---|---|---|
| evangelists | 46.6 | individual decision | 69.4 |
| father | 28.9 | deliberate choice | 71.4 |
| mentors | 52.9 | step of faith | 70.6 |
| mother | 55.8 | personal Bible study | 69.1 |
| other family members | 42.5 | | |
| pastors | 74.3 | **Divine agency** | **Agreement** |
| prayer partners | 48.4 | direct encounter | 77.5 |
| spouse | 52.4 | | |
| worship leaders | 58.8 | | |
| youth pastors | 25.9 | | |

| Christian media | Agreement |
|---|---|
| Christian teaching on DVDs | 26.4 |
| church music | 69.1 |
| Christian music on CDs | 62.3 |
| Christian media | 37.2 |
| sermon recordings | 36.3 |
| Christian literature | 47.8 |

To obtain a sense of the strength of individual items within the sample as a whole, it is interesting to observe basic agreement with individual measures by displaying agreement in percentage terms by adding measures 4 (much) and 5 (very much) on the Likert scale together (valid %). Table 4 shows the extent to which the respondents agree with the various socialization factors in terms of their influence upon an experience of a relationship of love with God. The reference group items indicate that close friends play the most important role, but small groups, church holidays, and camps play a much lesser role. Pastors are by far the most significant factor for significant others, followed at some distance by worship leaders, then mothers, mentors, and spouses. The low scores for youth pastors and fathers in particular should be noted and suggest further exploration, especially in relation to age and gender. Music is the most significant factor for Christian media, whereas all the secular media items produce low scores. Similarly the physical environment of the church building does not play an important role. All of the personal agency items score high, suggesting that this is a very important factor. These must be interpreted alongside the direct encounter with God item, which is the single highest-scoring item and suggests a very high perception of divine agency within the experience. Therefore, at the center of this socialization process there is recognition by respondents that there is a two-way process whereby individual agency and divine agency (at least in terms of perception) are both important for experiencing a relationship of love with God.

## Conclusion

It can be said that the theory of socialization is an important lens through which to view religious life and that it provides insight into how specific factors influence the acquisition of beliefs and values, including specific experiences. Using the contribution of socialization theory to investigate theological attitudes can provide an important context in which to place these findings. The contribution of this research to the study of Godly love suggests that experiences are indeed mediated through key factors such as the reference group, significant others, and Christian media. However, what emerges is the finding that personal agency is the strongest factor; combined with the perception of direct divine encounter, it suggests possible explanations for the acquisition and sustenance of benevolence. In other words, individual differences as much as social processes contribute to the expression of benevolent action in the world. To explain this finding more fully, it can be suggested that personality theory could be used to test how different traits that explain specific attitudes and practices are associated with Godly love. For example, one might expect those scoring high on the extraversion scale and low on the psychoticism scale to act more benevolently toward others. This has relevance for socialization, because those people who score low on the psychoticism measure are known to be influenced by others more readily than those who score higher.[44] This has potential significance for understanding how pentecostals learn to love and thereby love to serve.

# Notes

1. Johannes A. van der Ven, *Practical Theology: An Empirical Approach* (Kampen, The Netherlands: Kok Pharos, 1993).

2. Chris A. M. Hermans and Mary E. Moore, eds., *Hermeneutics and Empirical Research in Practical Theology: The Contribution of Empirical Theology by Johannes A. van der Ven* (Leiden: Brill, 2004).

3. Mark J. Cartledge, "Empirical Theology: Inter- or Intra-Disciplinary?" *Journal of Beliefs & Values* 20:1 (1999): 98–104; Cartledge, *Practical Theology: Charismatic and Empirical Perspectives* (Carlisle, UK: Paternoster, 2003); William K. Kay, "Empirical Theology: A Natural Development?" *Heythrop Journal: A Quarterly Review of Philosophy and Theology* 44:2 (2003): 167–81.

4. James Fulcher and John Scott, *Sociology*, 2nd ed. (Oxford: Oxford University Press, 2003).

5. Stephen J. Hunt, *Alternative Religions: A Sociological Introduction* (Aldershot, UK: Ashgate, 2003).

6. Peter Berger, *The Social Reality of Religion* (London: Faber and Faber, 1969).

7. George Furniss, *Sociology for Pastoral Care: An Introduction for Students and Pastors* (London: SPCK, 1995).

8. Berger, *Social Reality of Religion*, 15.

9. Furniss, *Sociology for Pastoral Care*, 37.

10. Meredith B. McGuire, *Religion: The Social Context*, 5th ed. (Belmont, CA: Wadsworth Thomson, 2002), 37.

11. Peter Berger and Thomas Luckmann, *The Social Construction of Reality: A Treatise in the Sociology of Knowledge* (London: Penguin, 1967).

12. Alan Aldridge, *Religion in the Contemporary World: A Sociological Introduction* (Cambridge: Polity, 2000).

13. Johannes A. van der Ven, *Ecclesiology in Context* (Grand Rapids, MI: Eerdmans, 1996).

14. Audrey I. Richards, "Socialization and Contemporary British Anthropology," in Philip Mayer, ed., *Socialization: The Approach from Social Anthropology* (London: Tavistock, 1970), 1–32.

15. Graham White, *Socialisation* (London: Longman, 1977).

16. Kurt Danziger, *Socialization* (Harmondsworth, UK: Penguin, 1971).

17. A. N. Oppenheim, *Questionnaire Design, Interviewing and Attitude Measurement* (London: Pinter, 1992).

18. William J. Samarin, "Glossolalia as Learned Behaviour," *Canadian Journal of Theology* 15 (1969): 60–64, and *Tongues of Men and of Angels* (New York: Macmillan, 1972).

19. Vern S. Poythress, "Linguistic and Sociological Analyses of Modern Tongues-Speaking: Their Contribution and Limitations," *Westminster Theological Journal* 42 (1980): 367–88.

20. Ibid., 369.

21. Mark J. Cartledge, ed., *Speaking in Tongues: Multi-Disciplinary Perspectives* (Carlisle: Paternoster, 2006).

22. Samarin, "Glossolalia as Learned Behaviour," 55.

23. Samarin, *Tongues of Men and of Angels*, 50–58.

24. Samarin, "Glossolalia as Learned Behaviour," 62.

25. William J. Samarin, "Glossolalia as Regressive Speech," *Language and Speech* 16 (1973): 77–89.

26. Mark J. Cartledge, "The Socialization of Glossolalia," in Leslie J. Francis, ed., *Sociology, Theology and the Curriculum* (London: Cassell, 1999), 125–34.

27. Mark J. Cartledge, *Charismatic Glossolalia: An Empirical-Theological Study* (Aldershot, UK: Ashgate, 2002); N = 633.

28. Cartledge, *Practical Theology*, 243.

29. Cartledge, *Charismatic Glossolalia*, 146, table 1.

30. Ibid., 181.

31. Ibid., 168–73.

32. Ibid.; Hans J. Eysenck and Sybil B. G. Eysenck, *Manual of Eysenck Personality Questionnaire (Junior and Adult)* (London: Hodder & Stoughton, 1975).

33. For details, see Cartledge, *Practical Theology*.

34. Mark J. Cartledge, "Socialisation and Empirical-Theological Models of the Trinity: A Study among Theology Students in the United Kingdom," in *Empirical Theology in Texts and Tables: Qualitative, Quantitative and Comparative Perspectives* (Leiden: Brill, 2009), ed. Leslie J. Francis, Mandy Robbins, and Jeff Astley, 269–90; Cartledge, "Empirical-Theological Models of the Trinity: Exploring the Beliefs of Theology Students in the United Kingdom," *Journal of Empirical Theology* 19:2 (2006): 137–62; Cartledge, "God, Gender and Social Roles: A Study in Relation to Empirical-Theological Models of the Trinity," *Journal of Empirical Theology* 22:2 (2009): 117–41.

35. Cartledge, "Socialisation and Empirical-Theological Models of the Trinity," 288–89.

36. Stephen G. Post, in Matthew T. Lee and Margaret M. Poloma, *A Sociological Study of the Great Commandment in the Pentecostalism: The Practice of Godly Love as Benevolent Service* (Lewiston, NY: Edwin Mellen Press, 2009), i.

37. Margaret M. Poloma and Ralph W. Hood, *Blood and Fire: Godly Love in a Pentecostal Emerging Church* (New York: New York University Press, 2008), 4.

38. Pitirim Sorokin, *The Ways and Power of Love: Types, Factors, and Techniques of Moral Transformation* (1954; reprint, Radnor, PA: Templeton Foundation Press, 2002); Matthew T. Lee, Margaret M. Poloma, and Stephen G. Post, "Researching Godly Love in the Pentecostal Tradition: A White Paper for the Flame of Love Project," University of Akron, Ohio (2008), 9–11.

39. Werner G. Jeanrond, *A Theology of Love* (London: T & T Clark, 2009), 2.

40. Ibid., 5.

41. Ibid., 173.

42. Ibid., 215–16.

43. Ibid., 242.

44. Leslie J. Francis and William K. Kay, "The Personality Characteristics of Pentecostal Ministry Candidates," *Personality and Individual Differences* 18, no. 5 (1995): 581–94; Lesley J. Francis and Susan H. Jones, "Personality and Charismatic Experience among Adult Christians," *Pastoral Psychology* 45, no. 6 (1997): 421–28.

# Ten

# TOWARD A GROUNDED THEORY

# OF GODLY LOVE

## Latino/a Pentecostals

### ARLENE SÁNCHEZ WALSH

This chapter offers two case studies of Latino/a pentecostal organizations as "exemplars" of Godly love, both viewing their ministries as extensions of their desire to extend God's love to the world. These two organizations offer us divergent views of how Latino/a pentecostals operate in terms of adopting a "love vs. law"[1] theological outlook as well as demonstrate how different generations view their mission as versions of Godly love. One might ask, What does the Love vs. Law debate have to do with Godly love? If these very limited case studies have anything to add to this question, it is that Latino/a pentecostals view Godly love differently depending on their ideological, generational, and cultural outlook.

Most Latino/a pentecostals, however, do not recognize that there is an inconsistency in their worldview. On the one hand, many Latino/a pentecostals have been deeply formed by what noted Catholic theologian Orlando Espín has identified as the traditionalist idea that God is omnipotent, omniscient, and omnipresent.[2] This idea is assumed by most Latinos/as, the majority historically and today coming from Catholic backgrounds. Yet it is this premodern disposition that allows for Latino/a Catholics to quickly adopt a pentecostal identity, because they both emphasize healing, prophecy, and other miracles. Thus, embracing supernatural religion, eschewing modernity and liberalism, fearful that "postmodernity" is code for "moral relativism," Latino/a pentecostals occupy a supernatural world filled with the miraculous. Yet, on the other hand, at least at the popular level, there is primarily not much of an awareness that this traditional view of God usually denies any genuine interaction between God and creation. This means that while pentecostals feel that the God described in scripture is literally capable of everything that is mentioned—healing, exorcism, and miracles of all kinds through the supernatural power available in Jesus and the Holy Spirit—this view sits at some odds with pentecostal instincts and sensibilities wherein God relates with free creatures to the point that at any time God can change situations, heal, answer prayer, and provide supernatural outcomes to the most intractable problems. In other words, pentecostal spirituality in some respects presumes a more open view of the world than that bequeathed by the premodern classical worldview.

Whether this premodern disposition has direct correlates to generational shifts is difficult to assess. While there are some studies of Latino/a religious attitudes that suggest this tie is very strong, there are others that make only anecdotal claims. What can be said with some certainty is that there are generational differences, and that they make a difference with regard to how Latino/a pentecostals experience things like Godly love. A brief historical overview of Latino/a pentecostal history is here in order.

## Historical Background

In its short history of just over one hundred years, Latino/a pentecostalism has already gone through several periods of growth and decline. In the early years of the movement, roughly 1906 to the 1930s, the fervor of evangelism, fueled by an equally fervent belief in the imminent Second Coming of Jesus, and an often overt anti-Catholic ideology, brought a steady stream of Latinos/as into pentecostal churches. Within these first 30 years, there was a broad swath of geographic as well as theological diversity that marked the movement. Churches sprang up all along the borderlands of the southwestern United States, in major urban areas of the Midwest and Northeast, and in areas like the Central Valley of California, where, as part of their initial attraction, pentecostal churches opened in places where Latinos/as worked. In the case of Central California, it was farmworkers that became part of the churches' first cohort of converts.

As the movement stabilized in growth, it also experienced many splits due to theological differences and also due to the perception among several major Latino/a ministry leaders that to stay under the auspices of white leadership in denominations such as the Assemblies of God would hinder the development of autonomous Latino/a leadership within those denominations. But the largest schism occurred between the Oneness and Trinitarian groups. Oneness pentecostalism began in white churches of the Assemblies of God, soon spread to the African American church, and eventually found its way to splitting the small group of Latino/a pentecostals who had converted in Southern California on the heels of the Azusa Street Revival. The split between the trinitarian pentecostal groups, chiefly the Assemblies of God and the Oneness (nontrinitarian) groups, occurred shortly after a revival held in Southern California in 1913, where an alternative baptismal formula was preached as being part of a new revelation. Soon thereafter, Oneness adherents began to rebaptize fellow pentecostals in the name of Jesus only, eschewing the traditional "Father, Son, and Holy Spirit" formula. One of those converts, Romanita Carbajal Valenzuela, converted in Los Angeles sometime shortly after the Azusa Street Revival, became a Oneness adherent, and went back to her native Mexico and helped found what today is the largest pentecostal group in Mexico, the Iglesia Apostólica de la Fe en Cristo Jesus (the Apostolic Church of the Faith in Jesus Christ). The American branch of the church, the Apostolic Assembly, is still one of the strongest Latino/a-majority denominations in the United States, expanding from the traditional areas of strength in the Southwest, to newer bases of expanded immigrant growth in the Pacific Northwest, rural Midwest, and rural Southeast.

This steady stream of converts, to both Oneness and Trinitarian varieties of pentecostalism, continued with modest gains from the 1940s through the 1960s. These years marked the emergence of the first English-dominant generation to be raised in Latino/a pentecostal churches and brought with it the challenges of how to retain second-generation children in the movement, and how far assimilation into the dominant culture would be necessary to keep their English-speaking kids in church.

In the 1960s the Jesus Movement not only began to reignite classical pentecostal churches (Assemblies of God, Foursquare, Church of God, Cleveland, Tennessee) but also launched a charismatic renewal in mainline churches. This diffuse movement introduced pentecostal spirituality and evangelical fervor to people in a less dogmatic, more accessible way. It also meant that Latinos/as who found pentecostalism through the Jesus movement were being nurtured in churches that were unable to reinforce their ethnic identity.

As the Jesus Movement faded, Latino/a pentecostalism began to find its own revitalization, much in the same way as it began, as a part of the religious expression of Spanish-speaking first-generation Latino/a immigrants from Mexico, Central and South America, and the Caribbean.[3] The second and later generations of these immigrants sought to obtain and maintain a vibrant charismatic religious identity that was not necessarily tied to traditional pentecostal denominations, was not dogmatic, and offered them a way to be pentecostal outside the confines of their parents' churches.

The theological diversity, autonomous leadership, and tremendous spike in the growth of the movement all occurred with this latest wave of adherents. It is this wave that many media observers have noted, often assuming that this surge, which began roughly in the early to mid-1980s, has received the bulk of attention by popular and academic observers alike. We now turn to placing Latino/a pentecostals within the existing framework of grounded theory.[4]

## Religious Worldviews

In fifteen years of interviewing Latino/a pentecostals, the author has found overwhelmingly that they have a religious worldview rooted in premodernity that creates an almost unconditional acceptance of the supernatural. Only one person in a survey and via an interview has been identified who was willing to admit he did not believe in miracles, was dissatisfied with church, and really did not know why he was involved in church at the same level that others were (he played in the worship band). All others defaulted to some level of a miracle motif, from serious life-threatening illnesses healed to more mundane things like luggage being found. One reason for this default is that Latino/a Pentecostals generally come to their faith through the process of conversion and, as such, need to go through a process of theological reeducation so that they can better acclimate to their new religious identity. Often this has included not only (un)healthy doses of mild to severe anti-Catholicism, but has also meant that the way they see the world has changed. One of the ways this worldview changes is that it now differentiates between a religious or a "Christian" worldview and the view portrayed by the "world." Now that their religious life has been righted by becoming pentecostal, embracing views seen as too worldly is simply incongruous with their conversion.

A further idea that will help us understand the case studies that follow is Espín's theological argument—in the already referenced volume—that suggests that Latinos/as historically and, it may be argued, with the political climate today, are a vanquished people, and thus it becomes easier to view Jesus as a locus of human experience and an ultimate symbol of vanquishment. How both of these religious organizations, Victory

Outreach and Latino Leadership Circle, experience, theologize, and liberate themselves and others from this vanquishment is the focus of the second half of this chapter.

Finally, perhaps one source for the uncritical Latino/a pentecostal adoption of the traditionalist worldview without any sense of how this sits in tension with their charismatic sensibilities is the funneling effect many Latino/a pentecostals go through when they continue their theological education. Often, they are channeled toward conservative theological views as well as conservative political views through their pastors, many of whom have received training in conservative seminaries or Bible institutes or have been self-educated through a vast array of media. Translated media of some of evangelicalism's most prominent people (James Dobson, Pat Robertson, and others) can be found in nearly every church the author has visited, either as an advertisement for selling items or as an encouragement to watch certain "acceptable" television shows.

### Love vs. Law

For Latino/a pentecostals, there appears to be a paradox that neither they, nor any other group that tends to be on the law side of the love vs. law debate, can reconcile. Because their overarching framework is premodern, and they are disposed to maintaining themselves as a last bulwark against encroaching theological and social liberalization, a generalization can be made about the legalistic tendencies of at least the immigrant and first-generation Latino church.[5] Those churches tend toward more legalism, as do certain kinds of pentecostal churches. One of the most recent analyses of survey research on Latino/a religious communities supports this anecdotal evidence that immigrant and first-generation Latinos, if they are Protestant at all (most are not, remaining Catholic and, in fact, replenishing American Catholicism), are the most conservative of the Protestant fold.[6] Churches that follow the Oneness tradition hold to the strict holiness codes of classical holiness pentecostalism. Among second and third generations, though, if the author's interviews of Latino/a youth are any indication, these English-speaking, highly Americanized generations wish to cast off the legalism of their parents as much as they want to cast off worshipping in Spanish with traditional hymns. It is these generations that also tend to leave the movement for many of the same reasons.

The paradox is that, for all the insistence on the law, Latinos/as, especially those in lower-income, marginalized communities, are surrounded by social pathologies that counter the strictness of their piety. They will acknowledge that church members have issues with drinking, spousal abuse, juvenile delinquency, etc., but they are loath to admit hypocrisy or complicity in such lax piety. A case study that serves us well as we study this paradox will be the Pentecostal drug rehabilitation ministry, Victory Outreach. What becomes most important is that the way one lives as a Christian, especially the particular reading of sexual mores and gender roles, needs to be encoded in the way every practicing church member lives his or her life. The other case study, the advocacy group Latino Leadership Circle, composed of second- and third-generation pentecostals, has seen as one of its tasks liberating Latino/a pentecostalism from its legalistic moorings and broadening the often insular vision of conservative immigrant and first-generation brethren regarding what kinds of ministry are viewed as proper for the church to engage.

Like any interaction between people and the sacred, religious identity is couched in cultural conditioning. Of particular interest will be the work of noted sociologist Pitirim A. Sorokin, especially his idea of "love-producing groups."[7] This chapter contends that Latino/a pentecostals view Godly love differently. Whether they are traditionalists such as Victory Outreach or reformers like the Latino Leadership Circle,[8] Latinos/as view Godly love in communal rather than purely individualistic terms. Thus, the meaning of benevolence—the outcome of Godly love—is determined by the very different experiences of distinct generational groups within the Latino/a community. The study of Godly love, therefore, cannot be conducted in a vacuum. Rather, it must understand the causes and consequences of the standpoints of those involved in Godly love interactions. There will be more on this later; for now, a brief description of the drug rehabilitation ministry Victory Outreach (hereafter referred to as VO) is provided.

VO was founded on the eastside of Los Angeles in 1967 by a reformed heroin addict and gang member, Cruz "Sonny" Arguinzoni, who converted to Pentecostalism under the auspices of the Assemblies of God's drug rehabilitation ministry, Teen Challenge. Arguinzoni built VO on the Teen Challenge model, with several crucial differences. Those needing help would not need to leave their neighborhoods to receive help, since VO placed its rehabilitation homes in inner cities. VO, unlike Teen Challenge, worked almost exclusively in Latino neighborhoods, staffed its rehab homes with reformed addicts and ex-gang members, and provided a career ladder of sorts for these reformed addicts if they wished to enter into the ministry.

The first years of VO found it trying to establish itself in the Latino neighborhoods of Southern California. From the 1980s to the 2000s, VO expanded its ministries to Asia, Africa, Latin America, and western Europe, staffing those rehab homes and churches, more often than not, with graduates from the U.S. programs. All the while, the focus of the ministry has been "the task of evangelizing and disciplining the hurting people of the world, with the message of hope and plan of Jesus Christ."[9] As such, VO should be categorized as traditionalistic. VO does not see social justice as an effective ministry path. VO operates much the same way as it did in 1967: it seeks out inner-city neighborhoods to open its rehabilitation homes, and it begins with house churches that double as rehab homes and continue to do so until it can reach a critical mass of congregants to move to larger quarters.

The author has written elsewhere that despite VO's protestations that it wants to be more than a Latino church,[10] the fact remains that VO began as a Latino/a church, specifically a Mexican American church, and that its strength, vitality, and own sense of ethnic identity emanate from its founding. As such, it is a Pentecostal social mission, seeking out various forms of liberation and restoration for a vanquished community. Despite VO's protestations in its writing, and in personal communications, VO serves as a "love-producing" group, which in turn serves "as an authentic consequence of their actual liberation from vanquishment"; Espín continues: "but not as the imposed result of ecclesiastical orthodoxy or of a deculturized evangelism."[11] VO brings people out of a marginal state, offers them a supernatural encounter with the Holy Spirit, and serves as an alternative family to those who have been cut off from nearly every mainstream organization and structure that people hope will be that last stopgap before total marginalization.

The author was not in the best situation when she finally purchased the last set of audiotapes at the Victory Outreach bookstore. The denomination made it clear that they no longer wanted her to conduct research at their churches, and asked that she stop interviewing church members. Hence, in purchasing the tapes she had to slip into the bookstore unrecognized and buy the entire series of tapes for the Women's Convention, covering the previous year and the most current one. In these tapes are found stories that illustrate Godly love in a traditional Latino/a Pentecostal context. This is not exclusive to Latinos/as, and no case is being made that it should be; but it is being offered to demonstrate that Godly love looks different, acts out differently, and certainly is perceived differently in different groups. Groups will vary in the degree of emotional experience present in the expression of Godly love, their understanding of God's will, and other commonly studied dimensions of religious life.

On one tape, a leader of one of the women's rehabilitation homes tells a rapt audience that true sacrifice is required in order to be a member of their denomination,[12] because that is what God has done for them through

Jesus in delivering them from a variety of life-controlling social pathologies. So if God was and is willing to do that, then they should be able to do the same. As proof of her level of devotion, she tells the audience that out of a desire to live out the principles of radical forgiveness she believed God calls her to, she allowed a convicted sex offender to live in their home while he began to repair his life after getting out of prison. It seems that her trust in his rehabilitation was misguided, since within weeks of his moving in with her family, he attempted to molest their young daughter. He was asked to leave and was reported to the denominational leaders. The gasps on the tape are audible. How does a mother allow a child predator into their house? How does one begin to forgive that type of behavior? She concludes her story with an exhortation to her shocked audience that if God brought her another "ex-con," she would do the same thing. Whether one admires or scoffs at her pronouncement of faith, or thinks that this whole episode smacks of naïveté, it does demonstrate several things about how belief in God's transcendent ability to radically alter one's station in life then becomes a catalyst for social transformation. Many Latinas come from depressed economic backgrounds. Nearly all of them have little to no postsecondary education. Some have felt the brunt of prison life and have been beaten at the hands of authorities charged to rehabilitate them, even by men and women who have claimed to love them. In these settings, Latinas decide to enact a radical call for rehabilitation without regard to personal safety or the safety of their children—they risk everything to follow God's call to help those who have been cast off. Such expressions of perceived Godly love occur within the context of individual encounters rather than structural change.

In the case of Victory Outreach, it may be that what they lack in material goods to offer as sacrificial demonstrations of Godly love, they make up for with a radical approach to rehabilitation. The woman who engaged in this experiment did seem aware of the radical nature of her gesture, since she mentioned on the tape that she understood the risk she was taking and that she would never subject her children to such potential harm if it were not for the fact that she believed God told her to make this grand gesture. That the roommate betrayed this gesture was something that was not questioned on the tape, nor was it questioned outside the confines of the church.[13] Using the categories mentioned above (generational shifts, worldviews, and ethnicity), it will serve us well to return now to the theme of Godly love and Latino/a Pentecostalism in general.

Generationally, the Pentecostals represented in the Victory Outreach belong to a U.S.-born group that has, if current surveys are correct, made a decision to become Pentecostal (the survey also includes evangelicals), as opposed to a decision to not belong to any religious community at all.[14] The findings show that as Latino/a Pentecostals/evangelicals grow into their religious faith, by the third generation, just as other factors of assimilation begin to take hold—chiefly, the exclusive use of English—the decision-making over religion is more dichotomous. Either Latinos/as choose from a variety of fundamentalist/evangelical faiths or they choose to disconnect from religion entirely. What this may say about the Victory Outreach members is that they are part of a religious community that exhibits an intensity due to a number of factors; the primary one, gleaned from observation and interviews, is that church members believe they have been saved from a life of drug addiction, gangs, prostitution, and prison by this church and, by extension, by God. Over the course of 16 months of fieldwork visiting churches, rehabilitation homes, and countless meetings, church leaders were heard asking members to offer themselves up for many different kinds of volunteer opportunities because they had been "snatched up from the pit of hell" by the church and its ministries and, therefore, the church and God deserve their time, finances, and loyalties.

For a group like Victory Outreach, love, as an energy, as a constructive force that offers some hope for transformation, emanates from a divine person. Godly love is very much rooted in a premodern worldview. This perspective suggests to them that they are on earth to do battle with the same evil forces that have adversely affected them throughout their lives, as gangs, drugs, prison, prostitution, and violence have impacted them. Godly love in this sense will be marked by the miraculous, by risk taking, and by engendering a sense that Godly love is mediated by the group, and that through this group one can get a larger dose of Godly love; for VO this is often shorthand for a life filled with things that global Pentecostals have been used to for over a century: a life filled with consistent, transformative encounters with the miraculous.

When Latino/a Pentecostals embrace modernity and even postmodernity, they usually do so when a number of demographic changes occur. Moving out of the first-generation/immigrant group (which has tended to be the most premodern), attaining some greater facility with the English language, attaining a higher level of education (most Latino/a immigrants average a sixth-grade education), and generally becoming more assimilated into contemporary American society—all combine to begin a process by which Latino/a Pentecostals' worldviews change. The Trinity survey supports the influence of Americanization, going further than most recent surveys to note that with assimilation come two stark choices: rapidly assimilated Latinos/as tend either to choose conservative Protestantism or to become secularized. The author's own work interviewing immigrant first- and second-generation Pentecostals supports this conclusion, since by the second and third generations, Latino/a Pentecostals tend not to be fluent in Spanish any longer, tend to move away from traditional modes of theological education in Bible schools in favor of seminaries, and as contemporary observations attest, tend to focus on a more holistic approach to ministry, not abandoning supernatural faith, but seeking to diminish the hypersupernaturalism of their parents in favor a more vibrant social justice agenda. Admittedly, the evidence is anecdotal, but it does not seem to stray too far from what surveys other than Trinity's uncovered.

A recent study by sociologist Edwin Hernández, who researched Latino/a evangelicals/Pentecostals and their social/political attitudes, found a correlation between assimilation and a tendency toward adopting more liberal political and social stances. Whereas immigrant and first-generation respondents were the most conservative on all issues, second- and third-generation Latino/a evangelicals/pentecostals tended to answer questions on abortion and homosexuality the same way assimilated Latino/a Catholics did, meaning that they had more accepting and even tolerant views. Such could not be said of either immigrant Catholics or (non-Latino/a?) pentecostals.[15]

Reasons for this shift vary: theological training that moves from conservative Bible schools to more refined seminary education, the desire for children of immigrants to adopt American popular culture, and the attendant views about social issues that mark a more tolerant, less "old-fashioned" perspective like that of their parents. The acquisition of more education—not simply theological, but in general—creates a different social location, so that second- and third-generation Latino/a pentecostals work in different jobs, go to different schools, and have different concerns than their immigrant parents. Returning to the idea of generational shifts and the concepts of "love vs. law," what can be said is that part of the outgrowing often involves a class-based shift as well. Along with the desire to acquire a different set of theological tools with which to make sense of their world, many of these reformers become convinced that the only way to acquire knowledge beyond the often insular confines of a traditionalist Latino Pentecostal church is to leave the established coterie of *institutos bliblicos* and what has become a cottage industry, the Bible school located right on church premises. Seeking to put some critical theological and geographic distance between their parents and themselves, these reformers are usually the first to go to what is considered a "liberal" seminary or, worse yet for their traditionalist families, a secular university. Returning to the pentecostal church, armed with a completely different outlook on how to see God acting (or not) in the world, these reformers seek to carve out their own theological space, and that does include to what extent God loves, and what that love in turn means for the community. While these speculations require much more discussion at a later time, what is clear is that Latino/a pentecostals adopt differing worldviews based on a variety of factors, and that this makes the interplay between their faith and their ethnicity an important variable when discussing the larger questions this study poses.

Social justice groups, if they are found at all, will be among second- and third-generation, seminary-educated Pentecostals who have been able to explore and develop a fuller social mission to their ministry. This is not to suggest that all Latino/a Pentecostals who are English-dominant and highly Americanized become social justice advocates. A barrier to this group tends to be a wholesale adoption of a conservative evangelical social and political agenda that is part of the cultural fabric of many contemporary English-speaking Pentecostal churches. Latino/a Pentecostals fit right into the existing categories the study found, where most exemplars sequester themselves in familiar and comfortable ministries such as healing and deliverance. Our second case study serves to develop some of these themes further.

The Latino Leadership Circle (LLC) "is a cohort of emerging ministers dedicated to theological reflection, mutual support, and social justice. Among the deep convictions of the LLC is that we have voice representing emerging Latinas and Latinos in the body of Christ. We feel called to find a nexus of understanding within our bi-cultural and spiritual identity."[16] Though the statement is brief, it differs from the VO mission statement in some striking ways. First, the LLC statement says little about traditional notions of evangelism. It makes explicit that their work is about social justice, which, in studying literally dozens of Latino/a Pentecostal mission statements and talking to over two hundred ministers and laity during fifteen years, the author has heard articulated only once or twice. The other difference that makes LLC distinctive is its explicit embrace of its ethnic identity. Again, this has been rarely, if ever, mentioned in the author's explorations of Latino/a Pentecostals, though, as the author has argued elsewhere, and continues to hold, the affirmation of one's ethnic identity should be viewed as an implicit act of resistance to the dominant culture alongside explicit declarations of resistance to assimilation.[17]

Although not like the direct, visceral, supernatural Godly love of VO, LLC can be understood as a "love-producing" group, since its creation was and is overtly activist, and since its outreach is rooted in benefiting the most marginalized of the Latino/a community—undocumented persons. If one were to bring Sorokin's examples and discussion of love-producing groups into contemporary context, it would seem that organizations such as LLC fit his paradigm for groups that generate some form of altruistic love. Sorokin is less optimistic about a group's ability to produce strong, pure, and long-standing love, because it rarely if ever circulates beyond the limited membership of the group.[18] This is where Sorokin's ideas, and contemporary scholarly notions of Godly love, especially among historically marginalized groups, should be revisited.[19]

A problem occurs when trying to describe LLC's work in the narrative and often dramatic terms that have been used to describe VO's work. There simply is no comparison. LLC's advocacy is policy-oriented, rooted in academic discussions, and abstract. As such, it does not make for a good story, and neither does it offer the same level of personal engagement. The narrative quality that often infuses people's religious lives is missing, and therefore the common response when one thinks of Godly love—of a transcendent moment when the divine radically alters the way one's life is going, a narrative that Christianity has relied on for over two millennia—is absent. VO's success has not been rooted in abstract arguments over ethics, or in the treatment of the least of these, but in the narratives of the miraculous. If we are to truly say Godly love is experienced differently among different groups of people, then the results of that Godly love may be expressed differently and possibly arrived at without the dramatic effects of a Damascus-like encounter with God.[20] Let us look at the five dimensions of love mentioned by Sorokin in relation to both LLC and VO in an attempt to explore how contemporary contextualized analysis can help shape how we can see Godly love in many different places.[21]

No one can doubt that the radical sacrifice, risk-taking, and personal intervention evident in the work of VO demonstrates the intensity, extensivity, duration, and adequacy of a love-producing group that has lasted, has transformed lives, and, more importantly for VO, has brought hundreds of people into the ministry and even more into Pentecostalism. Problematic, for VO as well as Sorokin's definition, is the one example offered above. Such a case of radical restorative justice, if the ethnographic sources are correct, may have been simply someone's misapplied zeal.[22] In that case, the love may have been motivated by ego, thereby making it impure. In the case of LLC, the five dimensions of love pertain more to the group than to the individual.

Within LLC, there is intensity, extensivity, duration, and adequacy of love expressed in the following ways: LLC has committed itself to maintaining its pentecostal faith within the Latino/a community because it sees itself as a voice for both the marginalized and for disaffected Latino/a pentecostals, especially from the second and third generations, who do not see their desire to be advocates being realized in the first-generation, traditionalist

Pentecostal church. LLC is seeking to reach out as a place of safety for hosts of Pentecostals who have left churches due to the ridigity of traditionalist theology and its legalistic mores. Duration requires some time measurement, and LLC's short life (founded in 2005) makes it difficult to judge at present whether it is committed to long-term transformation. Purity and adequacy are, like the first three dimensions of love, subjective and often completely arbitrary. Who really knows whether the motives of an organization or, moreover, the motives of individuals in those organizations are pure or not completely driven by ego? In its short existence, LLC has advocated for immigrant rights, sought to extend Latino/a theological education, and served as a political and theological virtual salon for reformist-oriented Latino/a Pentecostals who would otherwise abandon the church for lack of a suitable outlet for their concerns. Communally, LLC is seeking to help the vanquished, the dispossessed, through means not often regarded as transcendent, unless one understands that the century-old marginalization of Latinos/as with regard to education, especially theological education, is slowly being eroded through efforts of groups like LLC. That group sees liberation as a holistic endeavor, encompassing the traditional notion of salvation through faith coupled with liberation through advocacy.

## Conclusion

Sorokin's section on love-producing groups ends on a pessimistic note, worth quoting for contextual purposes: ". . . besides, such love tends to circulate mainly or exclusively among the members of the group, often followed by the generation of hate and animosity toward some [community]."[23] After reading Sorokin's examples of individuals and groups that served as exemplars, it should be noted that a significant number of those people beyond their generation failed to influence anyone outside their community. That groups that once produced love will eventually turn on others and revert to the Hobbesian state of nature seems less the pessimistic conclusions of a sociologist than the cold-eyed reality every historian understands as the record of human encounters. For Latino/a pentecostals, if one were to view VO as exemplary of that rarest of events— a transcendent breaking in of the Divine so life-altering that it redirects the normative human desire for comfort, security, and achievement—one would be impressed to a point. When faced with the devastated parents of that young child, one might think again whether this radical acceptance of living with dangerous people to prove the radicalness of God's redemptive grace is actually God at all. Similarly, LLC's actions and intellectual pursuits are impressive to a point, but they feel cold when compared to the blood and tears of what VO ministers face on a regular basis. While there is admiration for LCC's intellectual acumen, there is no sense among many Latino/a pentecostals, particularly traditionalists, that LLC is "preaching the gospel." For that, LLC will continue to suffer the almost inbred class bias many pentecostals harbor toward intellectuals. LLC's leadership was trained at places like Drew University and Princeton Theological Seminary, and for that very reason, their brand of liberation, of bringing the transcendent love of God to a vanquished people, will not be viewed in the same light as VO's. Renewing of one's mind may be a command of God, but it is not a reliable barometer of Godly love, at least not for many Latino/a pentecostals.

## Notes

1. This discussion has been explored more deeply in Lee and Poloma's work on Godly love. The authors see "love vs. law" as one of the tensions that become part of studying Godly love, and to some extent the authors find that with regard to how people view God, whether they see God as a rule giver or a grace provider, is shaped in some part simply by growing up. The authors assert that people sometimes outgrow their initial religion's doctrines, which they learned as children or young adults, because their experiences with God have changed. See Matthew T. Lee and Margaret M. Poloma, *A Sociological Study of the Great Commandment in Pentecostalism: The Practice of Godly Love as Benevolent Service* (Lewiston, NY: Edwin Mellen Press, 2009), 115.

2. Orlando Espín, *The Faith of the People* (Maryknoll: Orbis Books, 1997), 142.

3. The historiography of Latino/a Pentecostalism is not extensive; it is fair to say that noting the following sources will cover just about all roughly one hundred years of the movement. For information on the Latino/a Oneness churches, see Daniel Ramiréz's article "Borderlands Praxis: The Immigrant Experience in Latino Pentecostal Churches," *Journal of the American Academy of Religion* 67:3 (1999): 573–96. This entire issue has some of the first scholarly work on Latino/a Pentecostalism, including helpful works by Luis León and Gastón Espinosa. For a broader look at the history of Latino/a Pentecostalism, see Arlene Sánchez Walsh, *Latino Pentecostal Identity: Evangelical Faith, Self, and Society* (New York: Columbia University Press, 2003).

4. Here note that people's faith narratives, their media productions, fieldwork, and other ethnographic data are all subject to active repositioning by the researcher, so much so that it is appropriate to call me the coauthor of these narratives and ethnographic data. As such, as a historian, I have adopted the social science methodology advocated by sociologist Kathy Charmaz, that all grounded theory would best be called constructivist. For further explanation of some of her key ideas, see Kathy Charmaz and Richard Mitchell, "The Myth of Silent Authorship: Self, Substance, and Style in Ethnographic Writing," *Symbolic Interaction* 19:4 (1996): 285–302.

5. Juhem Navarro-Rivera, Barry A. Kosmin, and Ariela Keysar, "U.S. Latino Religious Identification 1990–2008: Growth, Diversity and Transformation," Trinity College, 2008. The survey findings help make the case that many scholars have known anecdotally for quite awhile, that Latinos/as who choose Protestantism tend to choose the most conservative denominations and tend to hold traditionalist views on most theological and social issues.

6. Ibid., executive summary.

7. Pitirim A. Sorokin, *The Ways and Power of Love: Types, Factors, and Techniques of Moral Transformation* (1954; Philadelphia: Templeton Foundation Press, 2002), 39.

8. These typologies, traditionalist and reformer, describe Latino/a Pentecostals and social action. Briefly, traditionalists hold to premodern worldviews, are often biblical literalists, and see themselves as holding the line against the continual erosion of traditional values, religious freedom, and morality. Reformers are Pentecostals who exhibit some loyalty to the brand, Pentecostal, but are trying to adopt a more holistic approach to things such as social justice activism and higher education. See Sánchez Walsh, "Christology from a Latino/a Perspective: Pentecostalism," in *Jesus in the Hispanic Community: Images of Christ from Theology to Popular Religion*, ed. Harold J. Recinos and Hugo Magallanes (New York: Westminster John Knox Press, 2009), 92–104.

9. From the Victory Outreach website, www.victoryoutreach.org.

10. See chapters 3–4 on Victory Outreach in Sánchez Walsh, *Latino Pentecostal Identity*.

11. Espín, *Faith of the People*, 24.

12. Rehabilitation homes are the primary way that VO operates its ministry. Pastors, all men, mostly married, are expected to live with their residents; eat, pray, and work alongside them; and then use that time together to begin the process of conversion.

13. Victory Outreach has historically kept a very tight rein on the operation of its rehabilitation homes and ministries. When a similar incident made local headlines in the first years of this century, the church immediately sought to distance itself from potential lawsuits and rested on the fact that they were doing the best to rehabilitate the most recidivist of ex-cons and sexual predators.

14. Trinity survey, 4–5.

15. Edwin Hernandez et al., "Faith and Values in Action: Religion, Politics, and Social Attitudes among U.S. Latinos/as," Institute for Latino Studies, University of Notre Dame, November 2007, 20–21.

16. From the information section of the Latino Leadership Circle's website, http://latinoleadershipcircle.typepad.com/about.html (accessed 09/12/10).

17. See the chapter on Victory Outreach in Sánchez Walsh, *Latino Pentecostal Identity*.

18. Sorokin, *Ways and Power of Love*, 39.

19. Arguably, civil rights and religious groups such as the Southern Christian Leadership Conference, the Student Non-Violent Coordinating Committee, and the Catholic Worker Movement are candidates for love-producing groups.

In fact, their collective actions have been substantial and raise questions about Sorokin's limited view that such groups are unlikely to produce "love" beyond their narrowly defined in-group.

20. Here, the author is indebted to the brilliant work of philosopher Mark Johnson, who seeks to recapture notions of God from the extreme desire of many Christians to see supernaturalism as its own religion—a form of idolatry, notes Johnson. If a more naturalistic definition can be applied to how God works, then Godly love can and should be allowed to accommodate that more naturalistic definition. See Mark Johnson, *Saving God: Religion after Idolatry* (Princeton, NJ: Princeton University Press, 2009).

21. Sorokin, *Ways and Power of Love*, ch. 15.

22. In 2004, a four-year-old girl was suffocated, allegedly by a female resident of a rehabilitation house run by pastors in Southern California. The pastors lived at the rehabilitation home and reported no problems with exposing their four-year-old to the oft-changing residents of the home. This tragedy resulted in no conclusive verdict of guilt or innocence, and the pastors left the ministry a year later. "Facing Tragedy, Pastors Put Their Faith on Hold," Clair Luna, *Los Angeles Times* (July 18, 2005).

23. Sorokin, *Ways and Power of Love*, 39.

# CONCLUSION

## AMOS YONG

This volume attempts to break new ground in two interrelated ways. Thematically, its focus has been on the new and emerging field of Godly love. Methodologically, it has sought to capture some of the energy devoted to bridging theology and the social sciences in the study of Godly love. The following set of concluding reflections focuses particularly on the questions related to the latter methodological issue by working backward through the two parts of essays in the book. We begin with an overview of the achievements of the methodological proposals by the social scientists (part II) and then step back to identify and critically assess the implications of the theological proposals (in part I) for the study of Godly love. The third section highlights additional methodological challenges confronting the study of Godly love, yet suggests how, from one theological perspective, this research program can proceed with theology and science as equal partners.

### The Study of Godly Love—Retrospect and Prospect

Many of the studies of Godly love have emanated from work funded through the Institute for Research on Unlimited Love (IRUL), established in 2001 by Stephen Post.[1] When collaborative discussions between him and sociologist Margaret Poloma began, Poloma's years of personal involvement in and research on pentecostal and charismatic renewal movements immediately registered the question, How might the study of Godly love be enhanced through a more specific focus on such movements, which

constitute an ever-increasing portion of the Christian religion, particularly as it has expanded across the global South during the last generation?
In further collaboration with another sociologist, Matthew Lee, funding
was obtained to explore precisely this question.[2]

As sociologists, Poloma and Lee naturally turned to the social sciences
in developing the methodological framework for this study. At the same
time, Poloma has long wrestled with methodological issues as a sociologist
and as a relative "insider" to the movements she has studied.[3] The result
has been the development, articulation, and prosecution of a social-scientific research program that has sought to include, rather than exclude,
the theological disciplines. If Ralph Hood, in his chapter in this volume,
documents the more or less recent reemergence of a "minority report,"
that represented by methodological agnosticism, amid the methodological atheism predominant in social-scientific research on religious matters,
Poloma has sought to formulate an interdisciplinary approach to the study
of pentecostal and charismatic movements that involves rather than toler-
ates, ignores, or rejects emic religious perspectives and the contributions
of theology. Needless to say, such a melding of theological and social-
scientific perspectives is fraught with challenges, especially in light of the
chasm between these two fields of inquiry practically since the emergence
of the modern university.

Following a number of recognized theorists, then, Poloma and Lee have
proposed an integrationist approach to sociology and theology for the
Godly love project.[4] By this, they mean to view the two disciplines as allies,
mutually interpenetrating and cross-fertilizing each other. As sociologists,
they recognize that their "home base" is in the social sciences, but they
have "endeavored to include theology as an equal partner," and to do so,
they have situated their research project "within the work of a particular
theological tradition," that of pentecostalism broadly defined, and attempted to pay attention to the self-understandings of the people they are
studying (through interviews and other means).[5] More than that, Poloma
and Lee have also tried to include, alongside the first-order testimonies recorded in the interview, second-order theological reflections such as those
provided by pentecostal theologians.[6] Their goal has been to produce a
grounded sociological theory that is deeply informed by pentecostal theological reflection—both first- and second-order accounts. Poloma and
Lee are to be commended for their efforts as sociologists to take theology
seriously across the spectrum of their research project: (a) locating their
research within a specific theological tradition; (b) inviting perspectives
from within that tradition to inform their theoretical frameworks; and
(c) allowing, even privileging, perspectives from within that tradition to

interpret themselves as well as inform project analyses and findings. At least part of the rationale has been that any social scientific study of Godly love must at least be sensitive to the divine variables identified in the label of what is being studied. The challenge has always been, of course, how to isolate and then test theological variables in scientific studies.

By and large, the authors in part II of this volume exploit the openings charted by Poloma and Lee to involve theological considerations in the social-scientific study of Godly love. Following Poloma and Lee's lead, Julie Exline suggests possible modes of integrating theology and psychology in the study of Godly love. Two overarching approaches are presented. Qualitatively, self-perceptions can be registered and then studied about how participants' perceptions of their encounter with Godly love have made a difference in their expressions of benevolent service to others. Here, it is the perceived effects of spiritual or religious experience that are being studied, regardless of what the researcher thinks about the participants' theological beliefs. A second step might be to develop some quantitative experimental measures that correlate spiritual or religious experiences and the beliefs about them with behavioral outcomes that are benevolent (socially healthy or edifying). Such a methodology would illuminate the effects of Godly love as manifest in the lives of believers.

Mark Cartledge adopts an approach similar to that of a practical theologian, albeit deploying in his chapter socialization theory and empirical survey methods, rather than the psychological sciences. His question, bluntly put, is how believers are socialized into the experience and expression of Godly love. The use of surveys as a form of self-report allows the registration of certain statistically significant variables that "combine to suggest possible explanations for the acquisition and sustenance of benevolence."[7] At the same time, such an approach does not produce definitive causal connections between key factors and benevolence: inevitably, the role of personal agency escapes quantifiable analysis. Cartledge's expert handling of these matters reflects the fact that, in the European context, the adoption of empirical approaches for theology has been standard for some time.[8] This Godly love project represents, at least in part, an attempt to engage an interdisciplinary conversation that brings the empirical methods of social scientists into dialogue with the theological methods of religious scholarship.

The socialization considerations highlighted in Cartledge's study flow from but yet also lead back to the grounded theoretical framework of this project on Godly love in the pentecostal and charismatic traditions. Arlene Sánchez Walsh's chapter in this book deepens such a theoretical model precisely by providing a case study of variables introduced by race/ethnicity (in her study of Latino/a pentecostalism) and generational differences (between first-generation immigrants and second- or later-generation who have assimilated into the American mainstream). As a religious historian, Sánchez Walsh is engaged less with the actual use of scientific measures or instruments than with documenting general historical trends that could generate hypotheses to be tested. Thus, emerging from her chapter, for instance, might be the following research questions. First, what specific theological views are correlated to either minimal benevolent action or with only certain types of benevolent undertakings? Second, what specific ethnic or cultural factors are correlatable with the various kinds of benevolent service? Last but not least, is there a strong or weak correlation between generational differences and various forms of benevolence, and what other variables might be involved?

Sánchez Walsh's chapter cautions anyone against rushing to "scientifically legitimated" conclusions based only on limited population samples. If in fact pentecostalism and the charismatic renewal are prevalent forms of global Christianity, then the kinds of factors introduced by her study suggest that other racial, ethnic, or cultural groups will focus attention on other variables. Let us look in three related directions. First, if generational shifts are indeed important, then might there be a way for studying Godly love historically? From a pentecostal point of view, this is not a moot question, especially not when it is documented that for the first generation of pentecostals at Azusa Street, the baptism in the Holy Spirit was as much a baptism into divine love as it was an experience of empowerment for witness.[9] While it may not be possible now to conduct straightforward social-scientific assessments of this group of early modern pentecostals, there may be sociohistorical cues here that could inform the ongoing study of Godly love. In other words, if it is possible to trace out benevolent behaviors in the lives of those for whom baptism in the Spirit was an experience of God's love, then that invites questions for other contemporary research projects such as: (1) To what degree have contemporary pentecostal and charismatic traditions retained such an understanding of Spirit baptism (and why or why not)? and (2) What has been the impact of this theological understanding on the practice of benevolent service in present-day pentecostal and charismatic movements?

The next section will return to explore further the use of historical methods in the study of Godly love. For the moment, however, Sánchez Walsh's case study is helpful for making a few observations about the tradition of African American holiness pentecostalism.[10] In the Afropentecostal tradition, the baptism in the Spirit understood as a baptism of divine love has long been correlated with a theological vision for social justice and racial reconciliation. In this respect, Godly love involves benevolent activities at the interpersonal level, particularly those that reach across the fundamental divides (of race and class) between human beings. In addition, however, Godly love involves social ministries directed to the alleviation of poverty or hardship and, in some cases, motivates the quest of social transformation and the enactment of social justice. These trajectories arguably represent expressions of the baptism of the Spirit as empowering interpersonal acts of love and kindness and the social witness of compassionate justice.

If an adequate grounded theory requires us to be attentive to the particularities of group identities and dynamics, then the next level of analysis requires us to dig down even deeper to assessments of individuals that constitute groups. Perhaps unexpectedly, of the essayists in part II, it is the sociologist Margaret Poloma who helps us to see how individual biographies can be helpful in the social-scientific study of Godly love. Recall that Poloma not only utilizes case studies—i.e., of Blood n Fire, outlining the rise and fall of this Atlanta-based ministry and what it has to teach us about the emergence, flourishing (at least for a time), and then disintegration of divinely motivated benevolence; and of the Assemblies of God, summarizing how the various forms of love experiences and expressions shape benevolent activity—but she also devotes a substantial portion of the latter half of her discussion to one exemplar of Godly love, Mother Teresa. The link between these organizational case studies and the narrative analysis is the role that ecclesiastical sanctions, or interdicts, played in the outworking of benevolent service. If ecclesial norms are more fluid in denominational movements like the Assemblies of God and if they were unevenly enforced in organizations like Blood n Fire, then their palpable presence especially in the global Catholicism present during the formative years of Mother Teresa's life shaped the "law of love" that motivated her ministry to the poorest of the poor in postcolonial India. While there are many interesting lines of thought opened up by Poloma's analysis, the result for our methodological purposes is her sketching and exemplifying a sociohistorical approach to the study of Godly love, one in which a grounded theoretical model is sensitive both to the particularities of a single narrative and to philosophical, religious, and theological variables underpinning the lives of individual exemplars.

The foregoing motivates a more global research project, one that is sensitive to the diversity of facts on the ground that inform human benevolence in general and those in pentecostal and charismatic movements in particular. Thus, Donald Miller and Tetsunao Yamamori have recently surveyed social engagement within these movements across the global

South.[11] The grounded theoretical framework proposed by Poloma and Lee, elaborated on by Sánchez Walsh, and then extended by Exline and Cartledge invites further social-scientific analyses of these developments. What we need to know is not only that these things are happening, but what the major variables are that correlate with expressions of Godly love, how benevolent actors are being socialized, motivated, and formed, and what the theological ideas are that can be linked with munificence across the global pentecostal community.

## Researching Godly Love—Theological Contributions?

We now turn to the chapters authored by theologians in part I, to ask how they might also contribute to the study of Godly love. By and large, these theological reflections have helped us to understand the nature of Godly love more than they focused on how theology informs research on Godly love. The exception is Tom Oord's chapter, to which we will return at the end of this section.

As should be clear by now, an important contribution that theology has made to the study of Godly love is the generation of hypotheses to be tested. Once these hypotheses have been tested, theology should also be involved in interpreting the meaning of empirical results and clarifying their relevance for specific religious groups. Michael McClymond's chapter does (at least) three things along these lines. First, it generates a theory of Godly love in dialogue with one of the most important American philosophers and theologians, Jonathan Edwards. Second, it allows us to compare how cognitive understandings of divine love (Edwards's theology) translate into benevolent and altruistic ways of life (here in the life of David Brainerd, a missionary colleague to Edwards). Third, it allows us to interpret the relevance of Edwards's ideas, as manifest in Brainerd's life, in a contemporary context (as applied to the ministry of an exemplary Pentecostal missionary to Africa, Heidi Baker). While McClymond's work has much to say to those considering afresh theologies of Godly love today, these methodological implications for the Godly love project are just as important for this nascent field of inquiry.

If McClymond inserts the historical ideas of Edwards into the discussion, Peter Althouse's and Paul Alexander's chapters identify a number of variables that invite social-scientific investigation. The former, a systematic theologian, presents a normative theological thesis, arguing that the Christian doctrine of kenotic incarnation provides a model of divine self-giving and self-emptying that simultaneously exemplifies how Christian believers, those who follow in the footsteps of the incarnate Son of God, should live. For Althouse, such a theological narrative inspires self-sacrificial benevolence on the one hand even as it provides a norm to evaluate putative altruistic activity: authentic altruism is discerned whenever people are motivated to empty themselves for no other acknowledged reason than that they wish to benefit others. However, researchers might wonder how Althouse's theological norm might inform social-scientific studies of Godly love. Perhaps it is possible to measure how groups exposed to the narrative of kenotic incarnation might respond altruistically to the needs of others. Alternatively, perhaps there is a statistical correlation between altruistic exemplars and certain theological beliefs regarding the self-sacrificial life of the Son of God.

Theological ethicist Paul Alexander also suggests a theologically normative portrait of Godly love, one derived from the life of Jesus as portrayed in the Gospel narratives. Writing as a Christian ethicist, Alexander observes a nonviolent Jesus and proposes that Godly love should be characterized by nonviolence. But how does this norm function? Does it mean that any act of violence reflects an absence of Godly love, or, on the other side, all acts of nonviolence reflect the presence of Godly love? Perhaps exemplars of Godly love will more consistently embrace a nonviolent worldview and way of life? Or is the suggestion instead that communities that are committed to nonviolence will inevitably reflect Godly love in greater purity, adequacy, duration, intensity, and extensivity than those that have not eschewed violence?

Stephen Post's chapter that opens this part of the book urges readers to carefully consider the importance of finding ways to nurture Godly love in a turbulent world. For purposes of studying Godly love, however, his comments at the end of his essay on how religious rituals might enhance Godly love are tantalizingly brief. What we need, Post suggests, are for the religions to "exhort, model, celebrate, and reward such [benevolent] actions of doing 'unto others,'"[12] since this itself will generate Godly love in unprecedented ways. Those looking to multiply human benevolence need to creatively implement this proposal. Researchers and others wanting to study Godly love, however, will ask at least some of the following questions: are there religious rituals that foster benevolent mentalities and behaviors, and if so, what are they and how do they accomplish these goals? Might community-formation activities within religious tradition foster the kind of orientations that enhance the service of others? Can we establish concrete statistical correlations between certain religious prayers—Post's example is the line from the Lord's Prayer "Give *us* this day *our* daily bread"[13]—and altruistic behavior?

Along related but distinct lines, Poloma and Lee have also deployed sociological ideas like interaction rituals, social capital, and bridge networks in their research on pentecostal Godly love.[14] Sociological research has helpfully illuminated the social processes through which religious realities are encountered, mediated, and effective in the lives of religious devotees. Rituals provide the core social (in theological terms: liturgical) contexts of religious practice, while social networks provide the broader communal (in theological terms: ecclesial) spaces for religious interaction. Put in generic sociological terms, religious devotees perceive the activity of the deity or transcendent realities in their lives when these are engaged in religious rites and social communities. Translated into the Godly love categories that Poloma and Lee have provided, Godly love in the lives of pentecostals is sociologically (i.e., liturgically and ecclesiastically) mediated and hence also sociologically (i.e., liturgically and ecclesiastically) measurable. Put in their own words, pentecostal expressions of Godly love are "produced, stored, and transmitted via social interactions that occur in a network that includes a perceived God and other people."[15]

From a pentecostal theological perspective, however, such sociological insights have important implications. For starters, the Godly love project challenges stereotypical pentecostal understandings of the Holy Spirit limited to its presence and activity in individual lives. Pneumatological categories like regeneration, sanctification, and Spirit baptism bequeathed by the broader Christian theological tradition have been reappropriated by pentecostals in individualistic ways. Thus, the concern for the work of the Spirit has inevitably, in pentecostal circles, been conceptualized in terms of what is done in the private hearts and lives of followers of Jesus. The Godly love research project, however, insists that we look at the social and communal realities within which pentecostals encounter the Spirit in order to more comprehensively identify the scope of the Spirit's work.

Thomas Oord's chapter presents the most sustained theological and philosophical rationale for how to scientifically measure Godly love. More precisely, Oord presents a metaphysical hypothesis—essential freewill theism, he calls it—that enables scientific measurement of divine action. If he is successful, he suggests, science would be able to affirm the effectiveness of God's action in any situation; translated into the Godly love idiom, if Oord were right, science would be able to discern the effectiveness of Godly love. How does Oord think science can ascertain such divine efficacy?

First, Oord's essential freewill theism assumes the following (much of it taken verbatim from Oord's chapter): (1) that God does not act coercively, but that God is always active in every event; (2) divine causation oscillates in the sense that it is dependent upon creaturely response; (3) divine causation is diverse, correlated to creaturely forms, capacities, situations, choices, and actions; and (4) love always characterizes God's causal influence. From this, Oord presents his scientific hypothesis: "divine causation is most evident in those events or things that express love, in the sense of promoting overall well-being. Divine causation is less effective, and therefore God's causal efficacy is less observable, in those events or things that undermine overall well-being."[16]

Oord's proposal basically says that behaviors or outcomes that foster love—overall well-being, in his terms—are indicative of the efficacy of divine action or divine loving. But this is a bit misleading and confusing, since such measurements really identify the degree to which creatures are responding to or participating in divine action/love. Oord anticipates this objection but responds that in cases where overall well-being is fostered, we can infer that the creaturely roles in fostering such well-being invite inference that in such cases, God's action is more effective than in cases where overall well-being is not fostered. Yet such an inference adds nothing to the theological assumptions already in place, since, as Oord already concedes, God's action "always runs at full throttle."[17] Thus, to say that divine action is more effective in cases where overall well-being is fostered does not explain how that happens; rather, what does the explanatory work here is that free creatures have responded differently. What causes such creatures to respond in ways that have increased overall well-being? Oord's theological answer is: divine activity. But this is circular if, as it appears to be in his project, the goal is to identify the efficacy of such activity to begin with. Hence, to put it bluntly, what makes the difference in overall well-being is not that God has acted more efficiently but that creatures have cooperated with God. In that case, the title of Oord's chapter is more accurate with regard to what his method accomplishes—which is the testing not of divine but creaturely action and love.

To be clear, there are no problems with Oord's theological or metaphysical assumptions. Everyone is entitled to their theological commitments. What is questionable concerns Oord's claim that there is a scientific means of testing the effectiveness of divine action, since his research program inquires into creaturely activities instead. If the foregoing is correct, then the question arises, Is theology, particularly our theological understandings of Godly love, constrained by social-scientific methods and findings? The simple answer is yes and no: yes in any project to bring theology and the sciences together in mutual inquiry, but no in the sense that the sciences, including the social sciences, do not exhaust the means of inquiry available to theologians. This final part of our reflections probes more deeply into the challenges revolving around such a dual response.

## Integrating Theology and the Social Sciences—
## A Pneumato-Theological Proposal

Our discussion so far might confirm the worst fears of those who wish to free theology from the grip of the secular and scientific—or at the worst, scientistic—imagination. John Milbank and the radical orthodoxy theologians, for example, have argued that theology as academic discourse has sold its soul to modernity and, in doing so, subordinated its theological voice and perspective to other disciplines in the wider academy.[18] There are two related claims being made here: first, that theology itself has been (and is or should be) essentially a meta-discourse or meta-narrative and that to reconsider theology otherwise already compromises the theological task; and second, that one of the ways modernity has struck the Achilles' heel of theology is to convince theologians that theirs is only one alongside many other valid and viable perspectives in the wider academy. This means that as soon as theology begins to view any of the other disciplines—e.g., the social sciences in general or even sociology in particular—as on equal footing with itself, then and there already theology has become incapacitated and impotent to make theological claims. This is because, for Milbank et al., the categories of sociology, for example (we focus on sociology since that has been central to the initial stage of the Godly love project), derive from an Enlightenment framework of secular reason and therefore are at best unconcerned with and at worst completely antithetical to a theologically informed worldview. In short, any effort to have theology and sociology as equal conversational partners already undermines the theological perspective.

We seem to be here at an impasse, yet perhaps not. While Milbank would be unwilling to consider sociology to be an equal dialogue partner with theology, the Godly love project as understood by most if not all of the contributors has taken extensive measures to minimize the effects of what Milbank considers "secular reason"—i.e., reductionism and scientism—in their social-scientific work. At the same time, so long as Godly love researchers view sociology and theology as equal dialogue partners in the quest for an integrated perspective on their topic, that still may be insufficient for Milbank and those in his train.

Pentecostal theologians, however, are looking for ways not to have to pick between radical orthodoxy and the Godly love project, even if such a path, if demarcatable, may not be convincing to both sides. In any case, the following still attempts to mediate this conversation and thus proposes a "pneumatological assist" to add into the mix. Of course, this proposal is theological, which represents the perspective and training of its author (who does not have an academic background in sociology, although he has an appreciation for what sociology can contribute to the work of theologians). In brief, the proposal is based on a pneumatological imagination informed by the central pentecostal narrative of Acts 2, in which the many tongues or languages each retained their particularity yet were capable of declaring the wondrous works of God.[19] By analogy, the many academic and scientific disciplines are capable of providing perspective on the world that God has created.[20]

The hope is that radical orthodoxy members and other kindred perspectives will be able to appreciate such a forthrightly theological stance. This is still a specifically pneumato-theological proposal wherein the wider academy and other scientific disciplines are accounted for within a theological framework. At the same time, there is a desire to recognize and honor the particular voices represented within the academy and the sciences, to listen carefully to what they have to propose, and to be willing to learn from (i.e., revise perspectives because of) them if necessary.[21] Hence, pneumatological theology not only allows but actually requires theologians to listen to (social) scientists and to treat them as equal partners, in turn, in an ongoing quest for truth.

Methodologically, there is probably no way to avoid posturing on both sides of the theology–sociology fence. Perhaps the best theologians can do is to treat their social-scientific colleagues as equals, while appreciating their extending to theologians the same courtesy. Social scientists have their various reasons for doing so, while theologians have their (specifically, pneumatological) rationale. With regard to the Godly love project that is focused on pentecostalism, the theological account provided, drawn as it is from the heart of the Day of Pentecost narrative, is arguably already internal to the framework of inquiry. Hence, there can be optimism that the "many tongues of Pentecost" metaphor not only invites the integration of theology and the various human and social sciences but also sensitizes researchers to the pluralism on the ground of any quest to study Godly love.

To be convincing, however, methodological implications of the Day of Pentecost metaphor have to be illuminating for the study of Godly love. The remainder of this conclusion sketches both how pentecostal theology can help to develop a grounded theory of Godly love on the one hand (this is pneumatology/theology's contribution to the social sciences) and how social science can inform pentecostal theological reflections on the other hand (this is the social-scientific contribution to theology).

So first, if theology and the social sciences are to be brought into mutual conversation, how might the theological disciplines inform social-scientific research on Godly love? More specifically, how might Pentecostal theology inform such a research project? As already seen, Poloma and Lee did consult the work of pentecostal theologians, and that is important. Beyond consulting the "pentecostal elite," however, the Godly love researchers have also made valiant efforts to thematize more intentionally the theological views of the pentecostals and charismatics they are studying and to utilize such perspectives in their construction of hypotheses to be tested.[22] This is important, since it is the rank-and-file whose benevolent activities are making a difference in the world.

In saying this, the desire is to build on the pluralism identified earlier in our discussion of how any grounded theoretical approach to Godly love in the global renewal movement needed to be attentive to the variety of expressions across racial, ethnic, class, and other lines. Here, though, the goal is to highlight also the diversity of fundamental pneumato-theological convictions and ideas informed by the Pentecost narrative. Put otherwise, perhaps the diversity of variables correlated with the pluralism of pentecostalisms expresses not only the many tongues of Pentecost but also a spectrum or range of views about the Holy Spirit.[23] For example, will Oneness understandings of the Spirit reject the communitarian and even social aspects of trinitarian theology so that, perhaps, Oneness pentecostals would exemplify Godly love in less communally and socially definable ways?[24] This in turn raises questions about the kinds of ministries thought to be prominent in pentecostal circles and from which the exemplars have been selected. As a counterhypothesis, perhaps Oneness adherents are more inclined to emphasize the *Holy* Spirit, so that their ministries might reveal Godly love as active in the process of intracommunity (i.e., intra-Oneness) building—otherwise known theologically as sanctification—rather than the kinds of ministries studied by the Godly love project.

In short, the preceding intends to push the study of Godly love in pentecostal and charismatic movements and traditions to identify their "objects" of study using not only phenomenological measures but also theological markers. What kinds of distinctive theological views are embraced by renewalists around the world, and how, if at all, do such beliefs and ideas motivate benevolent behavior in what environments or what forms?[25] Only by asking and then pursuing these kinds of questions will we be able to distinguish benevolent activity in its pentecostal and charismatic modality from generic Christian benevolence.

But second, if theology and the social sciences are to be equal dialogue partners according to the Day of Pentecost metaphor, then not only should theology inform social-scientific work, but the social sciences should also be able to influence theological reflection. How might this occur? In the end, the social sciences will impact the theological academy to the degree that theologians are convinced that social-scientific results are relevant for their work. My claim is that as social-scientific methods illuminate the diversity of theological views on the ground, not only in terms of content but also in terms of function, theologians will not be able to avoid the theological implications.

The following traces out a hypothetical scenario about how this might unfold. We have already seen how Althouse and Alexander, for example, both provide normative theological guidelines for the recognition of Godly love. What is being proposed in addition is that more specific theological criteria should also be enacted, particularly among pentecostal and charismatic groups or exemplars. One of the results of following out both research trajectories is that researchers will gradually be able to identify both quantitative and qualitative differences between pentecostal/charismatic and non-pentecostal/charismatic manifestations of Godly love. The distinguishing marks may be related to the relatively unique spiritual (or pneumatic) experiences that mark pentecostal and charismatic piety. Thus, any grounded theory of Godly love among pentecostals should thematize the work of the Spirit so that it is registered in quantitative and qualitative ways. Then, comparative data can be drawn from nonpentecostal groups to measure the difference that specific encounters with the Holy Spirit, as well as their concomitant theologies (or pneumatologies), make.

It is also possible, however, to gain more than just these minimal theological results. Social-scientific research might in the long run be able to correlate specific beliefs with benevolence and malevolence. Those that foster the former in individuals, groups, and whole movements are harbingers of the reign of God in all its goodness, beauty, and truth. Kenotic self-emptying and nonviolence might indeed be inviolable norms that anticipate the kingdom of God.[26] But surely there are other norms as well, even emerging ones amidst the lives of pentecostals and charismatics around the world.

In short, if research on Godly love among the fastest-growing group of Christians in the world is to advance, perhaps more pneumatologically specific variables need to be identified, and perhaps a pneumatological hypothesis about the specific role of the Holy Spirit in the lives of pentecostal exemplars of Godly love can be presented and tested. In the process, such a pneumatologically driven research project may inform the grounded theory, and it may not be too outrageous to propose that such a theory would eventually lead pentecostal, charismatic, and even other Christian theologians to rethink their pneumatology (not to mention their theology of Godly love).

## Conclusion

For scholars of religion in general and for those interested in pente-costals and charismatics in particular, the research program outlined in this volume should be a priority. If in fact there is a God and if in fact such a God is essentially love, then there is much at stake in how such "love energy" is mediated to and effective in the world. In a real sense, there may be no more important set of questions for the human species than those about how to identify such love and how to foster it. And if the social sciences might provide us with some windows into this reality, then the dialogue between theology and the social sciences needs to be engaged more intentionally, rigorously, and strategically. Both sides can only benefit from such a mutual project, and human creatures just might become more adept through this process of inquiry about how to serve as better conduits for the manifestation of divine love in the world.[27]

## Notes

1. Post has authored and edited many volumes related to Godly love; the one that most explicitly unfolds the aims of IRUL is his *Unlimited Love: Altruism, Compassion, and Service* (Philadelphia and London: Templeton Foundation Press, 2003).

2. Although this initial phase of the Godly love project has focused on pentecostalism, broadly defined to include charismatic and other related movements, there is every intention to pursue the study of this phenomenon with regard to other Christian and even non-Christian groups, funding permitting. In the more theological reflections at the end of this conclusion, more comments address specifically some of the issues related to pentecostalism, in part because a few of the chapters in this volume have focused on pentecostal themes but also, more importantly, because of the author's own overall pentecostal theological orientation. At the same time, the implications of this interdisciplinary study are certainly not confined to the pentecostal tradition but have wider relevance for religious movements in general.

3. There are probing self-critical reflections on method in almost all of Poloma's books. See an overview of her thinking about these matters in her "Is Integrating Spirit and Sociology Possible? A Postmodern Research Odyssey," in *Science and the Spirit: A Pentecostal Engagement with the Sciences*, ed. Amos Yong and James K. A. Smith (Bloomington: Indiana University Press, 2010), 174–91. For further discussion of Poloma's work and methodology, see Yong, *The Spirit of Creation: Divine Action and the God–World Relationship in the Pentecostal–Charismatic Imagination* (Grand Rapids, MI: William B. Eerdmans, 2011), ch. 2.

4. See Matthew T. Lee and Margaret M. Poloma, *A Sociological Study of the Great Commandment in Pentecostalism: The Practice of Godly Love as Benevolent Service* (Lewiston, NY: Edwin Mellen Press, 2009), esp. ch. 1.

5. Lee and Poloma, *A Sociological Study of the Great Commandment in Pentecostalism*, 15.

6. Drawing especially from Frank D. Macchia, *Baptized in the Spirit: A Global Pentecostal Theology* (Grand Rapids, MI: Zondervan, 2006).

7. See chapter 9 in this book.

8. As a self-identifying "empirical theologian" in the charismatic tradition, Cartledge has been one of the leaders from across the Atlantic in the social-scientific study of pentecostalism—e.g., Mark J. Cartledge, *Charismatic Glossolalia: An Empirical-Theological Study* (Burlington, VT: Ashgate, 2002), *Practical Theology: Charismatic and Empirical Perspectives* (Waynesboro, GA: Paternoster Press, 2006), *Testimony in the Spirit: Rescripting Ordinary Pentecostal Theology* (Burlington, VT: Ashgate, 2010), and an edited volume, *Speaking in Tongues: Multidisciplinary Perspectives* (Waynesboro, GA: Paternoster Press, 2006).

9. This thesis is convincingly demonstrated by Kimberly Ervin Alexander, "Boundless Love Divine: A Re-evaluation of Early Understandings of the Experience of Spirit Baptism," in *Passover, Pentecost, and Parousia: Studies in Celebration of the Life and Ministry of R. Hollis Gause*, ed. Steven Jack Land, Rickie D. Moore, and John Christopher Thomas, Journal of Pentecostal Theology Supplemental Series 35 (Blandford Forum, UK: Deo, 2010), 1–32.

10. The following considerations are informed by previous work—Yong, "Justice Deprived, Justice Demanded: Afropentecostalisms and the Task of World Pentecostal Theology Today," *Journal of Pentecostal Theology* 15:1 (2006): 127–47. See also Amos Yong and Estrelda Alexander, eds., *Afro-Pentecostalism: Black Pentecostal and Charismatic Christianity in History and Culture*, Religion, Race, and Ethnicity Series (New York: New York University Press, 2011).

11. See Donald E. Miller and Tetsunao Yamamori, *Global Pentecostalism: The New Face of Christian Social Engagement* (Berkeley: University of California Press, 2007).

12. See chapter 1 in this book.

13. See ibid.; emphasis in original.

14. See Lee and Poloma, *Sociological Study of the Great Commandment*, esp. 38–45.

15. Lee and Poloma, *Sociological Study of the Great Commandment*, 61.

16. See chapter 5 in this book. Oord has also argued this thesis in two recent books: *Defining Love: A Philosophical, Scientific, and Theological Engagement* (Grand Rapids, MI: Brazos, 2010), and *The Nature of Love: A Theology* (St. Louis: Chalice Press, 2010).

17. See chapter 5.

18. See especially John Milbank, *Theology and Social Theory: Beyond Secular Reason* (Malden, MA: Blackwell, 1993).

19. The theological details here are in Yong, *Spirit-Word-Community: Theological Hermeneutics in Trinitarian Perspective* (Aldershot, UK: Ashgate, and Eugene, OR: Wipf & Stock, 2002), part I.

20. A more detailed argument for this position is presented in Yong, "Academic Glossolalia? Pentecostal Scholarship, Multi-Disciplinarity, and the

Science-Religion Conversation," *Journal of Pentecostal Theology* 14:1 (2005): 63–82.

21. Sociologists have adopted a similar stance with regard to interdisciplinary engagement; see Lee and Poloma, *Sociological Study of the Great Commandment*, 57.

22. E.g., Margaret M. Poloma and Ralph W. Hood Jr., *Blood and Fire: Godly Love in a Pentecostal Emerging Church* (New York University Press, 2008); and Margaret M. Poloma and John C. Green, *The Assemblies of God: Godly Love and the Revitalization of American Pentecostalism* (New York: New York University Press, 2010).

23. Clearly, certain pre-understandings of the Spirit lead to certain interpretations—e.g., Edward E. Decker Jr., "Meaning-Making and Religious Experience: A Cognitive Appraisal Model of Pentecostal Experiences of the Holy Spirit," in *The Spirit Renews the Face of the Earth: Pentecostal Forays into Science and Theology of Creation*, ed. Amos Yong (Eugene, OR: Pickwick Press, 2009), 191–209; the question, however, concerns not just the interpretations, but the resulting practices or even way of life.

24. Oneness Pentecostals reject the classical doctrine of the Trinity; for an overview of Oneness Pentecostalism, see David A. Reed, *"In Jesus Name": The History and Beliefs of Oneness Pentecostals* (Blanshard Forum, UK: Deo, 2007).

25. Lee and Poloma (*A Sociological Study of the Great Commandment in Pentecostalism*, 98–107) do identify various types of pentecostal ministries—what they call servers, renewers, and changers—which is an important step toward thematizing the difference that theology makes.

26. See here Ada M. Isasi-Diaz, "Kin-dom of God: A Mujerista Proposal," in *In Our Own Voices: Renditions of Latino/a Theology*, ed. Benjamin Valentin (Maryknoll: Orbis Books, 2010), 171–90, who contests the hierarchical and patriarchal connotations of the traditional English "kingdom."

27. Thanks to graduate assistant Timothy Lim Teck Ngern for proofreading this chapter, and to coeditor Matthew Lee for his feedback on a previous draft of it.

# CONTRIBUTORS

**Paul Alexander** is Professor of Christian Ethics and Public Policy at Palmer Theological Seminary of Eastern University in Wynnewood, Pennsylvania, and author of *Peace to War: Shifting Allegiances in the Assemblies of God.*

**Peter Althouse** is Associate Professor of Religion and Theology at Southeastern University, Lakeland, Florida, and author of *Spirit of the Last Days: Pentecostal Eschatology in Conversation with Jürgen Moltmann* and *The Ideological Development of "Power" in Early American Pentecostalism.*

**Mark J. Cartledge** is Director of the Centre for Pentecostal and Charismatic Studies at the University of Birmingham, UK; he is the author of a number of books in the field, including *Testimony in the Spirit: Rescripting Ordinary Pentecostal Theology.*

**Julie J. Exline,** an Associate Professor of Psychology at Case Western Reserve University in Cleveland, Ohio, specializes in research on spiritual struggles and forgiveness.

**Ralph W. Hood Jr.** is Professor of Psychology at the University of Tennessee at Chattanooga, a past editor of the *Journal for the Scientific Study of Religion,* and senior author of the *Psychology of Religion: An Empirical Approach,* 4th ed.

**Matthew T. Lee,** Associate Professor of Sociology at the University of Akron in Akron, Ohio, is coauthor of *A Sociological Study of the Great Commandment in Pentecostalism* and author of *Crime on the Border.*

**Michael J. McClymond** is Associate Professor in Theology at St. Louis University in St. Louis, Missouri, and editor of the *Encyclopedia of Religious Revivals in America* and *Embodying the Spirit: New Perspectives on North American Revivalism.*

**Thomas Jay Oord** is Professor of Theology and Philosophy at Northwest Nazarene University in Nampa, Idaho, author of *Defining Love* and *The Nature of Love*, and author or editor of more than a dozen other books.

**Margaret M. Poloma,** Professor Emeritus of Sociology at the University of Akron in Akron, Ohio, has written extensively about religious experience in contemporary American society, including pioneering studies of pentecostalism, prayer, and divine healing.

**Stephen G. Post** is President of The Institute for Research on Unlimited Love and Professor of Preventive Medicine, Head of the Division of Medicine in Society, and Director of the Center for Medical Humanities, Compassionate Care and Bioethics at Stony Brook University in New York; and the author of seven books on self-giving love, including *The Hidden Gifts of Helping.*

**Arlene Sánchez Walsh,** Associate Professor of Church History and Latino Church Studies in the Graduate School of Theology at Azusa Pacific University in Azusa, California, is author of *Latino Pentecostal Identity: Evangelical Faith, Self, and Society.*

**Amos Yong** is J. Rodman Williams Professor of Theology at Regent University School of Divinity in Virginia Beach, Virginia, and the author or editor of more than 20 books, including most recently *Pentecostalism and Prosperity: The Socio-Economics of the Global Charismatic Movement.*

# INDEX

Abrahamic faiths, 17–18, 20–22, 25

agnosticism, methodological. *See* methodological agnosticism

Alexander, Paul, 9, 223, 229

Alexander, Richard, 104, 105

Althouse, Peter, 222, 229

altruism, 7, 11, 27, 28, 61, 101, 104, 105, 117n7, 124, 223

atheism, methodological. *See* methodological atheism

Augustine, 42, 52n6, 53n16

Azusa Street Revival, 202

Baker, Heidi, 49–51

baptism in the Holy Spirit, 220, 221

Barbour, Ian, 106

Barth, Karl, 57, 59–63, 65, 67, 73n21

Batson, C. Daniel, 98–99, 117n7, 152

Beloved Community, 17–19, 23

Benedict XVI, Pope, 169

benevolence, 3–12, 35, 116, 197, 205, 217–23

    acts of, 57, 63, 67, 69–71, 161–62, 167, 174

    definition of, 40

    universality of, 17, 20

Berger, Peter, 121–22

Big Bang, 80–82

bin Laden, Osama, 19

Blood n Fire (church), 161–62, 167, 221

Boff, Leonardo, 69

Bosch, David, 67

Brainerd, David, 45, 46, 49

Browning, Don, 33–34, 52n2

Butler, Joseph, 38

*caritas,* 40

Calvin, John, 58–59

Carey, William, 46

Cartledge, Mark J., 219

Church of God (Cleveland, Tennessee), 192, 194

community, 40–43

cosmology, 92n15

creation *ex nihilo,* 80–81, 92n15, 118n42

Damasio, Antonio, 103

Damasio, Hanna, 103

destructiveness, 18–20

Diamond Model of Godly love, 6–12, 165–66, 174, 177

dignity, 21

dispensationalism, 93n29

Dittes, James E., 122–24

divine action, 114–15

divine causation, 109–10

Edwards, Jonathan, 35

Eisenberg, Nancy, 103
Espín, Orlando, 200, 203
eudaemonism, 40
evolution, 80–82
evolutionary sociobiology, 101
exclusivism, 28
Exline, Julie, 219

Flame of Love project, 5–8, 10–13, 50, 70, 142, 144, 159, 192
free will, 81
freewill theism, 107–11, 118n42
Freud, Sigmund, 124–25, 128–29, 130–34
Full Gospel Business Men's Fellowship, 188
fundamentalism, 20, 21, 26

glossolalia, 187–90
God, 7, 8, 60, 108
    image of, 9
    nature of, 190–92
    self-giving, 63–66
    self-humiliation, 63–66
Godly love: *see also* Diamond Model
    definition of, 5
    origins of the study of, 3–6, 217–18
    scientific study of, 217–22
    theological contributions to the study of, 222–25
Great Awakening, 44
Great Commandment, 6, 25
Green, John C., 165–67
group selection theory, 101

hatred, 21, 29
Hegel, G. W. F., 74n34
Hick, John, 134
historiography, Latino/a Pentecostal, 213n3
Hitchens, Christopher, 172, 174, 177–78
Holl, Karl, 52n6
Holy Spirit, 142, 194, 228
Hood, Ralph W., 161–62, 165, 192, 218
Hopkins, Samuel, 35, 39
Hume, David, 38
humility, 4, 71

inclusivism, 26
indeterminacy, 81
individualism, 61
inspiration, theory of, 89
Institute for Research on Unlimited Love, 23, 217
interdisciplinarity, 4–5, 12–13, 121, 159, 219
International Society for Empirical Research in Theology, 183
Irenaeus, 58, 73n6

James, William, 23
Jeanrond, Werner G., 193–94
Jesus, 78–80, 86
Jesus Movement, 202
John Paul II, Pope, 171
Johnson, Mark, 215
Johnson, Rolf, 159–62
Jones, Rufus, 128
justice, 86–88

LaBarre, Weston, 132, 135
Langford, Joseph, 170–171
Latino Leadership Circle, 210–13
Lee, Matthew, 218–19, 223–24, 227, 232n25
liberation theologies, 61, 68
love: *see also* Godly love
    *agape,* 36
    appreciation-love, 160, 174–76
    care-love, 160, 177–79
    definition, 95–96
    *eros,* 36
    experimental approaches to study of, 150–53
    faces of, 159–61
    *philia,* 36
    scientific research on, 96–105
    scientific testing of, 111–12
    *storge,* 36
    union-love, 160, 173–74
Luther, Martin, 39, 58

Macchia, Frank, 12, 14n9, 110
Marsden, George, 45

McClymond, Michael, 222
McGrath, Alister, 62, 73n21
meditation, 30
methodological agnosticism, 56, 218
methodological atheism, 56, 121, 122, 124, 125–26, 134, 218
methodological naturalism, 105–7
methodological pluralism, 228
Milbank, John, 89, 226
Miller, Donald C., 221
Mills, C. Wright, 158, 159
mission studies, 66
Moltmann, Jürgen, 11, 65, 66, 68, 75n39
Mother Teresa, 168–79, 221
Murphy, Nancey, 81

natural theology, 62
Niebuhr, Reinhold, 78
Nygren, Anders, 35, 37, 47
obedience, 44
Oliner, Pearl, 102
Oliner, Samuel, 102
Oneness Pentecostalism, 202, 204, 228, 232n24
Oord, Thomas Jay, 13, 48, 55n59, 90, 92n15, 224–25
Origen, 58, 72n5
Outka, Gene, 54n35

Paul, the Apostle, 25, 31
Pentecost, Day of, 227, 228
Pinnock, Clark, 11
Pius X, Pope, 178
Poloma, Margaret, 135, 192, 217–19, 221, 223–24, 227, 232n25
Porpora, Douglas V., 122–23, 134–35
Post, Stephen, 37, 42, 47, 149, 217, 223
Poythress, Vern S., 187
prayer, 30
psychoanalysis, classical, 129–30, 130–133
psychological methods, 143

quantitative methodologies, 144–45

Ramsey, Paul, 53n19
reason, 72n3

religion, theory of, 130–33
Rieff, Philip, 166, 168, 175
Roman Catholic Church, 34
Roosevelt, Franklin Delano, 31
Roughgarden, Joan, 82, 92n18

Samarin, William J., 187, 188
Sánchez-Walsh, Arlene, 9, 10, 13, 219, 220
Saunders, Cicely, 23, 24
scientific method, 107–11
Shoemaker, Samuel M., 157, 158
Smith, Christian, 11, 70
Sober, Elliott, 101
social constructionism, 131–33
Sorokin, Pitirim, 26–30, 61, 70–71, 158, 162–65, 192, 211–12
suffering, 82–86
supernaturalism, 106
Swartley, Willard, 79, 85, 93n26

Teen Challenge, 205
Theresa of Lisieux, 178
Thomasius, Gottfried, 64, 65
Tillman, J. Jeffrey, 33, 34, 52n2
Torrance, T. F., 73n21
tribalism, 22

Vacek, Edward, 34, 47
Vaillant, George, 102
van der Ven, Johannes A., 184
Victory Outreach, 205–8, 210–13
violence, 23
Volf, Miroslav, 69, 77, 83–84, 91n3
von Balthasar, Hans Urs, 63, 72n4

Wesley, John, 46
Wilson, Bill, 157
Wilson, David Sloan, 101
Wilson, E. O., 104

Yamamori, Tetsunao, 221
Yoder, John Howard, 78, 79, 93n29